Talking Sense about Politics

Talking
Sense about
Politics

How to Overcome
Political Polarization
in Your Next Conversation

Jack Meacham

Q

Quaerere Press

Jack (John) A. Meacham
is SUNY Distinguished Teaching Professor Emeritus
at the University at Buffalo–The State University of New York.

Quaerere Press, Oregon
meacham@buffalo.edu
© 2017 by Jack Meacham
All rights reserved. Published 2017.
Printed in the United States of America

23 22 21 20 19 18 17   1 2 3 4 5

ISBN 978-0-9992976-0-5 (cloth)
ISBN 978-0-9992976-1-2 (paperback)
e-book ISBN 978-0-9992976-2-9

Epigraph courtesy of Guardian News & Media Ltd.

People are tired of simple things.
They want to be challenged.

—Umberto Eco

Contents

Tables

Introduction

How to Have a
Conversation about Politics

Americans come together the fourth Thursday of November to share a traditional Thanksgiving dinner, setting aside everyday concerns and enjoying the comfort of familiar food and the security of being at home. We tell stories and share memories of good times with family and friends; that is, until the conversation turns to the economy and jobs, government programs, or foreign policy and the national and state elections held only three weeks previously.

Someone casually and perhaps innocently casts the first bait across the table:

"Global warming is real." Others still smarting from the election results take the bait:

"Humans aren't causing global warming."

"Democrats want to spend other people's money." Soon voices are raised and people are talking over each other:

"The Constitution is the law, not the Bible."

"Republicans spend more money than Democrats."

"The Constitution is the law, not the whims of liberal judges." Still nursing wounds from last year's Thanksgiving dinner, someone throws out a well-rehearsed one-liner:

"Labor unions built this country—," and is immediately silenced with "Business owners created the jobs," and is just as quickly defended with "Corporations are not people!"

Not everyone at the Thanksgiving table participates in this exchange of one-liners, zingers, put-downs, quips, and comebacks. One or two people with more tact, and wishing to maintain family harmony, try to turn the conversation back to football or ahead to who would like pumpkin pie and who would like mincemeat and who would like some of each. Two of the combatants, still loyal to their cause, are unwilling to yield unless they can have the last word:

"FOX News isn't real news; it's a hateful, right-wing propaganda machine."

"MSNBC isn't real news; it's the propaganda machine of the liberal loony left."

The tactful mediator tries again to turn the conversation: "Let's just agree to disagree and move on."

Meanwhile, others have detached themselves from the conversation and sit quietly or have already moved to the kitchen to start cleaning up. They may have strong social and political views but don't want to offend others, or they don't want to get drawn into an argument and risk being hurt. Yet, shouldn't a gathering of family and friends be a time to be comfortable with who you are and what you believe, not to censor yourself? Shouldn't you be able to express your views openly and have others respect what you say?

The holiday dinner ends with *loyal* winners and losers, *tactful* but frustrated mediators, and a *detached* and withdrawn few in the kitchen. The *caring* sentiments of this national holiday--President Ronald Reagan, in his 1988 Proclamation of Thanksgiving Day, asked Americans "to remember the sacrifices that have made this harvest possible and the needs of those who do not fully partake of its benefits. The gratitude that fills our being must be tempered with compassion for the needy;" and President Barack Obama, in his 2014 proclamation, said, "I encourage the people of the United States to join together . . . and give thanks for all we have received in the past year, express appreciation to those whose lives enrich our own, and share our bounty with others"--have been forgotten.

A similar conversation is taking place year round in our communities and workplaces, in the media and nationally. The tone is tense and alarming. Americans' views on political issues have become increasingly polarized. The share of Americans who are consistently liberal or conservative has doubled in the last two decades. Most Democrats are more liberal than most Republicans; most Republicans are more conservative than most Democrats.

Critical challenges for America's future that should not be political—education, health care, infrastructure, technology, and energy—are recast by politicians, pundits, and the media to appear intensely partisan. A third of Republicans say that Democratic policies threaten the nation; a third of Democrats say the same about Republican policies. Close to half of Democrats view the Republican Party in strongly negative terms, and vice versa.

Among colleagues at work and neighborhood friends, any casual comment can lead to a heated exchange. Each side is firmly loyal to the obvious truth of its personal position. Neither side listens with an open mind to what the other is saying. Engaging in a thoughtful and tactful conversation, establishing common ground, and finding workable solutions to America's problems is impossible in our current polarized national conversation.

Meanwhile, many Americans have detached themselves from talking about the challenges facing America. They, too, are concerned about America's future but see only political brawls, gridlock, and ineffectiveness in Washington, DC. They make it a point to avoid getting involved in political discussions and heated arguments. Feeling that their views aren't represented by the major political parties, they drop out of America's civic discourse, lose trust in government, and stop voting. Yet, doesn't America's ability to address its looming problems depend on everyone feeling they are free to speak out, their ideas will be listened to, and they can contribute potential solutions?

The American political scene now consists of *loyal* and triumphant winners and disheartened losers, a *tactful* few hoping to find common ground, and an increasing number of angry, frustrated, and *detached* Americans. The vision of America as a *caring* nation has faded from view.

Political polarization is dangerous for the United States. Complex issues become oversimplified when forced to fit within only two opposing political positions. Simplistic and misleading representations of issues become obstacles to crafting workable solutions to move America forward. A climate of angry political polarization undermines the open and respectful exchange of ideas among neighbors, coworkers, and citizens that is essential for America to function and endure as a democratic society.

America's major political parties now focus on message wars and symbolic votes; for example, on guns and climate change, while failing to enact legislation critical for the country's future. Political image and partisan branding have become more important than facts, loyalty to party more important than to country. Commenting on "the feeling of many Americans that our politics are totally stuck," Pulitzer-Prize winner and columnist for *The New York Times* Thomas Friedman has written, "The nonstop fighting between our two political parties has left many Americans feeling like the children of two permanently divorcing parents. The country is starved to see its two major parties do hard things together again."

The negative consequences of political polarization and divisiveness, including legislative paralysis and declining trust in government and democratic political processes, will continue to threaten America's promise and stability far into the coming decades. Harvard historian Jill Lepore, writing in

The New Yorker in 2013 on extremist voices in the media and on the internet, notes, "What's really going on could be anything from party realignment to the unraveling of the Republic."

Why do we continue to take the bait at Thanksgiving dinner and elsewhere and get drawn into these polarized and polarizing arguments? The conversations we observe on talk radio, cable television, and internet streaming provide poor models. Hot talk or shock talk features a host who dominates exchanges with listeners who call in. Comments—frequently one-liners—can be rude, disrespectful, and hit-and-run, with the host disconnecting a caller or a caller hanging up on the host. Partisan hosts and panelists spin their remarks, talk over one another, and play to the audience.

In contrast, conversations with family, friends, and colleagues are grounded in personal relationships that have been nurtured over many years. At the dinner table, ideal hosts are models for how to be tactful, express views carefully, draw others into the conversation, listen thoughtfully to what others say, and strive to articulate a common ground that all can agree to. The stakes are high. A careless comment can shatter long-term bonds of respect and affection among family members and friends.

Yet, some of us naively believe that if our one-liners or Facebook comments or 140-characters can set forth just one critical connection—"It's the business owners who create the jobs"—or provide just one key fact—"The carbon dioxide level in the atmosphere exceeds 400 parts per million"—our opponents will quickly perceive the truth and wisdom of our position and change sides and join together with us. Yeah, good luck with that.

One-liners, comebacks, and even indisputable, hard facts rarely persuade people to change their positions because they are always interpreted and accepted or rejected from the underlying perspectives that people bring to the conversation. Consider, for example, how a quick solution to the following riddle is made difficult by the perspective that many of us hold. A father and his son are in a bad car crash. The father is killed. The son is rushed to a hospital where the surgeon exclaims, "I can't operate on this boy—he's my son!" How is this possible?

The implicit perspectives that we hold—our points of view—have enormous power to shape how we think, speak, and act. They strongly influence our decisions about which facts are relevant and what weight to give them. Many of us fail to consider that the surgeon in the riddle might not be a man but a woman. Unfortunately, it can be difficult to perceive the underlying perspectives that influence our thinking and the diverse perspectives that others may hold. The car crash riddle might be resolved quite differently if the boy has two gay men as fathers, or a biological father and an adoptive father, or a biological father and a stepfather. So there are four possible perspectives on this riddle and perhaps several more.

Overcoming the riddle of political polarization requires recognizing that the reality of American history and political thought is far more complex than only two opposing perspectives: my personal perspective, the right one, and someone else's perspective, the wrong one. It's a mistake to crush everyone's thoughts and opinions into only two positions, right versus left, conservative versus liberal. Indeed, there is no consensus among Americans or even scholars on what these labels really mean. Let's start over with some familiar terms that we all do understand.

As shown in the chapters that follow, there are in fact not two but four American perspectives—Loyal, Tactful, Detached, and Caring—that people hold regarding how they view themselves, how they view others who are different, how they expect to live and work together with each other, and what they believe on critical issues confronting American society.

Why does this matter? Consider, for example, a business owner and a civic leader who differ in their power and privilege and who disagree on an issue in their town. Only two conversations are possible: first, a dialogue between a *small* business owner and a *strong*, entrenched civic leader; and second, a dialogue between the city's *major* employer and a *weak*, recently elected civic leader. Now imagine three perspectives on the issue, those of the business owner, the civic leader, and now a poet. With differences in power and privilege among the three, there are now six possible dialogues. If a fourth perspective is added, for example, that of a social worker, the number of possible dialogues is increased from two to sixteen (as shown in chapters 4 through 8).

Recognizing that there are four American perspectives and as many as sixteen possible dialogues on any issue greatly expands the public space and the diversity of voices for discussion and debate on matters of importance for America's future. Thoughtful Americans who have felt frustrated as their ideas and values were misrepresented and blocked by the two dominant political parties can feel empowered to re-engage in public discussions, talk sensibly about politics, and argue openly and convincingly for their positions.

When I began to write this book and talk with friends, the most common question was, what are the other two perspectives? They assumed, as I did initially, that the tired and simplistic dichotomies of right versus left, conservative versus liberal, or Republican versus Democratic were two of the four. As I thought and wrote further, I was surprised to find that I was forced to a different conclusion. Readers will also be surprised and challenged as they consider which of the four perspectives they personally hold and how these perspectives explain America's polarized political conversations and disturbing and stressful Thanksgiving conversations.

We will not overcome political polarization in America by focusing on who people are and their age, gender, race or ethnicity, and geography. We cannot change who we are nor the demographics of our extended families, coworkers, and fellow American citizens. And, to be honest, there are many good people in these social and cultural categories whom I enjoy being with and would like to keep as friends—even though we may happen to disagree from time to time on certain political issues.

Far more urgent and promising is to learn how to communicate with people who do not share our views without getting drawn into divisive arguments. A first step towards better communication is knowing that Americans hold not two but four perspectives—Loyal, Tactful, Detached, or Caring—that determine how they listen, think, and speak. The second step is recognizing which of these perspectives we ourselves hold and which perspectives others might hold and how these perspectives shape our conversations about political issues. The way to overcoming political polarization in America is to focus on how to have a better conversation about politics.

The chapters of this book are organized into three sections. Part I (chapters 1-4) sets forth the conceptual framework for all that follows. Chapter 1 shows how four perspectives have been present throughout American history and the present. Chapter 2 illustrates the Loyal and Tactful perspectives with examples from American history including George Washington, Henry Clay, and Franklin D. Roosevelt. Chapter 3 illustrates the Detached and Caring perspectives with the examples of Daniel Boone, Henry David Thoreau, and Jane Adams. Why are there four American perspectives and not three or five? Chapter 3 answers this question and defines the perspectives in terms of their underlying assumptions: first, how our identities and relationships are understood; and second, whether our intentions are to control and win or to understand and cooperate. Chapter 4 introduces sixteen dialogues between people holding the four perspectives and having more or less power and privilege.

Part II (chapters 5-8) presents the sixteen dialogues as models for how to have conversations about politics anywhere and any time of year. The dialogues are illustrated with current issues including minority and women's rights, immigration, cheating in sports, religious freedom, bullying, inequality, foreign policy, climate change, homelessness, freedom of speech, gun control, and more.

Part III (chapters 9-12) shows how American politics and the attitudes of American voters are more understandable and more fascinating when we resist worn out, polarizing dichotomies and instead recognize that there are in fact four American perspectives. Chapters 9 and 10 focus on the political scene in Washington, DC and how the Republican and Democratic parties reflect coalitions of people holding strongly to each of the four perspectives. What might be the future for civil discourse and democracy in America? Chapters 11 and 12 argue that we can overcome political polarization by recognizing the four perspectives and so changing how we think and talk about the issues.

My hope is that those who read this book will find the four familiar American perspectives a useful tool for understanding and rejecting the stale and misleading partisan dichotomies of left versus right, liberal versus conservative. My hope is that readers will use the sixteen dialogues as a guide towards making more focused and coherent presentations of their personal positions on political issues. Of course, good communication also requires listening more carefully to what others have to say and understanding better the nuances of their positions. Our conversations about politics and the issues confronting American society can become less often occasions for anger or defensiveness or tuning out and more often opportunities for spirited engagement and joy in discovering what others have to contribute that we had not thought of. The reward for overcoming political polarization will be rediscovering the great breadth of what we as Americans do believe and value in common.

Part I

Four American Perspectives

1

Four Americas:
Loyal, Tactful, Detached, Caring

Americans are increasingly frustrated, angry, and frightened at the surge of political polarization between left and right, liberals and conservatives, Democrats and Republicans. *E pluribus unum*, the historic motto appearing on our nation's Great Seal, once captured how people with diverse backgrounds and views work together to build a strong, dynamic, and shared society. But now Americans are concerned that we have become two tribal Americas, with conflicting beliefs about what is wrong and what is strong, the rights and responsibilities of citizens, the purposes and limits of government, and America's place in the world in the twenty-first century.

Yet the reality is there are not two Americas but four Americas. These four Americas are not geographical regions or personality types or categories of people or reflective of particular occupations. Instead, the four Americas are different perspectives or points of view that people hold regarding how they view themselves, how they view others who are different, how they expect to live and work together with each other, and what they believe about the significant challenges facing American society today.

Consider, for example, Tom Venn, a businessman in early twentieth-century Alaska, at first selling supplies to gold miners, later managing a salmon fishery and cannery, and eventually rising to become president of his company. On numerous occasions, Venn put his loyalty to the company and protection of the company's interests ahead of other considerations. As a cannery manager, he focused on controlling labor costs, taking advantage of his Native American, Filipino, and Chinese workers, to increase his company's profits. Venn took personal credit for the mechanical innovations of one of his Chinese workers. His goals of working hard, gaining promotions in the company, and moving to the Seattle headquarters led to abandoning his first love, a Native American woman, and marrying his boss's daughter. As company president, Venn worked closely with a lobbyist to promote the commercial interests of Seattle industries and banks over the welfare of the people of Alaska and their drive for statehood.

Somewhat different is the perspective of John Whipple, a businessman and plantation owner in nineteenth-century Hawaii. Whipple's life goal was to work for himself, earning enough to buy the things he wanted. He got his start in business by selling supplies to whaling ships and eventually became the owner of a sugar plantation. Whipple respected the abilities and intelligence of others and recognized that his own success depended in part on their efforts. So he argued for the fair treatment of Chinese who had been brought to Hawaii as laborers. He believed they were destined to become accountants and mechanics, schoolteachers and bankers and to demand a voice in governing Hawaii. Whipple understood Hawaii would be stronger when everyone was able to work to their fullest potential. Just as Whipple was determined to better himself, he was pleased to see others who were determined to better themselves. He recognized the interdependence of the various Hawaiian communities and that everyone working together would lead to their mutual success.

In contrast, John Klope, a gold miner in early twentieth-century Alaska, had difficulty talking with others or making friends and did not form business partnerships. On one occasion, as a member of a group trekking fifty miles through deep snow and bitter cold, Klope volunteered to follow last to look after those too exhausted to care for themselves. Yet on arriving safely at their destination, Klope shunned attention and gave credit to others for the lives he saved. Klope was a drifter, self-contained and independent, working and living alone, yet persistent and hard working. When he eventually found gold, he shared his wealth with the three friends who had been close to him when life was difficult and he was struggling.

Maxwell Mercy, an army captain stationed in Colorado in the nineteenth century, did not pursue money or other gains for himself. Instead, he was motivated by a caring concern for others and by an interest in justice. Assigned to accompany emigrants across the Great Plains, he tried to assure them they would have little to fear from Native Americans. When their guide assumed approaching Native Americans would be hostile, Mercy argued they would be peaceful and knocked the guide's rifle away to prevent needless shooting. In later years, Mercy worked to arrange treaties between Native Americans and the American government, ensuring open land and buffalo herds for the former and farmland close to rivers for settlers. He was confused and distressed when the American government voided treaties he had helped negotiate. Mercy argued for providing relief for Native Americans who were starving and against brutal government policies that would lead to their extermination.

These four individuals—Tom Venn, John Whipple, John Klope, and Maxwell Mercy—are fictional characters. Their stories are told more fully by the American novelist and Pulitzer Prize-winner James Michener. Among his many novels are several following diverse families through centuries of American history: *Hawaii, Centennial, Chesapeake, Texas,* and *Alaska.*[1] The perspectives of these four people have little in common. Do their points of view represent only these people and the particular events of their lives? Or can these same perspectives be found among others in American history and today?   Consider the perspectives of four more of Michener's fictional characters:

Rosalind Steed was a plantation owner in eighteenth-century Maryland. She was remarkable for her mastery of how to grow tobacco and sell it for a profit in London or Bristol, of when to buy and sell slaves and how best to put them to use, and for her oversight and expansion of the family holdings. These included what might be found in a small, self-contained town: weavers, tailors, tanners, cabinetmakers, caulkers, sawyers, carpenters, rope makers, fishermen, coopers, and more. Steed had a controlling role in her extended family, rejecting young women's potential suitors and arranging for families to move away and settle new land. It was Steed who pursued the pirates who attacked the family's ships and insisted they be hung. Her daughter, Emily, summed up and described Steed's life as always pursuing some enemy. Steed agreed she had been hard, but insisted this was the right thing to do. All that mattered, for Steed, was to become the best person possible, to build the best life possible, and to be loyal to herself and her family.

Rosalind Steed's perspective on herself and others is similar to that of Tom Venn (the Alaska businessman). They share an intention to control others in order to maximize their own gains. Venn lacked understanding and empathy for his workers, as did Steed for her slaves. Their efforts were focused primarily on what they wanted for themselves and those closest to them. Steed was strongly loyal to her family, just as Venn was to his company. Their perspective on themselves and others will be termed "the Loyal perspective."

Paul Garrett was a rancher and civic leader in mid-twentieth-century Colorado. His strengths included staying connected with diverse interest groups and remaining flexible and open-minded when negotiating among them. Through being a good listener and diplomatic in discussions with ski resort owners, Garrett arranged an agreement balancing their commercial interests with protection of the nearby mountain environment. As Garrett looked to the future of Colorado, he saw huge challenges in balancing protection of forests, trout, and elk against growth in population, industry, and agriculture and, in particular, the need to wisely apportion water in order to maintain all of these. Garrett felt strongly that if people had shaken hands on a deal, then honor required that they never break their word, for this was essential for maintaining long-term working relationships.

Paul Garrett and John Whipple (the plantation owner in Hawaii) are similar to Venn and Steed in their intention to control others to maximize their own gains. Yet Garrett and Whipple also appreciated that their continued success required working together and getting along with others. Negotiating and compromising are important in reaching short-term agreements, and trust and honor are important in maintaining a shared community. This will be termed "the Tactful perspective," to call attention to being considerate and dealing fairly with others.

Amos Calendar was a cowboy in Colorado in the second half of the nineteenth century. Shy and sparing of words, Calendar preferred living alone. With his gun, his bedroll, and his horse, he lived a self-contained life on the prairie. His skills included making his own bullets and cartridges and stalking and shooting deer. He took odd jobs in small towns only to earn enough to care for his guns. When he was young, Calendar worked with others on cattle drives. When he was older, he herded sheep because he preferred working by himself. Yet on one occasion Calendar recruited others to avenge the murder of one of his few friends.

Self-contained and independent, Amos Calendar and John

Klope (the Alaska gold miner) share what will be termed "the Detached perspective." They are similar to Venn and Steed in focusing on themselves rather than on working together with others, yet they do not share Venn and Steed's intention to control others and maximize personal gains. Calendar and Klope understood well the lives they had worked out for themselves, living in relative isolation on the Colorado prairie and in the Alaska mountains.

As a young woman, Missy Peckham was a social worker in charge of a church charity in Chicago. In the 1890s, she joined the Klondike gold rush and then remained in Alaska, where she consistently advocated for the rights of the downtrodden, for Native Americans and farmers arriving from the Midwest. She fought battles against injustice and ignorance, in her own words "among the hopeless, but never without hope." An early advocate for statehood, Peckham envisioned an Alaska not controlled by powerful commercial interests in Seattle, but instead able to draft its own laws and govern itself. She argued strongly that Alaska should have schools for all its children, good housing for Native Americans, opportunities for immigrants to own their own farms, and local jurisdiction over roads and hunting and salmon fishing.

Missy Peckham shared with the soldier Maxwell Mercy what will be termed "the Caring perspective." They were always engaged with others, whom they found worthy of respect, and humble and aware of their own shortcomings. Their Caring perspective is similar to the Tactful perspective of Garrett and Whipple, in the interdependence of their own lives and the lives of others. But Peckham and Mercy focused less on their personal needs and wants and more on understanding and looking out for the needs of others, including those whose backgrounds and experiences were quite different from their own.

In summary to this point, there are four perspectives— Loyal, Tactful, Detached, and Caring—that describe how we view others and ourselves. There are similarities among them. The Loyal and Tactful perspectives, for example, share an intention to control other people and events; and the Tactful and Caring perspectives recognize the interdependence of our own lives and the lives of others. Yet each of these perspectives is unique. Michener's novels provide additional examples of these four perspectives making clear that not all family members necessarily think the same way.

Floyd Rusk, living in Texas in the first half of the twentieth century, illustrates the Loyal perspective. As a young man, Rusk bought a gun and soon joined with other men to force Black families, Jewish shopkeepers, and Catholics to move away from their small Texas town, eventually becoming the group's leader. Later these vigilantes forced the town's liberal newspaper editor and church minister to leave as well. By Rusk's middle adulthood, oil had been found on his land and the focus of his life became controlling the tricky deals involving land and oil and his rapidly increasing wealth. Later, Rusk joined with other wealthy oilmen to support the town's high school football team. They searched for the most brawny young linemen and the fastest runners, and then arranged jobs for their fathers in nearby oil fields so they could move to town and enroll their sons at Rusk's local high school. It didn't matter that many of the players whom Floyd Rusk procured were already in their twenties; all that mattered was that his football team win all of its games.

Floyd Rusk's father, Earnshaw Rusk, illustrates the Tactful perspective. Working in the 1860s as a government agent among Native Americans, Rusk gave sanctuary to a band being pursued by US soldiers, for he felt the band had peaceful intentions. Faced with contrary evidence, Rusk reversed himself and asked the soldiers to punish the band for their crimes. Years later, Rusk supported a candidate for the US Senate who, having served in the Confederate army, represented much that Rusk, a pacifist, opposed. Nevertheless, realizing that the other candidate was arrogant and deceitful, Rusk chose to work with the former, whom he felt was the better of the two. On another occasion, he was committed to fencing his water hole, but when cattle being driven north needed water, Rusk considered the other person's problem, saw that his own position was wrong, and cut and opened his fences. In an effort to bring a railroad spur to their town, Rusk formed a coalition with a man who had previously tried to steal his land. Rusk understood that in the game of building Texas, people who had worked against each other could also work together for their common good.

Because he wanted to live openly as a Catholic rather than under the control of the Protestant majority, Edmund Steed immigrated from England to Virginia early in the seventeenth century. He soon left Jamestown in a boat he had built and settled by himself on a small Chesapeake Bay island where he traded with Native Americans for beaver pelts, raised corn and tobacco, and established a self-sufficient and prosperous plantation. In his later years, a quiet and withdrawn Steed reluctantly took on the role of revolutionary leader. He argued forcefully for the principle that the laws of Maryland should be drafted by ordinary men who had settled there, and not imposed by men with wealth and privilege in London. Others came to regard Steed, who insisted "we are to be free men in a free society," as their leader in the defense of their liberties. Edmund Steed's views are an example of the Detached perspective. The examples of Tactful Earnshaw Rusk and Loyal Floyd Rusk, and Detached Edmund Steed and Loyal Rosalind Steed, make clear that particular perspectives do not necessarily reoccur within families.

Michael Healy was captain of a revenue cutter, charged with enforcing customs regulations and catching smugglers, sailing off the coast of Alaska in the late nineteenth century. The son of an Irish father and an African-American slave mother, Healy had an explosive temper. Despite his temper, however, his goal was to bring order to the seas and to educate. Many of his actions illustrate the Caring perspective. He pursued and fined men who were selling alcohol to Native Americans. He was successful in mediating disputes between Native Americans and newcomers over fishing rights. When the catch of seals and whales by Native Americans was insufficient, Healy provided food and medical supplies. On one occasion, Healy joined with his crew to construct a church for Christian missionaries. A significant decision by Healy was to conceal his discovery of cannibalism among a group of shipwrecked sailors he had rescued. One of the sailors later praised Healy for giving no sermons or lectures and instead for understanding that all people are alike and sometimes forced to make difficult choices.

These four perspectives—Loyal, Tactful, Detached, and Caring—are ways of looking at oneself and others. The perspectives are not personality types or categories of people or reflective of particular occupations; indeed, one individual may on different occasions hold two or more of the four perspectives. Consider, for example, Nyuk Tsin, brought from China to Hawaii as a young woman in the mid-nineteenth century. When her husband was exiled to a leper colony on the island of Molokai, she volunteered to accompany him although she herself did not have leprosy. After her husband died, she stayed on in the colony, caring for leprosy patients who were neither Chinese nor her own family members. In respecting and engaging with others, Nyuk Tsin demonstrated the Caring perspective. Throughout much of her life, however, Nyuk Tsin also illustrated the Loyal perspective. Her priorities were providing for her sons by growing and selling vegetables, maneuvering for their acceptance into the best schools, arranging marriages with women who brought land as part of their dowries, and managing the marital and financial prospects for her extended family.

In her later years, Nyuk Tsin gave sound advice to her sons and grandsons on how to work together with others in Hawaii. Following the Honolulu Chinatown fire in 1900, she encouraged her son not to press financial claims for his own family but instead to speak strongly in support of the entire Chinese community. Nyuk Tsin understood that if her son did not serve on the board distributing money, others would in the end be more generous in providing relief for her extended family. On another occasion, she advised her grandson to always pay a little more for land than what the seller might hope for, so the seller would not feel cheated and would maintain their long-term relationship. In her practical wisdom about establishing positive roles for her Chinese family members within the broader Hawaiian community, Nyuk Tsin was demonstrating the Tactful perspective.

Hans Brumbaugh is a second example of someone who held more than one of the four perspectives. A German immigrant to Colorado in the mid-nineteenth century, Brumbaugh pioneered the use of irrigation to provide water for growing potatoes and sugar beets. Because of the importance of water for farming in this dry region, Brumbaugh was aggressive in hiring lawyers to change the laws so he could gain control of water resources and exclude others. In giving priority to the control of water resources in order to expand his own farm, Brumbaugh was showing his Loyal perspective. However, in later years he provided substantial assistance to Russian, Japanese, and Mexican farmers in the region, including loaning money so they would be able to purchase land and co-signing their mortgages. Thus Brumbaugh was also able to adopt the Caring perspective.

Some readers will wonder which American perspective is the "good" perspective, the one they will agree with and identify with, and which three are the "bad" perspectives, the ones they will disdain and reject. Unfortunately, this is how political polarization too often works: if we can determine whether a politician's views are left or right, liberal or conservative, then we can readily lock onto what we now believe to be right or wrong, without having to bother listening to all sides, weighing the evidence, and thinking further. As the examples of Nyuk Tsin and Hans Brumbaugh illustrate, however, people can hold any of the four American perspectives on different occasions. Thus, it would be too simplistic to align any political parties or leaders with the four American perspectives without a more complete and careful consideration of context (the subject of chapter 9).

In conclusion, four perspectives or points of view have persisted throughout American history and today: Loyal, Tactful, Detached, and Caring. Questions may arise in the minds of readers. Perhaps these four American perspectives are merely ad hoc and anecdotal. What assumptions underlie these perspectives? Why are there four perspectives and not three or five? How can I know which perspective I am holding on an issue, or which perspective someone else is holding? These questions are pursued in chapters 2 and 3 showing in greater detail how each of the four perspectives is unique and differs from the other three.

2

The Loyal and Tactful Perspectives

How do you introduce yourself, for example, on a first date, on a job interview, or at a business meeting? Of course, make eye contact and smile, listen to the other person, and ask questions. But how do you respond when someone says, tell me about yourself?

You might describe your interests, abilities, and accomplishments, focusing on your independence. "I earned my degree in business, I'm hard-working and successful at what I do. I jog every morning to stay in shape." Or you might describe your connections with other people. "I grew up in a close-knit neighborhood. My family and school friends are still important to me. Now I lead a team at work that is responsible for marketing. After work my friends and I play together on a soccer team."

How we introduce ourselves is a reflection of our identities; that is, our conceptions of ourselves. The Loyal and Tactful perspectives share an intention to control others and be successful. They differ, however, in how identity and relationships are understood. From the Loyal perspective, identity is viewed as a separate, independent, and distinct entity; that is, self-contained. From the Tactful perspective, identity is understood as connected with others; that is, interdependent. To draw this distinction sharply: from the Loyal perspective, one strives to win without regard for the other, as armies fight each other in wars; from the Tactful perspective, one strives to win while maintaining respect for the other, as teams play each other in sports.

The Loyal Perspective: Being in Charge

What feelings arise for many Americans as they celebrate on the Fourth of July the independence of the United States, as together they sing the closing words of the national anthem, "The Star-Spangled Banner"—"o'er the land of the free and the home of the brave"—or "America the Beautiful"—"God shed his grace on thee, and crown thy good with brotherhood from sea to shining sea"? These feelings include satisfaction and pride in the hard-won achievements of Americans and of America as a nation, beginning with success in the War of Independence and establishing a Constitutional system of government that has been widely imitated. These achievements continued in the nineteenth century with the extension of the American spirit of progress and ideals of freedom and justice across the North American continent, exploding into the twentieth century with American victories in two World Wars and astonishing advances in industry, education, science, medicine, and technology.

The achievements and progress of the American nation seem to have been inevitable and to constitute clear and sufficient proof that God has indeed always been on our side. The nineteenth-century doctrine of Manifest Destiny, according to which the United States had the right and the duty to expand across the continent, has matured and been transformed into the contemporary view that our nation and what it stands for are both pragmatically and morally superior. America rightly occupies a privileged position among the nations of the world. A continuation of American progress, power, and leadership is indeed our natural and God-given destiny.

Of course, others advance alternative interpretations of American history or provide a less optimistic assessment of the standing of the United States among the nations of the world. Nevertheless, most Americans recognize that this image of the United States as a nation destined to become and remain powerful and morally superior is widely held, regardless of whether they personally agree with it. To construct, believe in, and sustain this powerful image of America requires, in part, that we be thinking about the United States not in terms of its relationship with other nations but rather as a unique, self-contained entity whose existence and virtues do not depend on anything outside of itself. When I am singing "The Star-Spangled Banner" I am not thinking of some other nation in addition to the United States.

What matters from this perspective is to be in control and in charge: a winner, number one, successful, the dominant nation. American progress and achievements imply that other nations have failed where America has been successful, that America has found the will and the means to do first what other nations will later merely imitate. This competitive ranking of nations is an important value and we assume the United States will continue to be the leader. (Such comparisons are, however, merely implicit; rarely is there consideration of the actual strengths and weaknesses of the United States relative to other nations.) This image of power and moral superiority is closely tied not only to feelings of satisfaction and pride in our country but also to a willingness to be faithful to, support, and defend the United States; that is, to feelings and acts of patriotism and loyalty.

In the previous chapter, the Loyal perspective in American history was illustrated with the example of Tom Venn, who started selling supplies to gold miners in Alaska and worked his way up to become president of a salmon canning company. For Rosalind Steed, the Maryland plantation owner, what mattered most was to be loyal to herself and her family. The Texas oilman Floyd Rusk, who started out with nothing and made himself wealthy by knowing when to buy and sell land, also illustrated the Loyal perspective. The paragraphs that follow provide a general description of the beliefs and attitudes that Loyal individuals hold toward themselves and others, and their typical mode of relating to others.

Loyal individuals and groups are proud of their community and its identity and feel righteous in its defense. For people holding the Loyal perspective, their way of life is the true and pure way, their aspirations and goals are correct, the trajectory of the community's growth is rising and unstoppable, and their community is not only better than other communities but also self-sufficient and not dependent on what others may believe, say, or do. Feelings of caring by Loyal people can be strong, but they extend these only towards others in their own family, group, or community, not to outsiders who are different.

These convictions provide the Loyal community with a rationale for refusing to yield resources, power, or privilege associated with its own identity and community. Furthermore, they provide a rationale for acting towards others with little regard for their lives and communities. Loyal people are likely to interpret many of the words and actions of others as potential threats to their own identity, community, power, and privilege, and so feel justified in guarding against and thwarting efforts by others to increase their own sense of control, power, and privilege. Other individuals and groups are viewed by the Loyal community as wrong in their beliefs and actions and as unworthy.

George Washington established the standard for loyalty and patriotism early in American history. Active in his support of the colonies during the French and Indian War, and increasingly opposed to British control of trade and government, Washington proclaimed his willingness to fight in support of the colonies by appearing before the Second

Continental Congress in 1775 in full military uniform. After serving as commander of the Continental Army, he resisted proposals that he put himself ahead of his country and be made king. Washington served as the first president of the United States and then, placing the interests of the nation foremost, he declined to run for a third term as president. A principal theme in his Farewell Address in 1796 was the danger to the United States of permanent alliances with other nations. Throughout his public career Washington's goals for the United States were independence, self-sufficiency, and competitive strength and placing the interests of the United States ahead of regional, political, or personal interests.

From the self-contained Loyal perspective, enduring relations with other individuals or groups are not necessary for self-understanding and integrity in life. Indeed, commitments to and entanglements with others can weaken personal self-sufficiency and independence. In general, other people are not seen as likable or as worthy of emulation, unless the imitation of certain behaviors can augment one's own power and privilege. Individuals holding the Loyal perspective are continually engaged with others in a struggle for control, power, and ultimately survival. The principal modes by which Loyal people relate to other communities include efforts to limit and control the other, to convert the other to one's personal identity, and to dominate, even destroy the other.

Relating to others can also involve stereotyping and the use of derogatory language. Even minor differences between groups can be perceived as having great significance. Identity and community are understood in an either-or manner, as opposed to a both-and manner: Someone can be a supporter of either my community or your community, but not both at the same time. A person is either loyal to the community or a traitor.

Sharing the facade of South Dakota's Mount Rushmore with George Washington is Theodore Roosevelt, the twenty-sixth president of the United States. A fervent nationalist who also greatly expanded the power of the presidency, Roosevelt was confident in his actions and often self-righteous. As assistant secretary of the navy, Roosevelt strongly favored a war against Spain so the United States could dominate the Caribbean region. In the course of the war Roosevelt led the Rough Riders in their assault on Kettle Hill in the Battle of San Juan. As president, Roosevelt worked to increase the strength of the navy, sending the "Great White Fleet" on a worldwide show of force and using the fleet as gunboat diplomacy to force the Chinese government to end a boycott of imports from the United States and other nations.

Roosevelt's vision for the United States was one of expansion and projection of power in the Pacific, the Caribbean, and Latin America, where under the Roosevelt Corollary to the Monroe Doctrine he assumed the right to intervene in the internal affairs of other, weaker nations. In the years following his presidency, Roosevelt called for further expansion of government welfare and regulatory efforts, encouraged preparation for the entry of the United States into World War I, and expressed reservations about the participation of the United States in the League of Nations. In putting the autonomy and power of the United States government foremost, both domestically and internationally, and in his belief that the United States as one of the superior nations had the right to dominate weaker nations, Roosevelt stands as a clear example of the Loyal perspective.

The loyalty of both Washington and Roosevelt to the United States was absolute, uncompromised by partial loyalties to other nations, regions, or causes. At the same time, both believed in the necessity of American dominance in the competition among nations. In the revolutionary America of Washington's era, the need was to be strong against the British. In the context of turn-of-the-century great power rivalries, Roosevelt saw the need to project the power of the United States throughout the Americas and across the Pacific towards Asia. Themes of nationalism, loyalty, and patriotism are significant and enduring themes in American history, important not only for presidents but for countless individuals. One of our best known patriots is Nathan Hale, captured and executed for spying against the British during the Revolutionary War. Hale ended his speech shortly before he was hung with the words, "I only regret that I have but one life to lose for my country. " Millions of men and women have demonstrated their loyalty to the United States, for example, through military service and as first responders.

The Tactful Perspective: Getting Along With Others

Do you know someone who depends on the Supplemental Nutrition Assistance Program (SNAP) to afford groceries? Almost 50 million Americans receive food stamps, with the largest numbers living in Tennessee, Louisiana, Oregon, Mississippi, and New Mexico. For individuals suffering chronic pain, would you like the cost of medical marijuana to be tax-deductible? If you live in California, Michigan, or Washington, the answer is likely yes. Agricultural subsidies for growing corn, cotton, wheat, and rice or for producing milk go to farmers, primarily in Texas, Iowa, and Illinois. Would you like the government to encourage an expanded market for fresh-cut Christmas trees? Perhaps yes, if you are a grower in Oregon, North Carolina, Michigan, or Pennsylvania.

These and other questions involving international trade, environmental conservation, agricultural research, food safety, and the well-being of rural communities were recently addressed by Congress in a single omnibus bill known as the farm bill. The previous farm bill had expired in 2012. After extensive discussion and debate, including $8 billion in cuts to SNAP, a new farm bill was passed as the Agriculture Act of 2014. How did Congressional representatives reconcile support for nutrition for families and price supports for farmers and the competing interests of their home states? In the end, the representatives and senators had to focus on playing well and getting along with each other.

Congress is the national legislative body of the United

States. The name stems from Latin words meaning to come together. Indeed, a great diversity of interests comes together in Congress, which includes representatives from large and small states, the Northeast, South, Midwest, and West regions, and cities, suburbs, and rural communities. Congressional representatives have widely differing experiences with wealth and poverty and, if they are of different generations, quite different senses of the culture of the United States as well as visions for America's future. And our representatives bring diverse views on religion and its place in public life, on regulation of business and protection of workers, on the role the federal government should play—or not play—in regulation of the economy, and on many other issues of importance for our country.

Given this great diversity of backgrounds, experiences, and views, we would not be surprised if each representative worked primarily to impose his or her own interests on the others, thus leaving Congress in a state of perpetual gridlock. Sometimes it does seem that this has happened. Nevertheless, Congress has endured as a strong and effective political institution. How has it managed to do this, despite the wide range of its constituents and interests? Many representatives recognize that working alone can accomplish very little, yet by working together in coalitions much can be accomplished. They realize that opportunities to work together extend over several years, and that an opponent on any particular issue might well be a key ally on some future issue.

An American statesman known for his ability to craft and gain acceptance of political compromises was Henry Clay, who served as Speaker of the House of Representatives, secretary of state, and a US senator from Kentucky. Clay secured passage in Congress of the Missouri Compromise of 1820, under which new states would be admitted to the United States in pairs, one slave state (Missouri) and one free state (Maine). As secretary of state and as a senator, Clay strived to overcome American regional interests with his American System, which included preservation of the Second

Bank of the United States (which he had earlier opposed), protective tariffs for American industries, and federal expenditures for improvements in the West.

Clay also played a constructive role in resolving the crisis brought on when South Carolina, fearing English retaliation against its cotton exports, declared that it would refuse to allow United States customs officers to collect tariffs on English imports. The crisis was resolved when Clay secured passage of the Compromise Tariff of 1833 that lowered tariffs and ended South Carolina's threat to nullify federal law and President Andrew Jackson's threat to use force against South Carolina. Clay is best known, however, for crafting the Compromise of 1850, which included stronger laws against fugitive slaves in the Northern states, the admission of California as a free state, and agreement that slavery would not be prohibited in the new, southern territories, thus dampening for another decade the secessionist movement among Southern states.

Thus, while it is reasonable for factions within Congress to strive to be successful in enacting the legislation they champion, at the same time it is extremely important that our representatives work together to protect and maintain a sense of community. In short, although the game Congressional representatives play is one of striving to control and win against each other, they must play according to the rules. This means having a good understanding of parliamentary procedures, earning the respect of colleagues by being honest and working hard, and being loyal to Congress as an institution and to its procedures. Congressional representatives regard being openly ambitious to attain the presidency or seeking support for legislation through the media rather than through discussion and debate with colleagues as not playing by the rules.

Congressional representatives can play within the rules while still employing winning tactics such as persuasion, coalition-building, negotiation, compromise, and logrolling (exchanging political favors and votes to achieve passage of legislation of interest to one another). Of course, these tactics are also familiar procedures in legislative bodies at the state and local level, in decision-making within government and business organizations, in town council and school board and community meetings, and in many other democratic bodies, both formal and informal. In all of these forums, individuals strive to win, yet they also strive to be tactful and preserve the body politic.

From the Tactful perspective, personal values and goals are worthy, yet those of other individuals and groups within the broader, shared community cannot be disregarded. In contrast to the Loyal perspective, the maintenance and strengthening of identity and community depend on a never-ending sequence of interdependent interactions with others intended to solidify and expand the individual's own resources, power, and privileges. In order to engage confidently in such interactions, people holding the Tactful perspective feel they have a practical intuition in dealing with and getting along with others. This intuition can include insight into and consideration of others' intentions as well as diplomatic skills in handling awkward situations without giving offense. As Earnshaw Rusk, the Texas rancher (chapter 1), might say, "You have to be flexible, be prepared for some give and take, and try to get along with people."

Tactful people are likely to regard others within the broader, shared community as rather unsophisticated, as lacking in the practical skills of diplomacy and negotiation, and as susceptible to manipulation and deceit. Tactful people feel that although they can be shrewd, astute, and cunning, they themselves are immune to being manipulated by others. From the Tactful perspective, people understand that they are inextricably bound to others, yet the goal is to be able to maintain control and gain as much as possible from the relationship while giving as little as possible in return. The worth of other individuals and groups and the decision whether to interact with others depends on how useful they might be for our own identity and community.

The attitudes and behaviors of Tactful individuals and communities are grounded in the assumption that groups are defined through their interdependent relations with other groups. This understanding of the nature of community is shaped by the assumption that the primary intention of humans is to control others. From the Tactful perspective, as from the Loyal perspective, relations with other groups involve control, power, and survival. Yet, to be members of a broader, shared community means that the course of any conflict should follow certain accepted conventions, rules, and principles that set limits on what one party might do to the other.

The Colorado rancher Paul Garrett might explain relationships from the Tactful perspective by saying, "I believe if you shake hands on a deal, then you should keep your word." For Tactful people the principle modes of relating to others include consideration of their views, negotiating, compromising, entering into agreements, and forming coalitions. One avenue is to deemphasize differences between groups and to focus instead on what all groups within the broader, shared community have in common. For example, the plantation owner John Whipple recognized the social and economic benefits that would flow when the various Hawaiian communities worked together.

As a master of the Tactful perspective, Franklin D. Roosevelt won the presidency on four occasions, each time by substantial margins. This is strong evidence of his ability to appeal to and unite diverse and competing interests. As assistant secretary of the navy, Roosevelt was able to listen to and balance the competing interests of senior navy officers, defense contractors, and labor unions. Roosevelt urged members of the Democratic Party to overcome regional and urban versus rural divisions. His ability to appeal to both urban and rural voters in New York State led to his election as governor in 1928. Roosevelt clinched the nomination for president by offering the vice presidency to a Congressional representative from Texas, thus overcoming the Eastern-urban versus Southern-Western-rural split within his party. Roosevelt's effort to bring the United States out of the Depression was a careful balancing of the interests of large corporations, commercial farmers, and small business owners, on the one hand, and union leaders and American workers, on the other, evoking criticism from the right that he was undermining individual liberties and from the left that he was being too cautious in attacking the Depression. Roosevelt learned through experience to compromise with Congress. He secured passage of legislation to create the Civilian Conservation Corps to provide work for the unemployed, fund the Public Works Administration to construct large-scale projects, raise taxes on the wealthy, shift control of monetary policy from bankers to Washington, DC, create the Works Progress Administration to distribute work relief funds, establish the National Labor Relations Board (which enabled workers to bargain collectively with management), and establish the Social Security program for the aged and disabled.

Most important for the future of the United States, Roosevelt worked earnestly to appease the isolationists in Congress and keep the United States out of the forthcoming war in Europe, and to provide military support to Britain and the Soviet Union in their struggle against Hitler's Germany. In the course of the war Roosevelt once again was able to balance competing interests, refraining from criticizing the colonialist and expansionist policies of Britain and the Soviet Union so that he could hold these nations together with the United States in an effective coalition against Germany and so win the war.

Both Clay and Roosevelt were highly competitive individuals yet both believed that the process that best ensured winning was one of working together with others, balancing competing interests, and negotiating and compromising, a process in which there was, in the end, a deal to be struck that included something for everyone. Thus, the lives and work of both Clay and Roosevelt may be taken as examples of the Tactful perspective. The conviction of most Americans that tactfulness is a good process leading to just outcomes is closely tied to their beliefs in liberty and equality for individuals. America provides opportunities for each person and group to strive hard and perhaps become enormously successful, yet for this success to be considered acceptable it must be earned while continuing to engage openly and fairly with other individuals and groups.

Similar beliefs and principles inform Americans' understanding of our economic system. The marketplace works best when there is competition among businesses and workers, each looking after his or her own interests, yet all agreeing to abide by commonly accepted practices as well as government regulations intended to ensure that relationships with one another remain fair. And similar beliefs and principles no doubt underlie the strong role of sports in American public life, in which individuals compete vigorously to win games and championships yet do so with a sense of fair play and good sportsmanship towards each other, with the expectation that next time they could be playing together not as opponents but as teammates.

Assumptions About Defining Ourselves and Our Relationship to Others

The 2016 US Olympic Team won 46 gold medals in Rio de Janeiro, 27 won by women, 19 won by men. Among the outstanding American athletes were the swimmers Michael Phelps, Katie Ledecky, Ryan Murphy, and Simone Manuel and the gymnast Simon Biles, now the most-decorated American gymnast. Competing primarily as individuals, their achievements reflected superior talent, determination, and competitiveness. In their commitment to demanding training regimens, their self-motivated drive to improve, and their individual performances these athletes can be described as self-contained.

Other outstanding American athletes were members of US teams that won gold medals: Kevin Durant on the men's basketball team, Diana Taurasi and Lindsay Whalen on the women's basketball team, and Ashleigh Johnson and Maggie Steffens on the women's water polo team. Their winning performances depended on the play and support of the other team members. Respecting fellow teammates, sharing successes and praise, admitting mistakes and taking responsibility, remaining optimistic in the face of adversity, and supporting each other like family are as essential for winning as athletes' personal talent and competitiveness.

How do we define ourselves in relationship to other individuals and groups? There are two contrasting assumptions in answer to this question. The first assumption is that we are self-contained, like the first group of Olympic athletes. There are strong psychological boundaries between ourselves and others. We believe that we have control over ourselves, without interference from others. We define our own identities—that is, our self-conceptions—without including others within our identities. The second assumption is that we are interdependent, like the athletes on Olympic teams. There are permeable boundaries between ourselves and others. We do not have complete control over ourselves. Control exists within social systems that are greater than ourselves. Our identities include other individuals and groups.

This distinction has been borrowed from Edward Sampson, the author of several books about social psychology and an emeritus professor at California State University, Northridge. He argues for two contrasting perspectives: first, self-contained individualism, characterized by firm self-other boundaries and a conception of self that excludes others from the definition of self; and second, ensembled individualism, characterized by a fluid self-other boundary and a conception of self that includes others within the definition of self. From the ensembled or interdependent perspective, Sampson observes, "Who I am is defined in and through my relations with others; I am completed through these relations and do not exist apart from them."

An example of the first assumption, a self-contained perspective, is a solo musician on the stage whose personal identity is that she is a violin player. An example of the second assumption, an interdependent perspective, is a musician within an orchestra, whose personal identity is that she is a member of an orchestra who plays a violin. Other examples of this second interdependent assumption are friend, parent, and team member. In these three examples, people understand their own identity only in relationship to others. One cannot be a friend without having a friend, one cannot be a parent without having a child, and one cannot be a team member by oneself.

The Loyal and the Tactful perspectives differ in how the relationship between self and others is conceived. From the Loyal perspective, the individual or group is understood as a self-contained entity, defining itself intrinsically and not through relations with other individuals or groups. From the Tactful perspective, the individual or group is defined extrinsically, through interdependent relations with other individuals and groups in a shared community.

So by now you've introduced yourself and responded to the "tell me about yourself" question posed at the beginning of this chapter. Next, how do you respond when someone asks, "So, what are your plans? What are you aiming for in life?"

You might say, "I intend to become successful by starting my own business. Someday I'd like to be very well off financially." The aims of Rosalind Steed, the Maryland plantation owner (chapter 1), were to manage her business and secure her family's long-term prospects. John Whipple, the Hawaiian businessman, also aimed to be successful in expanding his business. Both aimed to be in control, to succeed, and to win in life. As described in this chapter, the Loyal and Tactful perspectives share this intention to control others.

Or you might respond, "I'd like to develop a meaningful philosophy of life and a better understanding of other people and cultures. And I'd like to contribute to strengthening communities and protecting the environment." John Klope, the Alaska gold miner, and Amos Calendar, the Colorado cowboy, understood well the isolated lives they had worked out for themselves. Maxwell Mercy, the Colorado army captain, and Missy Peckham, the Alaska social worker, focused less on their own lives and more on understanding and looking out for others.

The Detached and Caring perspectives share this intention to understand. These perspectives are described in the next chapter, showing how they differ from each other and from the Loyal and Tactful perspectives. In addition, the next chapter concludes with a conceptual framework that serves to articulate and integrate these four American perspectives.

3

The Detached and Caring Perspectives

Imagine hiking through the mountains on a summer day and, just after climbing a small rise and rounding a bend in the trail, coming on a herd of deer grazing in the sunlit meadow just beyond the woods where you remain hidden in the shade. What is your intention now, your plan of action? Perhaps you quietly remove your backpack and unsling your rifle, slowly move toward the edge of the woods to have a clear shot, and then carefully aim at the buck with his spreading antlers. What a trophy this will make! And what a credit to your mastery of the woods and your skill in stalking your prey. Well, perhaps you don't have a rifle. However, you can still throw a rock or clap your hands or give a hearty shout and watch the deer startle and flee across the meadow and into the far woods as a result of your intention to intervene and control their behavior.

Or perhaps you quietly remove your backpack and take out your camera, slowly move toward the edge of the woods, and then consider carefully how to frame the photo in order to capture the beauty and mood of the scene. As you watch the deer from your hiding place in the shade of the trees, you admire the strength and grace of the muscles in the shoulders and legs of the deer, you discover differences in the color and texture of their coats, and you speculate on the significance of occasional grunts, snorts, head bobs, foot stamps, and tail flicks. Well, perhaps you neglected to bring your camera. However, you can continue to watch, striving to impress the scene into your memory. After a few minutes, you have stopped thinking about the deer and instead are reflecting on your relationship with nature and your hopes for the future. Then you notice the deer have moved to the far side of the meadow, so you now resume your hike without disturbing them, enriched in your new understanding of the deer and nature and yourself.

As shown in the previous chapter, the Loyal and Tactful perspectives share an intention to control others and be successful; for example, intervening and attempting to control the behavior of the deer. The intention of the Detached and Caring perspectives, in contrast, is not to control others but to understand and cooperate; for example, to better understand the deer, nature, and ourselves. The distinction already introduced in chapter 2, between viewing oneself as a self-contained entity versus being interdependent with others, continues to be useful: from the Detached perspective, the focus is on understanding and cooperating with those who are like ourselves; from the Caring perspective, the focus is expanded to include those who are different from ourselves. To draw this distinction sharply: from the Detached perspective, we strive for self-understanding; from the Caring perspective, we strive for understanding of both ourselves and others.

The Detached Perspective: Working It Out Myself

In 1893 the historian Frederick Jackson Turner read a paper at a meeting of the American Historical Association in which he noted that the 1890 census had shown every part of the United States had been settled and so the American frontier was now closed. The previous two centuries of American growth and development had been, in large part, a story of relentless movement toward the West, of pushing the frontier of settlement ever farther from the Eastern seaboard. The advance of American pioneers and settlers into the wilderness was not a coordinated, national effort; instead, the leaders and the heroes pushed forward as individuals— backwoodsmen and mountain men seeking adventure and independence and, later, farmers seeking new land and self-sufficiency. What is impressive in the accomplishments of these eighteenth- and nineteenth-century pioneers is not only what they were able to do but also more significantly that for the most part they did it alone.

Armed with little more than a rifle and an ax and rumors and hopes of game to be hunted, furs to be trapped, and fertile land to be farmed, small numbers of men passed in the mid- to late 1700s through the Cumberland Gap and into Kentucky, Tennessee, and Ohio. In the early 1800s they crossed the Great Plains and moved into the Rocky Mountains. What these men had in common was their independence, either traveling alone through the wilderness or, later, settling on a self-contained, self-sufficient farm with their pioneer wives and children. They struggled and competed not against each other, but against the forces of nature—dense forests, rugged mountains, wild animals, blizzards, droughts, and floods. From this they gained a keen understanding of themselves and human nature and the natural world in which they lived.

Daniel Boone stands as an exemplar of the American frontiersman, his reputation enhanced by Lord Byron's 1823 tribute to Boone in his narrative poem "Don Juan," and by James Fenimore Cooper's incorporation of details of Boone's life into stories of his fictional hero Leatherstocking. As a youth Boone developed expertise in hunting and trapping that served him well in his excursions in the 1760s and 1770s into what would become eastern Kentucky. Boone repeatedly left his family behind to venture farther into the wilderness.

At his happiest exploring new regions until he knew them well, Boone was saddest when the new countryside began to fill with settlers. Leaving Kentucky in dismay in 1798 because of the increasing population, Boone became one of the early settlers in what is now Missouri. In his later years Boone's exploration took him along the Missouri and Platte Rivers and into the Yellowstone region of Wyoming. His reputation included fearlessness, self-sufficiency, and simple wisdom.

Three individuals from chapter 1—John Klope, the Alaskan gold miner; Amos Calendar, the Colorado cowboy; and Edmund Steed, the Maryland farmer—also illustrate the Detached perspective in American history. Despite Turner's pronouncement of the closing of the American frontier, these eighteenth- and nineteenth-century frontier values and images of American independence, initiative, self-reliance, freedom, individualism, and self-sufficiency persist in American mythology, literature, music, film, and the political rhetoric of the present.

For Detached individuals and communities, the primary goal is to be left alone so they can pursue self-understanding. Constructing meaning and significance in life, and achieving and maintaining coherence and integrity in identity and community, are highly valued. These objectives can best be achieved through contemplation, reflection, introspection, and disengagement from others, not through engagement with other individuals and groups. For this reason, self-contained Detached people often regard interactions with others as threatening to their personal goals and sense of identity and community. Thus, the feeling of detachment is less one of being isolated and more one of being besieged. Detached people tend to regard themselves as quite insightful into their own intentions.

Whereas Daniel Boone sought detachment by venturing farther to the west, Henry David Thoreau sought detachment by withdrawing to a small cabin he built in the 1840s near Walden Pond outside Concord, Massachusetts. Thoreau's development of a philosophy of individualism had been influenced by Ralph Waldo Emerson's urging American scholars to become independent and self-reliant through following the precepts "Know thyself" and "Study nature." Thoreau's aim in living for an extended period by himself at Walden Pond was to simplify his life and gain time for reflection, observing nature, and writing. "A man is rich," Thoreau wrote, "in proportion to the number of things which he can afford to let alone."

During his two years at Walden Pond Thoreau wrote *A Week on the Concord and Merrimack Rivers* and *Walden*, the latter of which secured his reputation as an observer of nature and ecologist. During the same period, after refusing to pay his poll tax as a protest against slavery, Thoreau wrote *Civil Disobedience*, in which he emphasized the ethical responsibilities of individuals and the need to violate unjust laws in order to bring about their repeal. This philosophy of following one's conscience and passive resistance against immoral governments influenced twentieth-century leaders such as Mahatma Gandhi and Martin Luther King, Jr.

From the Detached perspective, other individuals and groups are of lesser interest. They may be tolerated, but there is neither antipathy (as is sometimes the case from the Loyal and the Tactful perspectives) nor strong sympathy (as from the Caring perspective). Detached people evaluate others from their personal perspective of detachment. Thus, the actions of others can be viewed as intrusive, bothersome, irritating, annoying, or troublesome. Because of their lack of engagement, Detached people may often lack an accurate understanding of others and even be insensitive toward the needs of others. This lack of empathic understanding can leave Detached people open to manipulation with stereotyped images and language.

From the Detached perspective, relations with others are not necessary for defining oneself or for self-understanding and integrity in life. Indeed, as from the Loyal perspective, commitments to and entanglements with others can be an impediment to personal self-sufficiency. Given that personal identity is self-contained, defined independently of relations with others, then from the Detached perspective we pursue self-understanding in relative isolation from others. The primary mode of relating to others is thus to be indifferent, to merely tolerate, and when possible to disengage.

The stance of Detached people is largely defensive, in contrast to the other three perspectives. When other people press their demands for interaction and disengagement is not possible, the Detached response can be to call for greater understanding between the groups. Often what greater understanding means is for the other to understand *me*, and in particular to understand my desire to be left alone. Emphasizing differences rather than similarities between self and others can become important as a rationale for not interacting.

The lives of Daniel Boone and Henry David Thoreau typify American values of independence and self-reliance, of knowing oneself well rather than becoming entangled with others, of living in accord with one's individual conscience and sense of personal responsibility, even if this means being viewed by others as unconventional, nonconformist, or eccentric. These values have provided the foundation and the inspiration for American pioneers as they settled the West, generations of writers, social critics, and reformers, diverse religious and secular movements advocating goodness, integrity, and simplicity, and occasional pacifist and isolationist themes in American foreign policy.

The Caring Perspective: Looking Out for Others

"Give me your tired, your poor, Your huddled masses yearning to breathe free, The wretched refuse of your teeming shore, Send these, the homeless, tempest-tost, to me, I lift my lamp beside the golden door!" These lines, written by Emma Lazarus in 1883, are inscribed on a bronze plaque inside the pedestal of the Statue of Liberty in the harbor of New York City. Lazarus' sonnet and the Statue of Liberty have been an inspiration for millions of immigrants to the United States, representing not merely the opportunities generations of new arrivals hoped to find in America but also the compassion, caring, and generosity that a bountiful America was able and willing to extend to the newest members of its communities.

America's compassion and caring is expressed through a wide range of federal, state, and local programs providing health care, housing, and food to those in need, including the aged, the disabled, the mentally ill, and poor families. In addition, many private charitable and philanthropic organizations provide direct aid to individuals and families in need, revitalize distressed neighborhoods, and expand training and employment opportunities. Fictional examples of the Caring perspective in American history from the first chapter include Maxwell Mercy, the Colorado soldier; Missy Peckham, the social worker in Alaska; and Michael Healy, the Alaska boat captain.

The founding of the Chicago social welfare center known as Hull House by Jane Addams in 1889 was a pioneer effort in caring for immigrants. The daughter of a prosperous merchant, Addams was inspired by learning of social reform efforts in Europe to strive for similar humanitarian reforms in industrial cities in the United States. Programs at Hull House served to facilitate the settlement of recent immigrants in America, through provision of a day nursery, a gymnasium, a community kitchen, boarding for working women, training in art, music, and crafts, and college-level courses in various subjects. Many social workers and reformers visited and worked at Hull House to learn about and borrow from these innovative programs.

Addams later became influential in campaigning for juvenile-court laws, tenement-house regulations, an eight-hour workday for women, safety inspections in factories, and workers' compensation. She wrote many articles and books, the best known of which is *Twenty Years at Hull House*. In 1931 Addams was awarded the Nobel Peace Prize in recognition of her many innovative contributions.

In the twentieth century the United States extended its caring and generosity outward through foreign-aid programs intended to provide relief from suffering as a result of wars and natural disasters and improvement of living standards for people in other countries. Shortly after the end of World War II, George Marshall, then secretary of state, called for a foreign policy directed against hunger, poverty, desperation, and chaos. Congress subsequently passed legislation funding the Marshall Plan for the reconstruction and economic development of a devastated Europe. American humanitarian concern for the peoples of other nations has also been expressed through the provision of disaster relief. For example, the Agency for International Development stimulates economic infrastructure and growth and agricultural self-sufficiency in developing countries through the provision of money, goods and services, loans to support specific social and economic projects, and technical assistance and training. Various private American organizations also provide substantial aid to other countries. For example, Ford Foundation funding assists developing nations to expand agricultural production, increase educational opportunities, and support and resettle refugees.

From the Caring perspective, people view their identity and community as defined by their commitment to the integrity of others' identities and communities. A better understanding of self depends on recognition of the interdependent nature of identity construction, expressed through an active engagement with and a caring commitment toward others. People achieve a profound self-understanding not by seeking to understand themselves in isolation, as from the Detached perspective, but rather by striving to understand themselves in the context of a broader, shared community of persons who are both similar to and different from themselves. As Edward Sampson notes, "When self is defined in relation, inclusive of others in its very definition, there is no separate self whose interests do not of necessity include others." Thus, it is essential to be informed about and take seriously the perspectives of others and to recognize and act on our responsibilities to broader communities, locally, nationally, and globally.

Like Jane Addams, Eleanor Roosevelt came from a prosperous, prominent family. As a young woman she worked with the poor in a settlement house in New York City, then during World War I with the Red Cross, and in the 1920s with the League of Women Voters and the Women's Trade Union League. In 1926 Roosevelt helped establish a furniture factory that provided jobs for the unemployed. She encouraged President Franklin D. Roosevelt's progressive initiatives and supported New Deal programs providing services for children and youth. Roosevelt's most notable public service, however, occurred in the years following the death of her husband. As chair of the Commission on Human Rights, she was instrumental in drafting the 1948 United Nations Declaration of Human Rights.

There are dimensions of respect, caring, and responsibility in the Caring perspective, and a commitment to striving to maintain and strengthen relationships. The definition of community may be changed when this serves the goal of becoming more inclusive, of structuring the community so that others with different backgrounds and experiences may feel genuinely welcome as members. Because of the respect accorded to others' goals, values, and views, those who hold a Caring perspective are likely to become aware of their own shortcomings, and to have and show feelings of humility rather than excessive pride. It is not easy to be caring, for this means continuing to respect, love, and accept responsibility for others, even when we are attacked, when we have been manipulated and deceived, and when our love has been rejected, not returned, or ignored.

The attitudes and behaviors of the Caring perspective are grounded in the assumption that individuals and groups are defined through their relations with others. In the Caring perspective, this understanding of the interdependence of individuals and communities has a significant interaction with the assumption that the primary intention underlying human action is to understand; that is, to construct meaning and significance in life. Understanding one's personal identity and community depends on recognition of the interdependent nature of identity construction, expressed through a caring commitment to others who are different from oneself. The principal modes of relating to other individuals and groups include cooperating, striving to understand the other, nurturing the other, and self-sacrifice. To be committed to the other is not merely to tolerate difference, but instead to respect, nourish, defend, and indeed to love difference.

Today millions of Americans not only support humanitarian efforts carried out by government and private organizations but also demonstrate their caring and compassion through personal contributions of time, effort, and money to local government service programs and to private charitable and service organizations. What all these efforts, both organized and personal, have in common is not a narrow concern for one's own community but rather a more general concern for the American public at large and for diverse peoples around the world. In short, the primary concern is not for self but for others, a concern growing out of the view that the self is defined through interdependent relations with others.

Assumptions About Intentions With Respect to Others

You are hiking in the mountains and come upon a herd of deer grazing in a meadow. What is your intention, your plan of action? Will you intervene and attempt to control the behavior of the deer? Or will this be an opportunity to better understand the deer, nature, and yourself? The Loyal and Tactful perspectives differ from the Detached and Caring perspectives in assumptions about intentions with respect to others. For the first two, the intention is to control others and achieve success; for the latter two, the intention is to understand self and others; that is, to construct meaning and significance in life.

These contrasting assumptions are borrowed loosely from the sociologist and philosopher Jürgen Habermas. A professor at the Goethe University Frankfurt in Germany, Habermas was elected a Foreign Honorary Member of the American Academy of Arts and Sciences in 1984. He distinguishes between first, instrumental and strategic action, both oriented toward controlling the world and achieving success; and second, communicative action, oriented toward reaching understanding.[1] The action that follows from the intention to control proceeds from an egocentric defining of what will constitute successful action. The action that follows from the intention to understand is based in the cooperation of the people who are parties to the action.

A perspectives matrix is formed by the intersection of two rows and two columns with contrasting assumptions (table 3.1). The contrast between viewing oneself as a self-contained entity versus being interdependent with others, introduced in chapter 2, defines the rows in the matrix. The contrasting intentions of controlling others versus understanding and cooperating with others, introduced in the present chapter, define the columns. Each of the four cells in the matrix represents a perspective that contrasts in significant ways with the other three.

It would be a mistake to focus on the name of each perspective—Loyal, Tactful, Detached, and Caring—in isolation from its relationships with the other three perspectives in the matrix. These names are provided merely to facilitate discussion of the four perspectives. Any names carry a multitude of connotations, but what is most important are the meanings that arise at the intersections of the rows and columns. To say it starkly, the four names are not as important as the underlying assumptions regarding identity and intentions—that is, the distinctions between the rows and between the columns. The names of the perspectives should not be taken as labels that can be affixed to particular individuals, personalities, or types of persons or groups. One person can hold two or more of the perspectives, as illustrated by Nyuk Tsin in Hawaii and Hans Brumbaugh in Colorado.

Table 3.1. The Perspectives Matrix

	Intention	
Identity	Control	Understand
Self-contained	**Loyal**	**Detached**
Interdependent	**Tactful**	**Caring**

The four perspectives are compared and contrasted in the following tables, which also summarize what has been presented in chapters 2 and 3.

The next table provides a brief overview of how people and groups holding each perspective view themselves (table 3.2). For example, those who hold the Loyal perspective often feel proud and self-righteous.

Table 3.2. Each Perspective's View of Self

Loyal	Detached
Proud	Besieged
Righteous	Self-sufficient
Tactful	**Caring**
Considerate	Engaged with others
Shrewd	Sympathetic

Table 3.3 is an overview of how people and groups holding each perspective view others. For example, those holding the Loyal perspective are likely to view others as wrong and unworthy.

Table 3.3. Each Perspective's View of Others

Loyal	Detached
Wrong	Intrusive
Unworthy	Bothersome
Tactful	**Caring**
Useful	Able
Unsophisticated	Enriching

Third, people and groups holding each of the four perspectives are likely to behave toward others in different ways (table 3.4). For example, those holding the Loyal perspective are likely to compete with others, those holding the Tactful perspective are likely to negotiate with others, those holding the Detached perspective are likely to disengage from others, and those holding the Caring perspective are likely to cooperate with others.

Table 3.4. Each Perspective's Behaviors Toward Others

Loyal	Detached
Dislike others	Indifference toward others
See differences between self and others	See differences between self and others
Compete with others	Disengage from others
Control others	Tolerate others
Aggress against others	Patronize others
Focus on self-improvement	Call for others to understand

Tactful	Caring
Use others	Love others
See similarities and differences between self and others	See similarities and differences between self and others
Negotiate with others	Cooperate with others
Persuade others	Respect others
Manipulate others	Nurture others
Form coalitions with others	Self-sacrifice for others

Fourth, each perspective is viewed similarly by individuals and groups holding the other three perspectives (table 3.5). For example, those holding the Tactful, Detached, or Caring perspectives are likely to view those holding the Loyal perspective as immature and aggressive.

Table 3.5. How Each Perspective Is Viewed by Others

Loyal	**Detached**
Immature	Aloof
Aggressive	Insensitive
Tactful	**Caring**
Manipulative	Naive
Threatening	Idealistic

If different people can hold any of these four perspectives, what happens when two people with different perspectives—or even the same perspective—meet and interact? If they were sitting at the same Thanksgiving table, would they be able to have a sustained conversation about politics in America? How would they understand each other? How would their conversation proceed? Would there be a clash of perspectives? These questions will be taken up in the following chapter, in which the focus shifts from the four American perspectives to communication, conversations, and dialogues.

4

Power, Privilege, and Sixteen Model Dialogues

Perhaps some will object to the descriptions in previous chapters of how people and groups holding each of the four American perspectives—Loyal, Tactful, Detached, and Caring—are likely to behave toward others (table 3.4). They could argue that how we behave depends not only on differences in our perspectives but also on other significant dimensions of our relationship. This argument would be correct and is the topic of the present chapter.

When I'm engaged in conversation with my family, how I present myself and how I respond to what others say often depends on whom I'm speaking with. Conversations with my parents and grandparents are different from conversations with my children and grandchildren. The same holds at work: conversations with my boss are different from conversations with my coworkers or those I supervise. These differences in how we communicate reflect differences in power and privilege. Some of the differences are positive; that is, some people have more experience, expertise, and understanding than others. Sometimes the differences can be harmful, when those with power and privilege stop listening and try to impose their views on others.

This is what politics is all about: conversations among interest groups competing for power and privilege. With political polarization, as in the United States now, the differences between interest groups are extreme. People no longer listen to each other and political conversations come to a halt. The key to overcoming political polarization is to get people listening and talking again, to focus on communication and dialogues among people holding the four perspectives rather than on people's personalities or types or categories of people. How people talk with each other is more important than who they are.

Suppose someone with a Loyal perspective (for example, the Texas oilman Floyd Rusk) strikes up a conversation with someone with a Caring perspective (Missy Peckham, the Alaska social worker)? Or suppose someone with a Detached perspective (Daniel Boone) starts talking with someone with a Tactful perspective (Franklin D. Roosevelt)? Would they understand each other? How would their conversation proceed? Would there be a clash of perspectives?

Power

One of the most common ways of describing relationships is to consider the relative strengths or weaknesses of the people involved and how these determine the course of the relationship. Often, concepts such as strength, resources, expertise, moral courage, authority, information, and privilege play central roles in characterizations of relationships. What do these and similar concepts have in common? In one way or another, they describe how power has been distributed and how much one member is able to exercise control and influence over the other.[1]

Power refers to the ability to obtain what one desires in a given situation. In other words, people with power are likely to get their way, regardless of challenges or resistance from others. Power is significant in social relationships because of variations in its distribution and magnitude. It is quite common to say one person or group is stronger than another. Individuals and groups vary in seven types of power they have and are able to exercise.

Physical strength is a type of power familiar even to children, who learn that the requests of their parents can be enforced by the parents' greater strength. Children also know that their parents' power can create a safe space of home and family. The power of the bully on the school playground, the power of the sports champion to compete against other athletes, the power of one nation to defend itself or to wage war against another—these are examples of power based in large part on physical strength. Physical strength is also an aspect of the power that is exercised in abusive relationships as, for example, when physical strength is directed against spouses and children.

Material resources is a second type of power that can be used to gain or maintain control in relationships. Possession of particular resources including jobs, property, credit, or wealth for purchasing goods and services may arise from birth into a family or community that has, historically, had control over them. Control over resources can also reflect the processes and decisions of institutionalized authority and access to food, housing, education, jobs, raises, promotions, credit, loans, health care, and more.

Emotional resources, the ability to give or withdraw love, affection, acceptance, and esteem, is a third type of power that can support the controlling person in a relationship. It can also be a foundation for building friendships in small groups, participating in community organizations, and identifying with ethnic, political, and religious groups. Individuals and groups strive to remain in relationships because the acceptance and esteem they receive can be an important component of the identity they have constructed for themselves. The relationship between parents and children is also grounded in the love and care each provides for the other.

Expertise of individuals and groups is a fourth type of power. Expertise may involve specialized knowledge, keen intuition or enlightenment, talents for doing something well, or skills acquired or developed through experience. A skill relevant to gaining and maintaining power is political skill, at which some people are more adept than others. Leadership abilities are a kind of expertise leading to power; people with exceptional leadership abilities are sometimes described as having charismatic power over their followers.

Determination or will, strength of character, or moral courage is a fifth type of power. Individuals and groups can gain this power through their understanding of and faith in belief systems that provide a guide to action. Examples are political belief systems such as democracy, economic systems such as capitalism, cultural systems such as prescribed gender roles, and systems of moral and religious beliefs.

Institutionalized authority is a sixth type of power; that is, when the distribution of power in society is agreed to by individuals and groups through chartering organizations, establishing governments, and passing legislation. As a result, certain individuals and groups are invested with legitimate authority to control the resources of the organization or the government. Institutionalized authority includes the power held and exercised by elected and appointed officials and bureaucrats. Others can share in this power to the extent that they have access to these officials and bureaucrats and understand how bureaucracies work. Enhanced access to institutionalized authority can occur when members of one's own gender or ethnic or religious community are elected or appointed to organizational and government positions.

Access to information is a seventh type of power that can include not merely having timely access to critical information but also the ability to gather, create, shape, and distribute information and to decide who will have access and who will not. This type of power affects how local, state, and federal governments make decisions and distribute resources, how small businesses, corporations, banks, and stock markets operate, and how the educational and health care systems function. The shaping of information can also include the ability of the news and entertainment media to represent individuals and groups positively or negatively, fairly and accurately or in terms of false stereotypes, and to render them invisible in society by neglecting to portray them at all.

Privilege

Powerful individuals and groups can often gain that which they desire not through the exercise of power but merely through the having of power. To be able to reap the benefits of being powerful without having to incur any of the costs of exercising that power is to have privilege. Privileges may be either privileges of doing, such as having access and controlling the agenda, or privileges of avoiding, such as exemptions and immunities. Privileges are not enjoyed by all, in contrast to rights, to which generally all individuals and groups may make a claim.

To be privileged brings benefits to powerful individuals and groups because less powerful people must be wary of the implicit threat to their own well-being by those whom they believe to be more powerful. They must be sensitive to the desires of those who are more powerful and perhaps try to accommodate or fulfill these. Or they may feel pressured to grant benefits, favors, or advantages to those who are privileged because they naively expect a reciprocal granting of benefits or favors in the future. Whether these sensitivities or pressures are right or just, however, depends on whether the privilege of the more powerful individual or group is a legitimate or earned privilege as opposed to an illegitimate or unearned privilege.

Some privileges are commonly accepted as legitimate or earned. In this category we may distinguish perquisites; for example, the benefits that come because of one's position or employment in addition to salary such as the use of a car. And we may distinguish prerogatives, the benefits and immunities held by people by virtue of a position they hold; for example, by being elected or appointed to a position of leadership. In these cases, the privileges are associated not with the person who benefits but with the position the person occupies and with the power of institutionalized authority. Prerogatives may be grounded either in law or in custom as, for example, the prerogatives of the president to be saluted by members of the armed services and to throw the first pitch at the opening of baseball season. And we may also distinguish earned privileges as, for example, those accorded to individuals and teams that have been exemplary in athletic, scholastic, military, or scientific competition.

In contrast, often individuals and groups benefit from illegitimate or unearned privilege. Illegitimate and unearned privileges reflect primarily custom, although such privileges may also be technically legal when the law has been written to conform to custom rather than to reflect rights. An example of illegitimate and unearned privilege would be the customs and laws of the long period of racial segregation in American history. People with white skin expected to receive, not through the exercise of their greater power but merely through the having of that power, both advantages and immunities with respect to transportation and hotel accommodations, service in department stores and restaurants, treatment under law enforcement and judicial systems, and opportunities for education, health care, and housing that people with dark skin could not expect to receive.

The line between legitimate and illegitimate privilege often is difficult to discern and, even when it occasionally becomes clear, continues to change because of the dynamics of power among individuals and groups in society. Consider, for example, the long-standing prerogative of the father of the bride to have the second dance on her wedding day. Many would argue that this is a legitimate prerogative, while others argue that it needs to be examined and changed. The contest for power among groups in American society, including groups defined by their gender, race, ethnicity, religion, and social class, and the question of what rights and privileges members of those groups should have, are among the issues discussed in the chapters that follow. In many sectors of American society, what have been assumed with little consideration to be established rights and privileges are now in question, as those who historically have had less power are now demanding the same rights and privileges as the more powerful.

Sixteen Model Dialogues

What is the relationship of power and privilege to the four American perspectives presented in chapters 1, 2, and 3? Individuals and groups holding each of the perspectives— Loyal, Tactful, Detached, and Caring—can be more or less strong with respect to power. We can contrast the institutionalized authority, the control over resources, and the political skill of George Washington and Theodore Roosevelt (both examples of the Loyal perspective) and perhaps conclude the former was more powerful than the latter (or vice versa). Similarly, we can conclude on the basis of control over resources, political skill, and leadership ability that Henry Clay was more powerful than Franklin D. Roosevelt (or vice versa), although both are good representatives of the Tactful perspective.

   Daniel Boone might be perceived as stronger than Henry David Thoreau (both representing the Detached perspective) in his expertise at hunting and trapping, whereas Thoreau might be perceived as stronger than Boone in his moral beliefs and ability to communicate those beliefs to others. Would

Jane Addams or Eleanor Roosevelt (both illustrating the Caring perspective) be considered the more powerful? Perhaps we would choose Addams as stronger on the basis of her leadership abilities or Roosevelt on the basis of her emotional resources, including acceptance and compassion.

Returning to the question with which this chapter began—what happens when two people holding the Loyal, Tactful, Detached, or Caring perspectives meet and interact?—we now see sixteen possible relationships, conversations, or dialogues between people holding these perspectives and having more or less power, as shown in table 4.1.

Table 4.1. Sixteen Dialogues and Thirty-Two Standpoints

Dialogue 1. Weak Loyal versus Strong Loyal
Dialogue 2. Weak Loyal versus Strong Tactful
Dialogue 3. Weak Loyal versus Strong Detached
Dialogue 4. Weak Loyal versus Strong Caring

Dialogue 5. Weak Tactful versus Strong Loyal
Dialogue 6. Weak Tactful versus Strong Tactful
Dialogue 7. Weak Tactful versus Strong Detached
Dialogue 8. Weak Tactful versus Strong Caring

Dialogue 9. Weak Detached versus Strong Loyal
Dialogue 10. Weak Detached versus Strong Tactful
Dialogue 11. Weak Detached versus Strong Detached
Dialogue 12. Weak Detached versus Strong Caring

Dialogue 13. Weak Caring versus Strong Loyal
Dialogue 14. Weak Caring versus Strong Tactful
Dialogue 15. Weak Caring versus Strong Detached
Dialogue 16. Weak Caring versus Strong Caring

Examination of the sixteen model dialogues reveals that an individual or group holding any combination of perspective and power can be in one of four possible conversations or dialogues. For example, someone holding the Loyal perspective and lesser power—the Weak Loyal standpoint—can be in dialogue with someone holding the Strong Loyal, Strong Tactful, Strong Detached, or Strong Caring standpoints, as shown in the dialogues numbered 1, 2, 3, and 4. If George Washington and Theodore Roosevelt were to have a conversation, this might be considered a Weak Loyal versus Strong Loyal dialogue (or vice versa). In this context, "weak" refers to relative power and is not intended to mean inadequate, ineffective, or undesirable.

How an individual or group in the Weak Loyal standpoint views others, and how others view someone in the Weak Loyal standpoint, will depend on which perspectives, weak and strong, are in dialogue with each other. Table 4.2 shows how each of the sixteen strong standpoints is viewed from the four weak standpoints; and table 4.3 shows how each of the sixteen weak standpoints is viewed from the four strong standpoints.

So, for example, in dialogue 2, the Weak Loyal standpoint views the Strong Tactful standpoint as wrong, unworthy, manipulative, threatening, and deceitful (table 4.2), whereas the Strong Tactful standpoint views the Weak Loyal standpoint as useful, unsophisticated, immature, aggressive, and rebellious (table 4.3). To make this particular dialogue concrete, consider a conversation between a Weak Loyal Theodore Roosevelt and a Strong Tactful Henry Clay and how each might view the other.

As a second example, in dialogue 15, the Weak Caring standpoint views the Strong Detached standpoint as enriching, able, insensitive, aloof, and apathetic (table 4.2), whereas the Strong Detached standpoint views the Weak Caring standpoint as intrusive, bothersome, naive, idealistic, and vexatious (table 4.3). Consider a conversation between a Weak Caring Jane Addams and a Strong Detached Daniel Boone and how they might view each other.

Table 4.2. How Weak Standpoints View Strong Standpoints

Weak Loyal		Weak Detached	
1 Strong Loyal	*3 Strong Detached*	*9 Strong Loyal*	*11 Strong Detached*
Wrong	Wrong	Intrusive	Intrusive
Unworthy	Unworthy	Bothersome	Bothersome
Immature	Insensitive	Immature	Insensitive
Aggressive	Aloof	Aggressive	Aloof
Corrupt	Patronizing	Dictatorial	Maladroit
2 Strong Tactful	*4 Strong Caring*	*10 Strong Tactful*	*12 Strong Caring*
Wrong	Wrong	Intrusive	Intrusive
Unworthy	Unworthy	Bothersome	Bothersome
Manipulative	Naive	Manipulative	Naive
Threatening	Idealistic	Threatening	Idealistic
Deceitful	Misguided	Powerful	Smothering

Weak Tactful		Weak Caring	
5 Strong Loyal	*7 Strong Detached*	*13 Strong Loyal*	*15 Strong Detached*
Useful	Useful	Enriching	Enriching
Unsophis-ticated	Unsophis-ticated	Able	Able
Immature	Insensitive	Immature	Insensitive
Aggressive	Aloof	Aggressive	Aloof
Tyrannical	Disengaged	Perplexing	Apathetic
6 Strong Tactful	*8 Strong Caring*	*14 Strong Tactful*	*16 Strong Caring*
Useful	Useful	Enriching	Enriching
Unsophis-ticated	Unsophis-ticated	Able	Able
Manipulative	Naive	Manipulative	Naive
Threatening	Idealistic	Threatening	Idealistic
Domineering	Forceful	Overbearing	Nurturing

Table 4.3. How Strong Standpoints View Weak Standpoints

Strong Loyal   **Strong Detached**

1 Weak	*9 Weak*	*3 Weak*	*11 Weak*
Loyal	*Detached*	*Loyal*	*Detached*
Wrong	Wrong	Intrusive	Intrusive
Unworthy	Unworthy	Bothersome	Bothersome
Immature	Insensitive	Immature	Insensitive
Aggressive	Aloof	Aggressive	Aloof
Deficient	Conceited	Unprovoked	Isolated

5 Weak	*13 Weak*	*7 Weak*	*15 Weak*
Tactful	*Caring*	*Tactful*	*Caring*
Wrong	Wrong	Intrusive	Intrusive
Unworthy	Unworthy	Bothersome	Bothersome
Manipulative	Naive	Manipulative	Naive
Threatening	Idealistic	Threatening	Idealistic
Presumptuous	Insignificant	Conspiratorial	Vexatious

Strong Tactful   **Strong Caring**

2 Weak	*10 Weak*	*4 Weak*	*12 Weak*
Loyal	*Detached*	*Loyal*	*Detached*
Useful	Useful	Enriching	Enriching
Unsophis-ticated	Unsophis-ticated	Able	Able
Immature	Insensitive	Immature	Insensitive
Aggressive	Aloof	Aggressive	Aloof
Rebellious	Alienated	Dogmatic	Indifferent

6 Weak	*14 Weak*	*8 Weak*	*16 Weak*
Tactful	*Caring*	*Tactful*	*Caring*
Useful	Useful	Enriching	Enriching
Unsophis-ticated	Unsophis-ticated	Able	Able
Manipulative	Naive	Manipulative	Naive
Threatening	Idealistic	Threatening	Idealistic
Gullible	Easy Prey	Petty	Promising

Tables 4.2 and 4.3 are not as complex as they might at first appear. The first four terms in each set merely repeat how from each perspective all of the other perspectives and standpoints are viewed (already shown in table 3.3) and how each perspective is viewed from all the other perspectives and standpoints (as shown in table 3.5).[2]

The fifth term in each set is unique for each of the thirty-two standpoints. For example, in the first dialogue, Weak Loyal versus Strong Loyal, Strong Loyal is viewed as corrupt (table 4.2), and Weak Loyal is viewed as deficient (table 4.3). Again, not to press the point, but merely to illustrate, consider a dialogue between a Weak Loyal George Washington and a Strong Loyal Theodore Roosevelt. As a second example, in dialogue 13, Weak Caring versus Strong Loyal, Strong Loyal is viewed as perplexing (table 4.2), and Weak Caring is viewed as insignificant (table 4.3). Consider a dialogue between a Weak Caring Jane Addams and a Strong Loyal Theodore Roosevelt.

To get more interesting, compare dialogue 7, Weak Tactful versus Strong Detached with dialogue 10, Weak Detached versus Strong Tactful. Both dialogues involve the same two perspectives, but the relative power of the standpoints has been reversed, leading to a substantial difference in how each standpoint is viewed by the other. In the case of dialogue 7, Weak Tactful views Strong Detached as disengaged (table 4.2) and Strong Detached views Weak Tactful as conspiratorial (table 4.3). However, when the relative power of the standpoints is reversed, in dialogue 10, Weak Detached views Strong Tactful as powerful (table 4.2) and Strong Tactful views Weak Detached as alienated (table 4.3).

To make the comparisons in the preceding paragraph concrete, imagine a dialogue between a Weak Tactful Henry Clay and a Strong Detached Daniel Boone. Henry Clay would view Daniel Boone as disengaged (table 4.2) and Daniel Boone would view Henry Clay as conspiratorial (table 4.3). Now imagine that the relative power of the standpoints is reversed, for example, a Weak Detached Henry David Thoreau in dialogue with a Strong Tactful Franklin Delano Roosevelt. Thoreau would view Roosevelt as powerful (table 4.2) and Roosevelt would view Thoreau as alienated (table 4.3).

In short, as in the example just given, a change in relative power can change the nature of the dialogue from disengagement and conspiracy, on the one hand, to alienation and power, on the other. The dialogue between these two people or groups will proceed quite differently as a function of the differential in power. With this example, we have come to the main contribution of this chapter: how people behave toward each other and how relationships develop depends on the perspectives of the observers and the observed and their relative power.

The terms shown in tables 4.2 and 4.3 may seem arbitrary at this point. Whether or not they are good descriptions of each standpoint will be tested in the following four chapters, where this framework of sixteen model dialogues will be illustrated with real world examples of interactions between individuals and groups rather than merely "what if" examples. In the first of these four chapters, concrete illustrations of each of the four Weak Loyal dialogues (dialogues 1, 2, 3, and 4)—with Strong Loyal, Strong Tactful, Strong Detached, and Strong Caring—will be provided.

Part II

Sixteen Model Dialogues

5

Being in Charge:
The Weak Loyal Dialogues

The two major political parties now focus on message wars and symbolic votes; for example, on guns and climate change, while failing to enact legislation critical for our country's future. Image and branding have become more important than facts, loyalty to party more important than to country. Issues that should be nonpartisan such as education, climate change, and infrastructure are now partisan. Among these now highly polarized and polarizing issues are how to provide good jobs for middle-class Americans, how to protect religious freedom for all Americans, and how men and women can navigate their changing roles in American society. These questions and more are addressed in the present chapter.

This chapter also presents the Weak Loyal dialogues. The Loyal perspective is defined by self-contained identity and intention to control; people and groups holding the Loyal perspective aim to compete and be in charge. From the Loyal perspective, we are proud of and committed to our own identity and community. Other people are viewed as less worthy and as threatening to ourselves. Examples from chapter 1 include Tom Venn, the Alaska businessman; Rosalind Steed, the plantation owner; and Floyd Rusk, the Texas oilman. Examples from chapter 2 include George Washington and Theodore Roosevelt.

There are four Weak Loyal dialogues, as people holding the Loyal perspective interact with those holding the Loyal, Tactful, Detached, or Caring perspective who also have greater power and privilege (table 4.1). In this chapter, current issues in American society are presented in terms of these Weak Loyal dialogues: first, how people holding each perspective perceive those holding the other perspective in the dialogue (tables 4.2 and 4.3); and second, how people holding each perspective behave towards those holding the other perspective in the dialogue (table 3.4). Readers will discover what people holding the Loyal perspective have in common across diverse contexts, and also how the perceptions and behaviors of Weak Loyal people and groups can be modified depending on which perspective—Loyal, Tactful, Detached, or Caring—they are in dialogue with.

Dialogue 1. Weak Loyal versus Strong Loyal
Small Business versus Big Business

You've Got Mail, the romantic comedy starring Meg Ryan and Tom Hanks and directed by Nora Ephron, neatly illustrates the dialogue of Weak Loyal together with Strong Loyal. E-mailing anonymously in a chat room, Ryan and Hanks are initially unaware that they are business rivals, she owning a small, independent bookstore and he representing a chain of large bookstores that will surely put her out of business. Ironically, as this movie was first showing in 1998, Amazon.com, started in 1994, was threatening the future of bookstore chains such as Barnes & Noble and Borders. Borders went bankrupt in 2011.

Small neighborhood businesses giving way to large national chains has become routine in recent decades, as tens of thousands of independently owned grocery, pharmacy, hardware, electronics, clothing, stationery, toy, and pet stores and restaurants have been replaced by national chains such as Walmart, Target, CVS Caremark, Rite Aid, Home Depot, Lowe's, Best Buy, Sears, J.C. Penney, Staples, Office Depot, Toys "R" Us, PetSmart, McDonald's, Subway, Starbucks Coffee, Pizza Hut, Domino's Pizza, and others.

The context for these changes in the business world is free market capitalism. In a capitalist economic system, businesses are privately owned and controlled. Their purpose is to generate and maximize profits by purchasing raw materials at low cost, minimizing the number of employees and their wages and benefits, creating and producing products and services, and then selling these at high prices. Profits can be invested in product research and development, new equipment and facilities, and compensation for workers and distributed as payments to owners, investors, and shareholders. In competitive markets, the interactions of supply and demand and of producers and consumers should lead to a consensus on fair prices for goods and services. An ideal free market is one without government intervention that might regulate working conditions and wages or encourage competition and influence prices for consumers.

Most businesses in free market capitalism illustrate the Loyal perspective: self-contained and responsible only to themselves, in conflict with their workers and in competition with similar businesses, striving to be free from government regulation, and with the singular purpose of controlling their growth and profit. The Loyal perspective underlies the values and actions of both small, independently owned neighborhood stores and large national chains, many of which began as single, independently owned stores that only later became the chain brands so familiar today. Examples include Barnes & Noble (first store in New York City, 1886), McDonald's (Des Plaines, Illinois, 1955), Pizza Hut (Wichita,

Kansas, 1958), Domino's Pizza (Ann Arbor, Michigan, 1960), WalMart (Rogers, Arkansas, 1962), Subway (Bridgeport, Connecticut, 1965), Borders (Ann Arbor, Michigan, 1971), and Starbucks Coffee (Seattle, 1971).

Interactions between individuals and groups who hold the Loyal perspective, because they do not differ in terms of the underlying assumptions, are essentially struggles over power (chapter 4): How can each party in the conflict best acquire, maintain, and increase its power over the other? Metaphors such as "winner-take-all," "two scorpions in a bottle," "zero-sum combat," and "no-holds barred" are appropriate, for both the Weak Loyal and Strong Loyal standpoints provide justification for dominating and even destroying the other party in the conflict. Each group feels proud and self-righteous, convinced that its own values and goals are worthy, and that the values and goals of the other are wrong, unworthy, and insignificant. This conviction provides a rationale for refusing to yield any of the power and privilege associated with one's own identity and community and for acting towards others with little or no regard for the integrity of their lives and communities.

From the Weak Loyal standpoint, the Strong Loyal standpoint appears aggressive and rightly to be feared. Weak Loyal, because it holds to the same underlying assumptions and the same perspective as Strong Loyal, understands well that this conflict is about power and dominance and ultimately about survival. So, for example, Meg Ryan understands that the survival of The Shop Around the Corner is at stake following the opening by Tom Hanks of a Fox Books chain store in her neighborhood. Weak Loyal is correct in believing that Strong Loyal would, if it felt sufficiently threatened, pursue almost any means to control, dominate, and even destroy Weak Loyal.

From the Weak Loyal standpoint, a dominant feature of Strong Loyal is its greater power. National chains can take advantage of efficiencies of scale, are able to undercut smaller competitors on price, have the floor space to display more products (for example, book titles), and can grow their market share by forcing competitors out of business. Bookstore chains have the market power to pressure publishers and wholesalers for favorable terms not available to independent bookstores. Weak Loyal views this power as corrupting, abusive, and oppressive, even though Weak Loyal would like to acquire more of the same power and privilege.

From the Strong Loyal standpoint, a dominant feature of the Weak Loyal group is its weakness, which can be taken as validation of the relative worth of the two groups. Nevertheless, Strong Loyal always regards Weak Loyal, despite its deficiencies, as a potential threat. At some level Strong Loyal recognizes that, if their situations were somehow reversed, Weak Loyal would strive to wrest power away from Strong Loyal. A small business would like to have the market share and profits of a competing big business. Yet in fact, Weak Loyal may be quite lacking in the resources needed to pose any serious threat to Strong Loyal's power, so this view of Weak Loyal can be merely a projection of Strong Loyal's own intentions onto Weak Loyal.

Weak Loyal Meg Ryan must calculate whether the threat that Strong Loyal Tom Hanks poses to her bookstore, identity, and community is sufficient that resources should be expended to resist. Some independent bookstores have come together in trade associations that lobby for enhanced government regulation to counter the power of large bookstore chains. Stereotyping and the use of derogatory terms to describe Strong Loyal—big-box store, megastore, category killer—can be defensive tactics against Weak Loyal's potential loss of identity and community.

An independent bookstore owner could also adopt the Tactful perspective and seek allies among owners of nearby neighborhood businesses. They might work together by promoting a buy-local campaign that keeps money in the local business community. They could point out that small businesses power the American economy, employing more Americans and creating more new jobs than large businesses.

Or a bookstore owner could adopt a Detached perspective, giving up the quest for control and profit and focusing instead on sharing and understanding great literature and the craft of writing and providing a personal touch in knowing the customers and serving their personal reading needs.

Or, adopting a Caring perspective, an independent bookstore could be transformed into a community-gathering place for citizens to share their views and concerns on local issues and organize themselves for community action. Of course, any of these actions might lead to a true change away from the Loyal to another perspective, as the independent bookstore owner begins to take pride in being part of and nurturing the local economy and community. Indeed, often it is the local retail landscape, including small and unique bookstores, that contributes to the color, vitality, and personality of a city or town. Consider the impact of, for example, J. Michaels Books, Powell's Books, City Lights, Book Passage, Kramerbooks & Afterwards, Politics and Prose Bookstore, Elliott Bay Book Company, Seminary Co-Op, Malaprop's Bookstore/Cafe, Astoria Bookshop, Trident Booksellers and Cafe, Joseph Fox Bookshop, and many more.

Strong Loyal must calculate whether the threat posed by Weak Loyal is large enough that resources should be expended to control and perhaps destroy Weak Loyal. Strong Loyal can rationalize its domination and perhaps the eventual destruction of Weak Loyal by emphasizing differences, rather than commonalities, between the two groups; that is, by building on the assumption of intrinsically defined identity. Using stereotyping and derogatory descriptions, for example, claiming mom-and-pop bookstores are dying, can heighten the psychological impact of minor differences.

A tactic Strong Loyal can pursue to prevent Weak Loyal from understanding its true intention is to masquerade as Tactful, Detached, or Caring. So bookstore chains now feature author tours with book readings and book signings, have modified their store layouts to include coffee and wine bars, overstuffed chairs, a more boutique feel, and free Wi-Fi access, and sponsor reading programs to promote literacy and book collections and donations for children. Alternatively, it can be in Strong Loyal's interest to attempt to convert Weak Loyal to its own identity and community. In the movie *You've Got Mail*, Meg Ryan closes The Shop Around the Corner and opens an alcove in one of Tom Hanks' Fox Books chain stores.

Dialogue 2. Weak Loyal versus Strong Tactful
Cheating versus Sportsmanship

The Tactful perspective is defined by interdependent identity and intention to control; the aim is to compete and be in charge. From the Tactful perspective, the nature, preservation, and strengthening of personal identity and community reflect agreements and alliances with other individuals and groups. Others are viewed in terms of relationships to be manipulated to increase one's own power. Examples from chapter 1 include John Whipple, the Hawaii plantation owner; Paul Garrett, the Colorado rancher; and Earnshaw Rusk, the Texas rancher. Examples from chapter 2 include Henry Clay and Franklin D. Roosevelt.

Sports competition provides a clear illustration of how, from the Tactful perspective, relations are interdependent in nature. Individuals and groups are defined not as self-contained entities but instead through their relations with others. An athlete or team cannot compete and win by playing alone; it is central to the nature of sports that there must be an opposing athlete or team to play against. Just as important as winning is to maintain good relations with our opponents, to have opportunities to play again in the future. Players are motivated to play fairly and according to the rules, so that their opponents will play fairly against them in subsequent games. As players advance through their professional careers and move from one team to another, this year's opponents might well be next year's teammates.

This Tactful perspective is evident in multiple examples of

good sportsmanship in both team and individual sports. To be a good sport is to play fairly and with respect for one's opponents, to be graceful both in losing and in winning, and to accept responsibility for our mistakes. For example, in 2005 Adam Van Houton, competing for the Ohio high school golf championship, realized one of his partners had written a five on Van Houton's scorecard when he should have written a six. Although he knew he would be disqualified from the state championship Van Houton, who had already signed the scorecard, still called attention to the error.

In 2008, J. P. Hayes, playing on the Professional Golfers' Association tour, realized he had mistakenly used a prototype golf ball not yet approved for competition. Hayes nevertheless reported the error to tour officials and was disqualified. Golf is unusual in the expectation that individual players monitor their own adherence to the rules, rather than relying on umpires or referees to police the players.

There are many examples of good sportsmanship in other types of competition. In 2008 during a Great Northwest Athletic Conference game, a player for Western Oregon University hit a three-run home run. However, in rounding first base she injured her knee and could not continue. Official rules prohibited her team members from helping her run the bases. At this point Mallory Holtman, the pitcher for the opposing Central Washington University team, asked permission from the umpires to assist. Holtman and her teammates carried the injured runner around the bases and to home plate. Western Oregon University won, four to two.

In an Ohio high school track meet in 2012, Meghan Vogel saw a competitor collapse in front of her. Rather than run by her, Vogel helped the exhausted runner run the remaining 20 meters and pushed her across the finish line ahead of herself. In the 2015 Australian Open tennis tournament, when a fan shouted inappropriately during his opponent's serve in a four-hour match, Tim Smyczek signaled to the umpire to allow his opponent another serving opportunity. Smyczek, who at one point thought he might win the match, lost in the end.

Consistent with the Tactful perspective, all of these athletes were fiercely competitive and among the very best in their sports. Yet they also recognized that as important as winning is playing fairly and honorably, respecting the efforts of their opponents, and upholding the integrity of the game. J. P. Hayes, asked about his decision to disqualify himself, said, "Everybody out here on the PGA tour would have done the same thing." Meghan Vogel commented afterward, "Any girl on the track would have done the same for me." Tim Smyczek said, referring to his opponent in the match, "I think he probably would have done the same thing if it was reversed." These athletes all viewed their opponents as people like themselves. They understood that maintaining a level playing field—playing by the agreed-on-rules—is central to the integrity of competitive sports and to the meaning of winning.

In contrast, the Weak Loyal perspective in sports competition is illustrated by the New Orleans Saints football team bounty scandal. From 2009 to 2011, a coach and two dozen players collaborated in a scheme to intentionally injure players on the opposing team, for which a Saints player could receive as much as $10,000 as a bounty. After the scandal broke, the National Football League fined the Saints franchise $500,000 and cancelled a portion of their draft picks for two years. Consistent with the Weak Loyal perspective, the Saints sacrificed their good relations with other teams and players to focus on their own team's identity and winning at any cost.

A second example of the Weak Loyal perspective in team sports is the use by bicyclist Lance Armstrong and his teammates of illegal performance-enhancing drugs from 1999 to 2005. Because of this scandal, Armstrong was stripped of his seven Tour de France titles and dropped by his sponsors. The use of illegal performance-enhancing drugs has been a long-term problem for major league baseball in the United States, according to the 2007 Mitchell Report. Further examples of cheating in sports include the 1996 knee-bashing of Olympic ice-skating champion Nancy Kerrigan by the husband of her competitor Tanya Harding and the 1980

Boston Marathon scandal in which Rosie Ruiz appeared to have won until it was discovered she had dropped out of the pack of competitors and taken the subway to a station near the finish line and then rejoined the race.

We turn now to the general features of the Weak Loyal versus Strong Tactful dialogue. From the Weak Loyal cheating standpoint, the values and goals of its own group are worthy, whereas the values and goals of the Strong Tactful sportsmanship group are not. Despite this, Weak Loyal is confronted with the fact that Strong Tactful represents a stronger community—for example, in material resources, emotional resources, expertise, or determination (see chapter 4)—that can potentially win against and harm Weak Loyal. The New Orleans Saints, Lance Armstrong's bicycling team, and numerous baseball players were faced with the fact that, unless they cheated, they would likely lose to more able competitors.

Weak Loyal cheaters regard sportsmanlike actions by Strong Tactful as a potential threat to their identity and community. They feel justified in guarding against efforts by Strong Tactful to increase its power and prestige at the expense of Weak Loyal; that is, they feel justified in cheating. Strong Tactful's assertions that both groups are, at some level, members of the same community and mutually dependent—sports teams competing fairly on a level playing field—will be difficult for Weak Loyal to hear and understand, given Weak Loyal's assumption of a self-contained, intrinsically defined identity.

Strong Tactful's attitudes and behaviors are grounded in the assumption that groups are defined through interdependent relations with other groups. For Strong Tactful athletes and teams, any competition is of course about control, winning, and success. Yet to be members of a shared community means everyone should follow certain accepted conventions, rules, and principles. Winning a sports competition at the cost of breaking the rules or engaging in unsportsmanlike conduct is not acceptable. Strong Tactful looks on Weak Loyal's assertions of a separate identity and community as naive, inappropriate, unsophisticated, aggressive, and rebellious (table 4.3).

From the Loyal perspective, the understanding of community is always an either-or understanding: one belongs either in this community or in another community, in my community or in your community, on my team or your team. From the Tactful perspective, the understanding of community is always a both-and understanding: one belongs both to this community and to other superordinate or subordinate communities, both to my own team and to the larger sports community. Therefore, in addition to the issue of power, the Weak Loyal versus Strong Tactful conflict can involve disagreement over the nature of community.

Dialogue 2. Weak Loyal versus Strong Tactful
Fundamentalism versus Secularism

In 2001 Alabama Chief Justice Roy Moore arranged for a two-ton granite block inscribed with the Ten Commandments to be placed in the rotunda of the Supreme Court building. The American Civil Liberties Union and other secular groups sued, arguing this was government endorsement of religion in general and Judeo-Christianity in particular. Moore argued, as Christian fundamentalists do, that God is the supreme authority over both religion and the state, the Ten Commandments are the moral and ethical foundation of American law, and the display of the Ten Commandments is therefore not illegal. Federal courts ruled against Moore and the monument was removed and, in 2003, the Alabama Court of the Judiciary removed Moore from his position as Chief Justice. Throughout, however, Moore received substantial public support from fundamentalist political leaders and thousands of participants at public rallies. In 2012, Moore was reelected as Chief Justice of the Alabama Supreme Court.

Christian fundamentalists feel they are a minority group

in the United States, marginalized and oppressed because of their religious beliefs and under assault by a secularist movement determined to destroy their religion and their communities. Fundamentalism is distinctive in its belief in the inerrancy of the Bible; that is, the belief that the Bible is the actual word of God and free from error. Fundamentalists view the Bible as the primary guide to what is true and to public morality, and they view Christianity as unique among all religions. For fundamentalists, an authoritative interpretation of the Bible is more compelling than the authority of the Constitution or the US Supreme Court. This is a Weak Loyal standpoint, focusing on one's own beliefs and community and viewing all other groups and their beliefs as less worthy and as threatening. (In dialogue 10 in chapter 7, religion is presented from a Weak Detached perspective.)

In contrast, secularism is the principle of government neutrality with respect to the religious beliefs and practices of individuals combined with the view that government decisions should not be influenced by any particular religious beliefs or practices. America's diverse religious groups as well as atheists exist in a complex tension with each other and with the government, as they strive to maintain and advance their particular beliefs and practices while at the same time continuing to live and govern together. Secularism has been a useful principle for negotiating these differences and reducing tensions among religious and atheist groups and between these groups and the government. The First Amendment and the principle of secularism reflect a Strong Tactful standpoint.

The US Supreme Court has, however, made several rulings that Weak Loyal fundamentalists interpret as defeats by an opposing Strong Tactful secularist movement. In 1963 the Supreme Court ruled that requiring a Bible reading or recitation of Christian prayers in public schools is unconstitutional. In 1968 an Arkansas law prohibiting the teaching of evolution, because this conflicted with the Bible, was ruled unconstitutional. In 1987 the Supreme Court ruled that a Louisiana law requiring the teaching of "creation science" in public schools is unconstitutional. A 1992 ruling prohibited public schools from holding religious prayers led by clergy during graduation ceremonies.

The reasoning underlying these and similar rulings is set forth in *Lemon versus Kurtzman* (1971): Whether a law remains constitutional, given the requirements of the First Amendment, depends on whether it has a legitimate secular purpose, does not have a primary effect of either advancing or inhibiting religion, and does not result in excessive entanglement of government and religion. Weak Loyal fundamentalists, however, argue that the "Lemon test" is vague and subjective and restricts their religious freedom.

Another illustration of Weak Loyal versus Strong Tactful conflict involves Kim Davis, a county clerk in Kentucky, who refused to issue marriage licenses following the 2015 decision by the Supreme Court that the Fourteenth Amendment guarantees to same-sex couples the right to marriage. Davis argued, consistent with the Weak Loyal fundamentalist standpoint, that such marriage licenses would conflict with God's definition of marriage as between a man and a woman, that she was acting "under God's authority," and that issuing such marriage licenses would violate her religious freedom and rights under the First Amendment.

Davis's supporters, including fundamentalist politicians, argued that the state of Kentucky should accommodate her religious beliefs and that her brief imprisonment was an attack on and a "criminalization of Christianity." Fundamentalists believe the authority of their religion and the Bible is supreme over the Constitution and a secular government should be constrained from interfering with their religious freedom. (Davis's supporters included Chief Justice Roy Moore, who ordered Alabama's probate judges not to issue same-sex marriage licenses. Following charges filed by the Judicial Inquiry Commission in 2016, Moore was suspended for a second time.) In public surveys, a quarter to a third of Americans said they supported Kim Davis in this controversy.

Ironically, Davis was using her religious freedom, guaranteed by the First Amendment, to argue that her religious beliefs were above the law. Davis argued that she was entitled to religious accommodation and not required to carry out the duties of her office and enforce the law if doing so would be in conflict with her religious beliefs. From the Strong Tactful secular standpoint, Davis was attempting to use her religious freedom to discriminate against gay and lesbian Americans. From the secular standpoint, religious accommodation means that the beliefs and practices of individuals should be protected from undue restraint or impositions by employers or the government. However, religious accommodation does not mean that individuals are entitled to hold their religious beliefs above the law, or to impose their beliefs on government or others. Americans who do not happen to share fundamentalist or other religious beliefs are protected as well by the First Amendment.

This long-standing tension between Weak Loyal fundamentalists and Strong Tactful secularists continues. Some Weak Loyal fundamentalists accuse secularists of attempting to privatize religion, keeping it out of public life in America. They argue, instead, that religious individuals and organizations have a responsibility and the right to take active roles in society and in politics. Recently, fundamentalist politicians have introduced religious freedom legislation in several states that would provide accommodations and exemptions and shield religious organizations and leaders from having to participate in or acknowledge same-sex marriages. This religious freedom legislation would also give businesses such as florists and caterers the right to refuse to sell products or services for same-sex weddings.

However, from the Strong Tactful secular standpoint, there is concern that such laws could have broader consequences. For example, opponents of same-sex marriage could be encouraged by such laws to deny social services, education, employment, or housing to gay and lesbian Americans. Furthermore, such laws could become a slippery slope towards enabling businesses and government to deny services and opportunities on the basis of race, gender, or ethnicity. Strong Tactful secularists argue that such laws are unconstitutional, both in their differential treatment of same-sex couples and, in particular, in their privileging of particular fundamentalist religious beliefs over other beliefs.

From the Weak Loyal fundamentalist standpoint, the values and goals of its own community are worthy, whereas the values and goals of the Strong Tactful secular group are not. Despite this, Weak Loyal is confronted with the fact that Strong Tactful represents a stronger community—for example, in political legitimacy and skill—that can potentially cause harm to Weak Loyal. Weak Loyal fundamentalists regard actions by Strong Tactful secularists, such as the various Supreme Court rulings, as a threat to their religious identity and community, and feel justified in guarding against efforts by Strong Tactful to increase its power at the expense of Weak Loyal. Assertions by Strong Tactful secularists that both groups are, at some level, members of the same community and mutually dependent will be very difficult for Weak Loyal fundamentalists to hear and to understand, given their assumption of a self-contained, intrinsically defined religious group identity.

The attitudes and behaviors of Strong Tactful secularists are grounded in the assumption that groups are defined in large part through their relations with other groups. This understanding of the interdependent nature of community is further shaped by the assumption that the primary intention for humans is to compete with and control others. For Strong Tactful secularists any conflict is about competition and control. Yet to be members of a shared community means, for Strong Tactful, that the course of conflict should follow certain accepted conventions, rules, and principles, particularly as set forth in the Constitution and in rulings by the US Supreme Court.

Strong Tactful secularists look on assertions by Weak Loyal fundamentalists that their particular religious identity, beliefs, and community stand apart from American society as naive, inappropriate, unsophisticated, aggressive, rebellious, and perhaps even threatening (table 4.3). From the perspective of Strong Tactful, all groups in American society are members in a broader, shared community. Nevertheless, while from the Strong Tactful secularist perspective the intention is to dominate, it is to dominate not through destroying the other but rather through engaging the other in hierarchical relationships in a community broadly conceived.

From the Weak Loyal fundamentalist perspective, the understanding of community is always an either-or understanding: one belongs either in this community—a faith community, a community of believers, God's eternal community—or in another community—a worldly and temporal community defined by the ideas and writings of imperfect humans, such as the Constitution. From the Strong Tactful secularist perspective, the understanding of community is always a both-and understanding: one belongs both to this community and to other superordinate or subordinate communities. A Strong Tactful secularist would argue that it is the Constitution and the principle of secularism that ensure that Weak Loyal fundamentalists are able to hold their beliefs and pursue their practices without interference from government. So in addition to the issue of power, the Weak Loyal versus Strong Tactful conflict will involve debate over the nature of community.

Weak Loyal fundamentalists are concerned over the possibility of being assimilated into Strong Tactful's secular community or of being used in Strong Tactful's quest to enhance its own community and power. For example, in campaigning for election to public office, secular candidates sometimes pander to fundamentalist communities merely to obtain their votes. For Weak Loyal fundamentalist groups, the best defense may be to strive vigorously to maintain their own separate identity. This defensive effort can include striving for self-improvement and clarification of one's own religious identity.

Dialogue 3. Weak Loyal versus Strong Detached
Bullies versus Bystanders

The Detached perspective is defined by self-contained identity and intention to understand; the aim is to disengage from others and work things out by oneself. From the Detached perspective, identity and community are strengthened by being isolated from others and striving for self-understanding. Others are of little interest. Examples from chapter 1 include John Klope, the self-contained, independent Alaska miner; Amos Calendar, the Colorado cowboy who preferred living alone; and Edmund Steed, who immigrated to Maryland to live freely as a Catholic rather than under a Protestant majority. Examples from chapter 3 include Daniel Boone and Henry David Thoreau.

From the Detached perspective, a primary goal is to be disengaged from others who are different, to be left alone, to not have to get involved. Not wanting to get involved was the reason given by several people who witnessed the assault and murder of Kitty Genovese in New York City in 1964 yet nevertheless did not intervene or call the police. Social psychologists have termed this the bystander effect: people are less likely to help a victim when they believe there are other onlookers. This effect has also been described as diffusion of responsibility; that is, the belief that others, including those perhaps better able to help, will voluntarily step forward to help a victim.

Whether bystanders get involved or not is central to understanding bullying behaviors, in which a person repeatedly abuses, intimidates, harasses, or dominates another. Bullying occurs in a wide range of contexts such as bullying of elementary and high school students, bullying of teens on the internet, bullying of gays and lesbians, bullying in the workplace, and bullying of disabled people. A quarter of

American students report having been bullied; three quarters report having witnessed bullying. The consequences can be devastating for the targets of bullying, including depression and suicide.

The characteristics of bullies reflect the assumptions of the Loyal perspective. Bullies view themselves as special and as having little in common with others and especially with their targets, whom they aim to control and dominate. Some bullies are arrogant and narcissistic and view themselves as powerful; others may come to feel more powerful through abusing and demeaning their targets. Bullies choose as their targets those who appear to be different on the basis of small size, being new in school, sexual orientation, physical or mental disability, being shy or timid, being bright and talented, or not conforming to peer norms.

Whether bullying behaviors persist or are discouraged depends critically on whether and how bystanders who witness or become aware of bullying respond. Bystanders can include peers, teachers, school administrators, parents, police, and others. Bystanders have the power to encourage the bully to continue, to come to the defense of the target, or to not get involved. This power can include leadership abilities, determination, moral courage, and legitimate authority (chapter 4). The failure of bystanders to confront and thus passively accept bullying is taken by bullies to be tacit approval of their behavior. Indeed, bullies often count on bystanders to look the other way, to not get involved. The failure of peers, administrators, parents, and other authorities to use their actual power to intervene against bullies and support their targets has compounded the tragedy of adolescent suicides. Thus, in understanding bullying the key dialogue is between Weak Loyal bullies and Strong Detached bystanders.

Here are the general characteristics of Weak Loyal versus Strong Detached dialogues: From the Weak Loyal bully's standpoint, one's own values and goals are worthy, whereas the values and goals of the Strong Detached bystanders are not. Despite this, Weak Loyal is confronted with the fact that Strong Detached represents a stronger community, one that stands in the way of Weak Loyal's interest in increasing its power and prestige and one that can potentially cause much harm to Weak Loyal. Bullies typically pursue their targets when adults, authorities, or others who might intervene and defend the target from the bully are not present.

From the standpoint of Weak Loyal's intentions of control and domination, it is surprising that Strong Detached is not more assertive in its claims to power and authority and in confronting and discouraging the bully's behaviors. Weak Loyal is likely to regard the resources and strengths of Strong Detached as unearned, undeserved, and only weakly defended. In short, it appears the Strong Detached bystanders are naive in not understanding that the conflict with the bully is about control, domination, and perhaps survival of the school or workplace community and its values.

For Strong Detached bystanders, the primary goal is to be left alone so that they can pursue self-understanding in the boundaries of their own community. Other individuals and groups may be tolerated, but there is neither strong antipathy nor strong caring towards others. The actions of the Weak Loyal bully are viewed as intrusive, self- serving, unprovoked, aggressive, and immature (table 4.3). Nevertheless, the actions of Weak Loyal may also be viewed as threatening if Weak Loyal has sufficient power and resources. Indeed, Strong Detached bystanders may be concerned that if they speak up they will draw attention to themselves and the bully will then retaliate and make them a target.

Therefore it is in the interest of Strong Detached bystanders to remain vigilant and not permit Weak Loyal bullies to become sufficiently strong to challenge Strong Detached. Because of their lack of engagement with other groups, Strong Detached bystanders may often be insensitive towards the needs of others who perhaps appear different and are often targets of bullying, such as new kids in school, gays and lesbians, and the disabled. Strong Detached bystanders may not have a good sense of their own power relative to other individuals. Bystanders fail to recognize that they have sufficient power to confront the Weak Loyal bully, whereas a target typically does not. While being privileged, Strong Detached bystanders may at the same time deny their own privileged status; that is, they fail to recognize they do have sufficient power to confront a bully.

Strong Detached's modes of relating to other individuals and groups include focusing on its own self-sufficiency and avoiding engagement with others. Teachers and school administrators too often ignore, deny, or minimize complaints of bullying, by saying "kids will be kids" or tacitly agreeing the target of bullying is different from other students (blaming the victim). Many teachers claim they do intervene to discourage bullying, but many students say they rarely observe this. The parents of eleven-year-old Carl Walker-Hoover and eleven-year-old Ty Field sought help from school officials on numerous occasions about the continual bullying of their sons. Carl committed suicide in Massachusetts in 2009, and Ty committed suicide in Oklahoma in 2010. These parents and many others believe their children's schools should be doing more to respond to and prevent bullying.

Consistent with the Detached perspective, bystanders are reluctant to get involved and use the power they have, and so Weak Loyal bullies are able to continue their bullying with impunity. Strong Detached bystanders often underestimate the power they can have if they would work together to find solutions to bullying. What is needed to reduce and eliminate bullying is for bystanders to reach out to each other, establish closer ties of friendship and support among themselves, recognize and accept that bullies and their targets are a part of the bystanders' community, and become defenders and allies of targets and work together with bullies to seek solutions. This can be difficult for to do, for it implies moving away from the self-contained, non-overlapping identities of the Loyal and Detached perspectives and towards the interdependent, community-oriented Tactful and Caring perspectives (for example, dialogue 2, Weak Loyal versus Strong Tactful, or dialogue 4, Weak Loyal versus Strong Caring).

Dialogue 4. Weak Loyal versus Strong Caring
Opponents versus Supporters of Women's Rights

The Caring perspective is defined by interdependent identity and intention to understand; the aim is to cooperate with others and look out for others. From the Caring perspective, our own identity and community depend on the welfare of others' identities and communities. Others are viewed as worthy and as enriching our own lives. Examples from chapter 1 include Maxwell Mercy, the army captain in Colorado; Missy Peckham, the social worker in Alaska; Michael Healy, the revenue cutter captain in Alaska; and Hans Brumbaugh, the Colorado farmer. Examples from chapter 3 include Jane Addams and Eleanor Roosevelt.

The persistent effort to gain the right to vote for women in America was part of a broader movement for women's rights, including the rights to education, to own property, to enter into legal contracts, to work outside the home, and to hold public office. In the seventeenth century in Europe, women were commonly regarded, consistent with the Loyal perspective, as less than human, inferior to men, with a status similar to children, slaves, and non-whites. By the nineteenth century, this view was challenged by the belief that all individuals, regardless of gender or other characteristics, have certain natural rights based on their common humanity. This latter belief is consistent with the Caring perspective.

"We hold these truths to be self-evident: that all men and women are created equal," reads the Declaration of Rights and Sentiments, the document written by the participants at the 1848 Seneca Falls Convention. At the urging of Elizabeth Cady Stanton, this document denounced the forced submission of women to laws in which they had no voice and the denial to women of the right to vote. For several decades, however, there was substantial opposition to guaranteeing the right to vote for women. It was not until 1920 that the Nineteenth Amendment, prohibiting denial of the right to vote on the basis of sex, was ratified by the thirty-sixth state and became law.

The controversy and debate over the Nineteenth Amendment was not a simple matter of men versus women. Both men and women advocated extending the right to vote to women, and both men and women opposed this. Central to the argument against women's right to vote was that men and women are by nature distinct and separate, consistent with the Loyal perspective based on the assumption of firm boundaries between self and other. In particular, women were said to be irrational and emotional and incapable of participating in government and making sound decisions.

Men, in contrast, were capable not only of governing but also of controlling and protecting women. From this Loyal perspective, women had no legal status apart from their husbands. Women could not, for example, sign contracts without their husband's approval. Therefore it seemed reasonable that it was the man's role to decide the family's position on public affairs and then to vote accordingly. If women were to have the right to vote, this would lead to divisions in families and weaken the power and control of men.

A second argument against voting rights for women also followed from the Loyal assumption that men and women are by nature distinct and separate. By this argument, women were not necessarily inferior to men. Instead, women had different characteristics such as modesty, patience, and gentleness and unique responsibilities in managing households and raising children to be strong adults. For women to become involved in politics would distract them from fulfilling these responsibilities at home, where they are needed. This argument appealed to many women as well as men.

Further, it was said, women would be sullied by the corruption of politics. Women should not get mixed up in the public men's world and instead should remain pure and committed to their homes and children. They should leave it to men to run the government and take care of the women. (A counter-argument was that, if women are so different from men, how can men know and represent their needs? Instead, women should be able to vote for their own representatives and make their own laws.)

A third argument from the Loyal perspective, advanced primarily by middle- and upper-class conservative women (in particular, financially secure urban women), was that equality between men and women—implied if the right to vote were granted to women—would mean the loss of the privileged positions these women currently enjoyed. These women felt that they had sufficient access to the men who held powerful political positions and argued that, as women, they already had important roles in philanthropy and charitable work without needing the right to vote.

Similar arguments, grounded in the Loyal assumption of differences between men and women, were advanced a century later against ratification of the Equal Rights Amendment. The ERA, guaranteeing equal rights for women, was passed by Congress in 1972 but ratified by only thirty-five of the necessary thirty-eight states. Reflecting a Weak Loyal standpoint, the opponents, many of whom were women, argued the ERA would take away existing rights and benefits for women, such as exemption from the draft and military service and separate public toilets for women. Opponents also argued the ERA was anti-family, for it would remove the responsibility of men to support wives who did not want to work outside the home. And, it was argued, the ERA would eliminate the presumption that women would receive alimony, child support, and custody of their children in divorce cases.

Although the ERA was not ratified, the Strong Caring arguments made in the 1970s in support of the ERA significantly advanced the understanding of women's rights by both men and women. Women's rights to serve in the military, have access to reproductive health and birth control services, be free from rape and sexual harassment and assault, and have equal pay for the same work are now broadly accepted.

From the standpoint of Weak Loyal's intentions for control and domination, it appears surprising that Strong Caring is not more assertive in its claims to power and prestige. Weak Loyal is likely to regard the resources and strengths of Strong Caring as unearned and as only weakly defended, if at all. In short, it appears that Strong Caring doesn't understand that the conflict is about control, domination, and perhaps survival. So, for example, those opposed to women's right to vote failed to understand how critical this issue was for the Strong Caring men and women who supported the expansion of women's rights.

The Strong Caring argument in favor of extending rights to women was grounded in the assumption that men and women are similar in nature and thus in their rights. This was an argument based not on the distinctiveness of men and women, but instead on the Strong Caring assumption of connectedness and interdependent relationships. For the same reason, many in the nineteenth century who were pushing for voting rights for women had also been involved in the movement to abolish slavery (and vice versa).

Further, the argument advanced in support of voting rights was not merely that this would benefit women. Jane Addams, for example, argued that in their roles as homemakers and mothers, women had insights into social problems such as child labor, poor housing, alcoholism, prostitution, and unsafe food practices. If women had the right to vote, they could contribute more to solving these problems and improving society as a whole, which would benefit both men and women. Of course, this Strong Caring argument was threatening to the Weak Loyal standpoint, and especially those who benefited from child labor and feared the temperance movement; that is, restrictions on the sale of alcohol and loss of profits.

The attitudes and behaviors of Strong Caring are grounded in the assumption that groups are defined through their relationships with other groups. Furthermore, from the Strong Caring standpoint the understanding of community is strongly shaped by the assumption that the primary intention for human action is to understand; that is, to construct meaning and significance in our lives. A better understanding of our own identity and community depends on recognizing the interdependent nature of identity construction, expressed through a caring commitment to others who are different from oneself. From the Strong Caring standpoint, there are dimensions of respect, caring, and responsibility towards other groups and relationships, as well as a commitment to strive to maintain and strengthen relationships.

Therefore those who supported women's right to vote rarely belittled men or advocated the separation of women from men. Instead, the argument was for improving society for both women and men and strengthening the relationship between women and men. The definition of community may be changed when this serves the goal of becoming more inclusive, of structuring the community so that other groups may feel genuinely that they belong. Strong Caring may consider the statements and actions of Weak Loyal to be self-centered, competitive, aggressive, narrow-minded, dogmatic, and immature (table 4.3). Nevertheless, Strong Caring advocates for women's rights regarded Weak Loyal opponents, both men and women, with affection and concern and were motivated to care for Weak Loyal opponents by involving this group in the broader, shared community.

From the standpoint of Weak Loyal opponents, the statements and actions from the Strong Caring standpoint about caring and community can appear naive, idealistic, and misguided (table 4.2). In addition, Weak Loyal may fear becoming entrapped in Strong Caring's notion of community and unable to define its identity and community separately and from its own perspective. Despite the inclusive intentions of Strong Caring, its statements and actions can be interpreted by Weak Loyal as hostile and designed to destroy its own identity and community. For example, *The New York Times* (which had first supported but later opposed women's right to vote) warned in a 1912 editorial that women would indeed get the right to vote "if the men are not firm and wise enough and, it may as well be said, masculine enough to prevent them."

In the next chapter, the four Weak Tactful dialogues are presented and illustrated. Readers will discover how changes in relative power and privilege can impact the dynamics of the dialogues. Compare, for example, dialogue 2, Weak Loyal versus Strong Tactful (illustrated in the present chapter with cheating versus sportsmanship) with dialogue 5, Weak Tactful versus Strong Loyal (illustrated in the next chapter with the debate over welcoming versus blocking immigrants to the United States). The two opposing perspectives are the same— Loyal and Tactful—but their relative power and privilege are reversed.

6

Getting Along with Others:
The Weak Tactful Dialogues

Should America continue to welcome new immigrants, including those whose ethnicity and religion may represent a break from America's historical culture and identity? Should there be restrictions on Americans' right to vote in order to prevent voter fraud and confusion at the polls? Are regulations aimed at protection of America's natural environment needlessly obstructing America's economic growth? These contentious political issues are addressed in the current chapter, where they also illustrate the Weak Tactful dialogues.

The Tactful perspective is defined by an interdependent identity, grounded in continuing relations with other individuals and groups. Yet, those holding the Tactful perspective also aim to compete with and control others. From the Tactful perspective, the nature, preservation, and strengthening of identity and community reflect negotiations, agreements, and alliances with others. Examples from chapter 1 include John Whipple, the Hawaiian plantation owner; Paul Garrett, the Colorado rancher and civic leader; and Earnshaw Rusk, the Texas rancher committed to working with others for the common good. Examples from chapter 2 include Henry Clay and Franklin D. Roosevelt. People and groups holding the Tactful perspective aim to get along with others.

In the current chapter, the four Weak Tactful dialogues are presented, as Weak Tactful interacts with Strong Loyal, Strong Tactful, Strong Detached, or Strong Caring. Each of these four Weak Tactful dialogues is illustrated with examples of contemporary issues in American society. Summary paragraphs describing the Loyal, Detached, and Caring perspectives are not repeated in this chapter. These paragraphs can be found in chapters 2, 3, and 5.

Dialogue 5. Weak Tactful versus Strong Loyal
Immigrants versus Nativists

In the 1840s in Philadelphia, rising tension between recent Irish Catholic immigrants and more settled Protestant residents became focused on which version of the Bible should be read in the public schools, the Douay version familiar to Catholics or the Protestant version. "Nativist" political leaders told more than three thousand people who had gathered at a rally, "This was and always will be a Protestant country." The following day, the nativist leaders moved the rally into the Catholic neighborhood. Heckling, pushing, and shoving led to gunfire and panic in which both Catholics and Protestants were killed. The Protestants returned the next day and, after a brief gunfight, set fire to many buildings and a Catholic church. Subsequently, they moved to downtown Philadelphia and, ignoring the pleas of the mayor, burned down a second Catholic church. The governor of Pennsylvania placed the City of Brotherly Love under martial law for a week.[1]

Similar tensions between immigrants and native-born Americans have persisted throughout American history, beginning in the seventeenth century with the push by European immigrants into the homelands of indigenous peoples. A surge of immigration in the mid-nineteenth century from Ireland, Germany, and elsewhere fueled the rise of the so-called Native American Party, also called the Know Nothing movement, which aimed to limit the immigration and influence of Irish Catholics and others. The late-nineteenth century saw another wave of immigrants from Italy, Poland, and Eastern Europe, including many Jews.

The nativist reaction included the Chinese Exclusion Act of 1882, the Immigration Act of 1924 setting restrictive quotas for Southern Europeans and Russians, and the rise of the anti-Catholic, anti-Jewish, and anti-immigrant Ku Klux Klan. The McCarran-Walter Immigration Act of 1952 reinforced the 1924 quota system favoring Northern Europeans. The Immigration and Nationality Act of 1965, however, opened the door to increased immigration from Mexico, India, and China. Opposition among native-born Americans to immigration has continued and has become a potent issue in American politics.

The attitudes and values of immigrants to the United States reflect the Weak Tactful standpoint. They are attracted to the United States because of our economic, political, and religious freedoms and the prospect of better lives for themselves and their families. In leaving their country of origin to settle in the United States, they know they will have to interact with others who may differ in language, religion, governance, and means of supporting themselves. Most immigrants arrive with good will and the expectation of working together with others, for they want to become Americans, to live the American Dream. But many immigrants lack vital material resources; for example, access to jobs, land, housing, and investment capital and access to information on how America works (as described in chapter 4). So as a group they are relatively weak. Immigrants know they will have to work hard to survive and get ahead, including mastery of English and acquiring American street smarts, competing with the many Americans who are already well-established.

Historically and currently, many in the United States have been quite welcoming of immigrants. From the Loyal and Tactful perspectives, immigrants—especially those whose ethnicity or religion is similar to one's own—can strengthen American communities. Many immigrants bring valuable skills and a strong work ethic and so they can be important additions to America's workforce, leading to increases in innovation, productivity, and economic output. Immigrants start new businesses at twice the rate of nonimmigrants. From the Caring perspective, the United States with its enormous resources has a responsibility to assist and care for those in need. This perspective is captured in Emma Lazarus' 1883 "Send these, the homeless" sonnet affixed inside the pedestal of the Statue of Liberty. Many feel it difficult to turn away immigrants—including undocumented workers and refugees fleeing violence—whose struggles remind them of their own ancestors' journeys to America.

Nativist opposition to immigration to the United States, however, reflects a Strong Loyal standpoint. Strong Loyal opponents to immigration emphasize the unbridgeable differences they perceive between themselves and immigrants. They see their own group as normative, as defining what it means to be a true American. They assume immigrants, because of differences in language or ethnicity or lack of occupational skills, can never be like themselves and can never be assimilated into American culture. Today's immigration opponents describe themselves not as nativists but as patriots, for they view themselves as the defenders of America's national identity. They believe immigrants can never be as loyal to America as they feel themselves to be. Some believe there is a danger of being outnumbered by new immigrants who will distort and corrupt American culture and values or even impose their own culture as a replacement.

An argument opponents of immigrants make is that America's resources—housing, land, social services, medical care, and educational opportunities—are no longer sufficient to provide both for those already here and for a large number of new immigrants. In particular, they hold concerns that the supply of good, middle-class jobs in America will not be adequate. They fear that immigrants will take jobs away from those who currently hold them or at least cause wages to fall, lowering the standard of living for native-born Americans. This can be a powerful argument when the economy is in recession and many Americans are anxious about their own economic security.

Given these arguments, many nativists feel their American identity and way of life is being threatened, feelings reflective of the Weak Loyal or Weak Detached standpoints, even though the position of native-born Americans is much stronger than that of immigrants, in terms of control over material resources, expertise, political skill, institutionalized authority, and access to information (chapter 4). Indeed, some politicians, past and present, have encouraged this feeling of being threatened, describing immigrants who are seeking a better life for themselves and their families as criminals, drug dealers, and freeloaders, as undesirable, unworthy, and less than human.

Anti-immigrant paranoia and hateful comments about immigrants make it more difficult for immigrants to find jobs and construct new lives in America. Some may feel forced to adopt a Detached perspective, becoming isolated in their own communities, neglecting the necessary efforts to acquire new social and occupational skills and to learn English, and making little or no progress towards engagement with American culture. Unfortunately, this change from the Weak Tactful to a Weak Detached standpoint can reinforce the view of Strong Loyal nativists that immigrants will never become assimilated into American life and identity. In short, the rejection of immigrants by Strong Loyal nativists can bring about the actual detachment of immigrants from American society, thus appearing to justify the initial rejection (discussed more fully in dialogue 9, chapter 7).

Let us now turn to some general features of the Weak Tactful versus Strong Loyal dialogue as illustrated with immigrants and nativists. The Weak Tactful standpoint of immigrants differs from the Strong Loyal standpoint not only in having less power but also in its assumption that groups are defined in large part through their relations with other groups. For Weak Tactful, these relations are based less on ethnicity or religion and more on shared values; for example, work ethic, individual responsibility, and concern for family.

Yet, both immigrants and nativists share the assumption that the primary intention for humans is to compete with and control others. Thus, for Weak Tactful immigrants the concept of community is not a goal in itself but rather a means towards the end of control and domination. Here, domination is understood not as destruction of the other but rather as engagement with the other in hierarchical relationships in a community, broadly conceived. To be members of a shared community means, for Weak Tactful immigrants, that any conflict should follow certain accepted conventions, rules, and principles that set limits on what one group may do to another. In short, the laws and norms of American society, the history and traditions of American institutions, and the rules of the workplace both explicit and implicit are to be respected and followed.

From the Strong Loyal nativist standpoint, the values and goals of its own community are worthy, whereas the values and goals of the Weak Tactful immigrants are not. This conviction provides a rationale for refusing to yield any of the power and privilege associated with its own identity and community and acting towards others with little regard for the integrity of their lives and communities; for example, in the debate over bilingual education (dialogue 9). From the Strong Loyal nativist standpoint, the aims of Weak Tactful immigrants are manipulative and presumptuous (table 4.3).

Strong Loyal nativists regard actions by Weak Tactful

immigrants—for example, reading from the Catholic Douay Bible in the 1840s—as a potential threat to their identity, community, power, and prestige, and feel justified in guarding against efforts by Weak Tactful immigrants to increase their power and prestige. Any assertions by Weak Tactful immigrants that both groups are, at some level, members of a broader, shared American society and interdependent will be difficult for Strong Loyal nativists to hear and understand, given Strong Loyal's assumption of its intrinsically defined, self-contained group identity.

From the Weak Tactful immigrant standpoint, shared membership in American society suggests the use of tactics including negotiating, entering into agreements, and asserting rights rather than more forceful means. Weak Tactful immigrants can strive to advance their position by pointing to what the two groups have in common, seeking to minimize differences between Strong Loyal nativists and Weak Tactful immigrants, arguing the imbalance in power and prestige is inappropriate in a shared American society, and seeking to negotiate with Strong Loyal for a more fair distribution of power and resources. In response, Strong Loyal's assumption that groups are defined intrinsically may lead to feeling offended by Weak Tactful's claim that both are members of the same, shared community. Strong Loyal nativists do not want to be associated with weakness or other presumed negative characteristics of Weak Tactful immigrants.

From the Strong Loyal nativist standpoint, certain aspects of the Weak Tactful versus Strong Loyal interaction can have the appearance of a Weak Loyal versus Strong Loyal interaction (as in dialogue 1, small business versus big business). Thus, Strong Loyal can be expected to engage in many of the same calculations and tactics as when Strong Loyal is opposed to Weak Loyal, including actions aimed at increasing psychological distance between the groups and dehumanizing the other. Weak Tactful immigrants will view such actions by Strong Loyal nativists as aggressive and tyrannical (table 4.2).

Furthermore, Strong Loyal nativists are likely to view Weak Tactful immigrants' attempts to define a community that includes Strong Loyal as a threat to the integrity of its conception of American identity and community. From the Strong Loyal standpoint, the understanding of community is always an either-or understanding: one belongs either in my self-defined community or in some other community. From the Weak Tactful immigrant standpoint, the understanding of community is always a both-and understanding: one belongs both to my particular community and to other superordinate or subordinate communities. Thus, in addition to the issue of power, the Strong Loyal versus Weak Tactful conflict will involve debate over the nature of communities and their boundaries. A Weak Tactful immigrant is comfortable saying, "I am both American and Irish." To a Strong Loyal nativist being American excludes other potential identities and loyalties.

Dialogue 6. Weak Tactful versus Strong Tactful
Expanding versus Restricting Minority Voting Rights

For the 2016 presidential primary voting in Maricopa County, Arizona, where there are a large number of Hispanic voters, elections officials quietly cut the number of polling places from 200 in the previous election to only 60. As a result, many minority voters were forced to wait in line for as long as five hours for their opportunity to vote. Unfortunately, many voters gave up, especially those who had to return to jobs for which they were paid by the hour or whose employers granted only thirty minutes leave from work. Similar disenfranchisement of minority voters, potentially changing the outcome of local, state, and national elections, has happened in other states where the white majority controls election procedures. Expanding and securing voting rights for minorities reflects a Weak Tactful standpoint; restricting minority voting rights reflects a Strong Tactful standpoint.

From the Tactful perspective, attitudes and behaviors are grounded in the assumption that groups are defined in large part through their relations with other groups. Both Weak Tactful and Strong Tactful are committed to the rule of law, as a procedural framework and a constraint on the competitive actions of individuals and groups living and working together in the same community. Both are committed to democratic government and, in particular, to voting as the procedure by which communities can change their laws or elect representatives who are empowered to change the laws. As a result, a principle arena of conflict has been the question of who has the right to vote in elections and who does not and, thus, which group has the power to change the laws with the aim of providing a further competitive advantage to itself.

Historically, only an elite group, typically upper-class men, had the right to vote, while minorities, women, and the poor were disenfranchised. In the United States the right to vote was gained for African American men by ratification of the 15th Amendment in 1870 and for women following ratification of the 19th Amendment in 1920. In the case of African American men and women, the right to vote has been strongly contested, from the nineteenth century throughout the twentieth century and continuing to the present. African American voters reflect the Weak Tactful standpoint, understanding they live in a society that has been majority white, but agreeing to work in the democratic system and play by the accepted rules; that is, to compete for desired outcomes through the process of voting and electing representatives and leaders.

In many regions the white majority, reflecting a Strong Tactful standpoint, circumvented and changed voting procedures in order to maintain and increase its power over African Americans. Following ratification of the 15th Amendment, most Southern state legislatures enacted a poll tax, requiring money be paid for voter registration. Although ostensibly poll taxes applied to everyone, white and black, the laws often included exemptions for men whose fathers or grandfathers had voted in a specific year; for example, 1864 and so prior to the 13th Amendment abolishing slavery in 1865, or 1867 and so prior to the 15th Amendment enfranchising blacks in 1870. Thus, although poll taxes were legal, their effect was to deny the right to vote to African Americans. A similar impact followed from the widespread use of literacy tests, often including arbitrary and obscure questions, as part of the voter registration process. Again, whites who could show they were descended from someone eligible to vote before the abolition of slavery were exempt. The impact of these and similar efforts to suppress black voting was extreme. As late as the 1950s, only a quarter of eligible black voters in the South were registered to vote.

In 1965 Congress, in an effort to enforce the voting rights guaranteed by the 15th Amendment, passed the Voting Rights Act. This act prohibited state and local governments from imposing voting restrictions, including poll taxes, literacy tests, knowledge requirements, or proof of moral character, that result in discrimination against racial or linguistic groups. The Voting Rights Act also provided for federal registrars to be sent to the South, for example, to Selma, Alabama, where only two percent of African Americans had been able to register. The immediate result was a substantial increase in the number of African Americans who were registered to vote and, in a few years, a marked increase in the number of African American state legislators and other elected officials. The Voting Rights Act also led to new laws encouraging people to vote; for example, registration at motor vehicle and public assistance departments, the option of registering and voting on the same day, and procedures for early voting in advance of election day. Overall, these changes in the law increased the participation of Weak Tactful minority voters, and women and the poor, in the democratic process.

The Strong Tactful white majority, however, soon pushed back. In 1966 the white-dominated Mississippi legislature passed several laws aimed at diluting the strength of black voters. These laws included manipulation of the boundaries of state and local election districts—gerrymandering—for example, consolidation of smaller black districts with larger white districts so white candidates usually win. Other Southern states quickly followed with similar changes to their own voting laws. In Arizona, election materials were printed only in English, despite the rapidly increasing Spanish-speaking population. It wasn't until 1982 that Congress passed amendments to the Voting Rights Act banning procedures that clearly had a discriminatory intent and impact, thus strengthening the voting rights of Weak Tactful African Americans and others, including Hispanic citizens.

Nevertheless, the Strong Tactful white majority continues to change voting laws to make it difficult for members of Weak Tactful minority groups to vote. Recent changes have included blocking voter registration drives, reducing the days and hours for early voting, eliminating registering and voting on the same day, purging people with Hispanic and Asian surnames from voter rolls, and requiring the presentation of only certain forms of identification in order to vote. For example, recently in Texas a student identification card issued by a university was not sufficient identification for voting, whereas a membership card from the National Rifle Association was acceptable. People who do not have the required form of identification must locate their original birth certificates, or pay for replacements, and then present these at a government office in order to be able to vote. This can be difficult for potential voters who are poor, disabled, or elderly or who live in rural areas.

From the Strong Tactful standpoint, the rationale for these and similar laws is that they will lead to cost savings in voting procedures, prevent fraud at the polls (although remarkably little voter fraud has been documented), and eliminate confusion and chaos on election days. In 2013 the Supreme Court in *Shelby County versus Holder* significantly weakened the Voting Rights Act, freeing states to make changes in voting procedures without federal oversight. The reduction in the number of polling places in Maricopa County, Arizona, in 2016 is an example. From the Strong Tactful standpoint, these changes are all legal and neutral in their impact. The Strong Tactful white majority is better able to compete with other groups and maintain its own power if it can limit the voting opportunities for minorities, students, the elderly, and the poor. Shortly before the 2016 elections, federal courts blocked new voting restrictions in several states, finding these were intended to depress voting by minority citizens.

Let us turn now to the general features of the Weak Tactful versus Strong Tactful dialogue. Weak Tactful minority voters regard the Strong Tactful group in power as manipulative, menacing, and a potential threat (table 4.2). From the Weak Tactful perspective, the fact of its own relative weakness is a problem that needs to be addressed. Weak Tactful minorities recognize that the Strong Tactful majority supports continuing stability in the existing situation, primarily because Strong Tactful finds advantages in having the relationship continue. Nevertheless, Weak Tactful's own concerns with control, domination, and survival require seeking ways to strengthen its position against Strong Tactful; that is, to compete for power in the context of democracy and voting for elected representatives and leaders.

From the Strong Tactful majority standpoint, a dominant feature of the Weak Tactful minority group is its relative weakness. Nevertheless, Strong Tactful will continue to regard Weak Tactful as manipulative and menacing and as a potential threat. From the Strong Tactful standpoint, the aim is through negotiations and agreements to maintain and strengthen its own power and prestige while yielding as little as possible in return. To maintain this expectation, Strong Tactful must view Weak Tactful as relatively unsophisticated in negotiations and even as gullible (table 4.3).

One possible action for Weak Tactful minorities is to seek an alliance with another strong group that can serve as a counter to the power of Strong Tactful. This is in fact what happened in 1965, as the Voting Rights Act was passed not merely through the efforts of Weak Tactful minorities, but also with the support of Caring civil rights allies. Another possible action is to enter into a coalition with several similarly weak groups whose combined strength may be sufficient to counter that of Strong Tactful (as described in chapter 9, the Caring and pro-government Tactful movement).

From the Strong Tactful standpoint, shared membership in a community suggests the use of tactics including negotiating, entering into agreements, and forming alliances. The negotiations are over issues of power, of course, for this is what primarily distinguishes the two groups. Yet, the negotiations are also over what it means to be members of a shared community; that is, the issue between them is not so much their separate identities but rather the issue of how they will relate to each other in the shared community. Because Strong Tactful recognizes the interdependent nature of its identity and community with that of Weak Tactful, Strong Tactful cannot have as an intended goal the destruction of Weak Tactful. Instead, the goal must be instead to dominate Weak Tactful while remaining in relationship with Weak Tactful. Both Strong Tactful and Weak Tactful are motivated to dominate the other, yet they both strive to maintain the relationship because each benefits from the continuing interdependency.

Dialogue 7. Weak Tactful versus Strong Detached
Disadvantaged versus Privileged

African Americans are a major ethnic group in the United States, about one of every eight American citizens. Historically, their prospects have been closely intertwined with those of other groups and especially dependent on the actions of the dominant white group. Following centuries of slavery and decades of forced segregation, the social and economic status of African Americans has now improved. African Americans value access to education and employment, working hard and competing with others in American society to improve prospects for themselves and their families. In recent decades, an African American middle class has emerged across much of the United States. Yet, many remain disadvantaged: income, housing, net worth, life expectancy, and other indicators are all substantially worse than for whites in American society. Disadvantaged African Americans, and other minority groups, represent a Weak Tactful standpoint.

In contrast, many whites in America enjoy the benefits of what Peggy McIntosh, senior research associate at the Wellesley College Centers for Women, has described as "white privilege." This term refers not to overt prejudice or discrimination by whites, but rather to the advantages whites continue to have because of centuries of oppression of blacks. As discussed in chapter 4, to be privileged means being able to reap the benefits of having greater power without having to incur any of the costs of exercising that power. Whites in America can assume their own life experiences are normative, have greater freedom to speak and act without being questioned or challenged, and enjoy a life of greater social status and economic benefits, even for those whites who happen to be poor. These privileges reflect a Strong Detached standpoint.

Although the 13th Amendment in 1865 ended slavery in the United States, oppression and discrimination against African Americans persisted for another century. The Supreme Court in *Plessy versus Ferguson* in 1896 upheld the constitutionality of laws requiring segregation of blacks and whites in public transportation, schools and colleges, restaurants, restrooms, drinking fountains, and elsewhere. The United States military and federal government workplaces were also segregated. In the Southern states, most African Americans were denied the right to vote (as described in dialogue 6). The Ku Klux Klan engaged in campaigns of terrorism and violence against blacks, including thousands of lynchings. African Americans who served in World War II were denied G.I. Bill educational and mortgage assistance because of discrimination by states and banks. For decades the Federal Housing Administration would not insure mortgages in "redlined" neighborhoods, restricting opportunities for black families to invest in home ownership and increase their family wealth. In these and other ways, African Americans were blocked from full participation in American society, including opportunities for consistent and gainful employment.

Despite the fact that African Americans were no longer slaves, the American dialogue of black versus white had changed very little: Weak Tactful blacks versus Strong Loyal whites. However, the dialogue between black and white Americans did change significantly in the mid-twentieth century. The Supreme Court ruled in 1954, in *Brown versus Board of Education*, that segregated public schools were unconstitutional. In 1964 Congress passed the Civil Rights Act, outlawing discrimination in restaurants, theaters, and public accommodations and by government agencies receiving federal funds. In 1965 the Voting Rights Act prohibited state and local governments from enacting laws requiring poll taxes and literacy tests that discriminated against minority groups. And in 1968 the Fair Housing Act banned discrimination in the sale, rental, and financing of housing.

Because of these judicial and legislative actions and the social, educational, and economic advances of African Americans, many white Americans have concluded that racism, prejudice, and discrimination are no longer barriers as in the past. These white Americans say they support the equality of blacks and whites and deny they personally discriminate. They believe there is now a level playing field. So, while they recognize that many African Americans continue to be disadvantaged, they believe whites in America are no longer responsible for this.

In short, in the past half century the standpoint of many whites has changed from Strong Loyal to Strong Detached. They continue to define their own group as self-contained, not depending on relations with others for a sense of identity. From the Detached perspective, it is difficult to see the impoverished lives of others who are assumed to be somehow different; that is, not members of one's own group. Even if it is acknowledged that many African Americans, as a minority group in America, continue to be disadvantaged in the quality of their schooling, medical care, housing, and opportunities for employment, from the Strong Detached standpoint there is no responsibility to deal with this.

These attitudes reflect the sense of entitlement and exemption from responsibility that have been described as white privilege. Peggy McIntosh gives these and many other examples of white privilege: Whites can arrange to be with people of their own race most of the time. They can watch television or read the newspaper and see people of their own race throughout. They can be confident that if they ask to speak to a supervisor, this will be a person of their own race. If they are stopped by the police or subject to a tax audit, they can assume they haven't been picked because of their race. Whites can assume if they need legal or medical help, their race won't work against them.

Here are the general characteristics of the Weak Tactful versus Strong Detached dialogue. For Weak Tactful disadvantaged blacks, to be members of American society means the course of conflict should follow certain accepted conventions, rules, and principles. Weak Tactful blacks may have difficulty understanding the rationale for the Strong Detached privileged group's lack of engagement in dialogue, negotiations, and the Tactful process. Not only does Strong Detached appear to be rejecting membership in a broader, shared American society, but Strong Detached also does not appear to understand that their interactions are really about control and success. From Weak Tactful's standpoint, Strong Detached appears unsophisticated, insensitive, aloof, and disengaged, yet nevertheless useful if an alliance or coalition can be negotiated around common interests (table 4.2).

For members of the Strong Detached privileged white group, the primary goal is to be left alone so they can pursue self-understanding within the boundaries of their own community. From the Strong Detached standpoint, other people are of little interest. The actions of Weak Tactful disadvantaged blacks are viewed as intrusive, self-serving, manipulative, menacing, conspiratorial, and unprovoked (table 4.3). One possible interpretation of Weak Tactful's actions is that the disadvantaged are immature, and so Strong Detached privileged whites may adopt a paternalistic attitude towards Weak Tactful individuals and groups, providing for their needs through charitable handouts without permitting them to have responsibility for their own actions and lives.

The actions of Weak Tactful disadvantaged groups may be viewed as threatening if Weak Tactful has sufficient power and resources, either on its own or through building alliances with other groups; for example, the Caring and pro-government Tactful movement (described in chapter 9). Thus, it is in the interest of Strong Detached privileged whites to remain vigilant and not permit Weak Tactful blacks to become sufficiently strong to challenge Strong Detached whites. Because of their lack of engagement with other groups, Strong Detached whites may be insensitive towards the needs of others. Given their disengagement and isolation, Strong Detached whites may not have a good sense of their own standing relative to other groups; for example, while being privileged they may at the same time deny their own privileged status. Strong Detached may overreact to the notion of implicit bias—even well-intentioned people can see the world as "us versus them"— by angrily denying they are racist (which is not at all the same as implicit bias). Weak Tactful's claim that "Black Lives Matter" is heard by Strong Detached not as "black lives matter, too," but as "black lives matter, white lives don't," and thus as a reverse racist statement by Weak Tactful.

From the Weak Tactful disadvantaged black standpoint, common membership in American society suggests the use of tactics including negotiating, entering into agreements, and asserting civil rights rather than using more forceful means. Weak Tactful blacks expect to advance their position by claiming membership in a common community with Strong Detached whites, seeking to minimize differences between themselves and Strong Detached whites, soliciting the support of Strong Detached whites against a common enemy, arguing the imbalance in power and prestige is inappropriate in their shared American community, and seeking to negotiate for a more fair distribution of power with Strong Detached.

In response, Strong Detached's assumption that groups are defined intrinsically may lead to feeling offended by Weak Tactful's claim that both are members of the same community. So, for Strong Detached, either black lives matter or white lives matter, but not both. Strong Detached whites do not want to be associated with weakness or other perceived negative characteristics of Weak Tactful blacks or to be engaged in a community defined more broadly than itself. So Strong Detached's belief and response to Weak Tactful is "we have nothing in common."

Weak Tactful, recognizing its relative lack of power and its vulnerability, may reasonably be looking for a stronger community to join. This may be quite advantageous for Weak Tactful in terms of gaining access to power and prestige, if it can negotiate the terms of joining the larger community successfully and not have to compromise too much on the integrity of its own identity and community. In orienting towards Strong Detached privileged whites, however, Weak Tactful disadvantaged blacks have chosen the group that is most difficult to join or to form coalitions with (they are in opposite corners of the perspectives matrix, table 3.1). The easiest course of action for Strong Detached privileged whites is to ignore Weak Tactful disadvantaged blacks; the problem for Weak Tactful disadvantaged blacks is how to get the attention of Strong Detached privileged whites.

Strong Detached's modes of relating to other individuals and groups include self-righteousness and avoiding engagement with others. Strong Detached whites are likely to try to erect barriers against interactions with Weak Tactful blacks, so they can live together in a separate yet peaceful coexistence. Strong Detached may also strive to prevent Weak Tactful from accruing additional resources and power, for example, by forming alliances with other groups. It may be in the interest of Strong Detached privileged whites to encourage conflict among Weak Tactful disadvantaged blacks and with other minority groups.

What can be the appeal of Weak Tactful disadvantaged blacks to Strong Detached privileged whites, especially if Weak Tactful is in the right? Strong Detached is open to responding to moral and emotional appeals by, for example, donating money or other resources to Weak Tactful groups. Yet, Strong Detached does this not out of motivations of charity and philanthropy, love for others, or to increase the well-being of others (the Caring perspective). Instead, Strong Detached often uses giving as a means of buying distance and of reinforcing its own separateness.

For example, Strong Detached gives money to a homeless person on the street merely to have the person go away, so Strong Detached may be freed of the implication that both are members of the same, shared community. The giving is merely paternalistic but not caring; it is not intended to foster the development of maturity, responsibility, and empowerment. Weak Tactful disadvantaged can increase its sense of power only by refusing to accept what Strong Detached has offered. In other words, Weak Tactful recognizes that the reason for the giving is to reinforce Strong Detached's feelings of greater power and separateness. Thus, Weak Tactful says, in effect, "I'll do without what you offer rather than accept the implication that we have no continuing relationship with each other."

Dialogue 7. Weak Tactful versus Strong Detached
Working Women versus Male Workplaces

Since the mid-twentieth century, reflecting in part an increase in office jobs no longer requiring heavy labor, more women have joined the workforce. Women now account for roughly half of the American workforce. Currently, more than half the adult women in America are working. The unemployment rate for women is now less than for men. Women are more likely than men to complete college and attend graduate school. Many women have earned degrees in business, law, medicine, and other professional fields. Close to half of working women are in management, professional, and related occupations, while smaller proportions work in sales and service occupations.

In the summer when it's hot the air conditioning is turned on in office buildings. Many women, however, feel cold in an air-conditioned workplace unless they wear an additional long-sleeve shirt, sweater, or sweatshirt or even bring a space heater to the office. The men, in contrast, are perfectly comfortable. What's happening here? The thermal comfort formula for office building temperatures, established in the 1960s when there were far fewer working women, was researched and standardized only for men's metabolic rate and men's typical work clothing.

The metabolic rate for women, who have smaller bodies and less muscle mass, is typically less than for men. In the summer women wear lighter clothing and sandals, in contrast to the long pants and suits that men wear year-round. For women to be as comfortable as men, air-conditioning temperatures have to be set as much as five degrees warmer. Instead, many women must compromise their comfort and how they dress as they try to adapt to the workplace and strive to do their best, to be productive and successful, and to compete and win clients, raises, and promotions. The situation of these women is consistent with a Weak Tactful standpoint. The men, in contrast, do not perceive or acknowledge the disparities in workplace conditions and care little about the discomfort of women, consistent with a Strong Detached standpoint.

In almost half of American families women are the primary or sole earners. For many single mothers, working is a necessity, not a choice. Long-term employment is a central dimension of identity for many women. They know they must work hard and do their best, competing against fellow workers, both men and other women, to hold onto their jobs, be given more responsibility, and earn raises and promotions. At the same time, being successful requires getting along well with others, including customers, clients, fellow workers, and supervisors, and in general being a good team player. Because women can be better listeners than men, more sensitive and skilled socially, less likely to dominate in conversations, and more comfortable asking for help, work teams that include women are among the most successful. Being able to compete while maintaining good relations with others reflects a Weak Tactful standpoint.

Nevertheless, many women continue to confront significant challenges in the workplace, particularly the gender pay gap. Women are paid on average only about four-fifths of what men earn. A further challenge is the "glass ceiling," barriers preventing women, despite being well-qualified, from obtaining the most powerful, prestigious, and high-paying jobs. Women hold roughly half of America's jobs and earn more than half of all master's degrees. Yet, women hold less than a fifth of corporate board memberships and less than a tenth of senior management positions. How are the gender pay gap and the glass ceiling to be explained? Yes, some men continue to be biased and discriminate against women, believing women should not be in the workplace and should not have benefits and opportunities similar to those of men (reflecting a Loyal perspective). But the reality of the challenges women face in the American workplace is more complex.

It begins with recruitment and hiring. In many workplaces, an unexamined assumption is that the ideal worker is someone who works full-time and maintains unbroken employment for many years. Recruiters and employers may believe women are likely to leave the workforce to have children or work only part-time while they are raising children. Studies have shown employers respond less often to identical resumes sent by women with children than by men with children. It wasn't until 1971 that the Supreme Court ruled employers may not refuse to hire women with preschool children while still hiring men with preschool children. These pervasive assumptions and stereotypes can lead to women being hired into positions with little opportunity for mobility and advancement and to women being hired for less pay than men.

A further obstacle to women being promoted or recruited into middle management and top leadership positions is that few women now hold such positions in business and government. Women in powerful and prestigious positions who can be models and mentors for younger women are rare. And the recruiters for these top positions are most often men who are embedded in informal social networks made up primarily of other men. Further, women can be passed over for promotion because of the assumption they are likely to leave the workplace to care for children. Some women do, of course, take extended breaks in their careers to have children. But when they return to the workforce, they are often offered lower positions and salaries than what they would have had if they had remained as full-time employees.

Many women continue to be employed in occupations that, because these have traditionally been women's occupations, have tended to pay less than occupations dominated by men. This happens even when women and men's occupations require similar amounts of education, levels of skill, and years of experience. Occupations in which women have traditionally worked—teaching, child care, nursing, social work, and nonprofit jobs—have been characterized as caregiving occupations. Many people, both men and women, assume caregiving activities are more natural for women than for men. Thus, for women to engage in caregiving is considered to be not really work, and so women in these occupations are expected to accept less pay than men. Caregiving, however, is real work, even though for no pay, no fixed breaks, and no vacation days.

The solution to these challenges—ensuring pay equity and breaking the glass ceiling—will require structural changes in the workplace itself and changes in the attitudes of many people in American society. These changes should include affordable and high-quality child care, so women who would like to pursue a career and have a family can have this opportunity on an equal basis with men. These changes should include school systems that provide meaningful after-school activities and school calendars that make sense for working families. These changes should include family-friendly workplace policies that include paid parental leave, an opportunity provided as a right for women and many men in all countries of the world except the United States, Lesotho, Swaziland, and Papua New Guinea. And these changes should include greater flexibility in work hours and scheduling, to accommodate both women workers who are responsible for caring for children or other family members, and a greater appreciation and respect for women and men who work in caregiving occupations.

It would be easy to blame men for the failure to introduce and support these changes in the workplace for the benefit of women. But to do so would assume most men are biased and discriminatory, motivated to control, compete against, and dominate women in the workplace, reflecting a Loyal perspective (see, for example, dialogue 4, opponents of women's rights). More likely, however, is that many men in the workplace are not aware of and not concerned about the gender pay gap or the glass ceiling or other negative features of the workplace, including the setting of the air-conditioning thermostats, that impact their fellow workers who happen to be women. These men are focused on themselves and their own situation in the workplace; they either can't see or do not want to see or get involved with what is happening to women workers. These attitudes reflect a Strong Detached standpoint.

The Strong Detached standpoint of men in the workplace features aspects of male privilege, even for men who have not attained positions of high pay or status. For example, in many American workplaces men, but not women, can assume that if they have children no one will question their commitment to their work. If they do the same task as a woman, others will assume the man did it better. Men do not have to be on guard against sexual harassment or assault in the workplace. If they are competing with a woman in hiring or promotion, the men will likely win; they will not be paid less only because they happen to be men. If they are not physically attractive or do not attend to their clothing and grooming, this will not disadvantage men in the workplace; higher-ups whom they need to impress are the same gender as themselves. When men speak they will not be interrupted by someone of the opposite gender. Furthermore, men have the additional privilege of not having to be aware of and responsible for their male privilege in the workplace.

The following paragraphs describe the general features of the Weak Tactful versus Strong Detached dialogue. To be members of the same community means, for Weak Tactful women, that the course of conflict should follow certain accepted conventions, rules, and principles. Weak Tactful women may have difficulty understanding the rationale for the lack of engagement by Strong Detached men in dialogue, negotiations, and the Tactful process. Not only do Strong Detached men appear to be rejecting membership in a broader, shared community, but also Strong Detached men appear not to understand that their interactions are really about control and domination. From Weak Tactful women's standpoint, Strong Detached men appear unsophisticated, insensitive, aloof, and disengaged, yet nevertheless potentially useful if an alliance or coalition can be negotiated around common interests; for example, meeting production and sales goals or ensuring the long-term success of the business (table 4.2).

For members of the Strong Detached men's group, the primary goal is to be left alone so they can pursue self-understanding within the boundaries of their own community. From the Strong Detached standpoint, other individuals and groups are of little interest. The concerns and actions of Weak Tactful women are viewed as intrusive, self-serving, manipulative, menacing, conspiratorial, and unprovoked (table 4.3). One possible interpretation of Weak Tactful's actions is that they are immature, and so Strong Detached employers and supervisors may adopt a paternalistic attitude towards Weak Tactful women employees, providing for their needs without permitting them to have responsibility for their own actions and lives.

The actions of Weak Tactful women may be viewed as threatening if Weak Tactful has sufficient power and resources, either on its own or possibly through building alliances with other groups of workers, for example, unionized workers. For women to become knowledgeable about gender discrimination as described in Title VII of the Civil Rights Act of 1964 may be viewed as threatening. Because of its lack of engagement with other groups, Strong Detached may often be insensitive towards the needs of others. Because of their isolation, Strong Detached men may not have a good sense of their own standing relative to women; for example, while being privileged they may at the same time deny their own privileged status.

From the Weak Tactful women's standpoint, common membership in a business and professional community suggests the use of tactics including negotiating, entering into agreements, and asserting rights rather than using more forceful means. Weak Tactful can advance its position by asserting the fact of common community at some level with Strong Detached, seeking to minimize differences between Strong Detached and Weak Tactful, arguing the imbalance in power and prestige is inappropriate in their common community, and seeking to negotiate for a more fair distribution of power and benefits with Strong Detached. In response, Strong Detached's assumption that groups are defined intrinsically may lead to feeling offended by Weak Tactful's claim that both are members of the same community. Strong Detached men do not want to be associated with weakness or other perceived negative characteristics of Weak Tactful women or be engaged in a community defined more broadly than the male community.

Strong Detached's modes of relating to other individuals and groups include self-righteousness and avoiding engagement with others; for example, not questioning the appropriateness of weekend golf outings restricted to male friends from work. Strong Detached is likely to try to erect barriers against interactions with Weak Tactful, so they can live together in a peaceful coexistence. Strong Detached may also strive to prevent Weak Tactful from accruing additional resources and power, for example, by forming alliances with other groups of workers. It may be in Strong Detached men's interest to encourage jealousies, competition, and conflict among Weak Tactful women and other groups.

What can be the appeal of Weak Tactful women to Strong Detached men, especially if Weak Tactful is in the right? Strong Detached men may be open to responding to moral and emotional appeals by giving money or other resources to Weak Tactful women. Yet, Strong Detached does this not out of motivations of charity and philanthropy, out of love for others, or to increase the well-being of others. Instead, Strong Detached more often uses giving as a means of buying distance and of reinforcing its own separateness. The giving is merely paternalistic, and is not intended to foster the development of maturity, responsibility, and empowerment of women.

There is considerable potential for each to misread the standpoint of the other, for the Weak Tactful and Strong Detached groups are opposed on both fundamental underlying assumptions (table 3.1). Weak Tactful women may misread Strong Detached men as Loyal, as prejudiced and discriminatory against women (as discussed in dialogue 4, opponents of women's rights), for the Detached and Loyal perspectives share the assumption that identity and community are intrinsically defined. This misreading may lead Weak Tactful women to adopt a more defensive posture or a more aggressive stance against Strong Detached men than may be justified, encouraging Strong Detached men to adopt an even more distanced, defensive, and isolationist stance.

Dialogue 8. Weak Tactful versus Strong Caring
Conservation versus Preservation of the Environment

The United States was once a land of enormous natural resources. The vast forests and abundant wildlife awed early European settlers. By the late nineteenth century, however, substantial deforestation had already taken place to provide wood for heating and building and to clear land for farming. Tobacco plants require rich soil and so, without fertilizer, every few years additional forests had to be cleared to provide new farmland. Extensive trapping of beavers to provide pelts for robes and hats led to steep population declines. The commercial hunting of passenger pigeons to provide cheap food for slaves and immigrants reduced the birds' numbers from billions to near extinction.

Similarly, the killing of buffalo for pelts, leather, and food, to eliminate grazing competition for domestic cattle, and to reduce the food supply for Native Americans and force them onto reservations left only a few hundred from herds once numbering 50 to 60 million. Overgrazing by cattle and sheep caused significant loss of native grasses and soil erosion. Mining for gold, silver, and other valuable minerals produced enormous tailings dumps and pollution of streams and rivers.

William Leiss, former president of the Royal Society of Canada and now at the University of Ottawa, has described the exploitation and destruction of natural resources for human use and profit as "the domination of nature." This nineteenth-century perspective also reflected the Loyal perspective.

These starkly visible environmental losses gave rise to the recognition that unrestrained exploitation of natural resources could not be sustained. Instead, the natural resources of the United States should be used wisely, conserved and not wasted, and managed properly for the benefit of humans. In 1872, in order to provide for the benefit and enjoyment of people, Congress established Yellowstone National Park, the first of many. In 1891 Congress authorized the designation of public lands as forest reserves; in 1905 these reserves became the core of the US Forest Service. Gifford Pinchot, the first forest service chief, promoted the efficient commercial management of forests to maximize profit and ensure human use in the future. Pinchot recognized humans could not live apart from nature and, instead, had to live in harmony with nature over the long-term. Thus, Pinchot's focus on conservation and stewardship helped move American attitudes from the Loyal to a Tactful perspective towards nature. A contemporary argument is that the Amazon rain forest may be particularly useful in harboring plants with rare enzymes that can lead to cures for human diseases.

At the same time, the naturalist John Muir opposed Pinchot's views. For Muir the beauty and grandeur of nature had spiritual and transcendent value beyond any short-term, material, and instrumental utility for humans. Muir wanted to understand nature as it is, rather than ask how we could use nature. For this reason, Muir argued for protection of nature from human intervention, use, and impact and for preservation of nature unspoiled in its natural state. In 1890 Muir and others persuaded Congress to pass legislation protecting California's Yosemite Valley, included in 1916 in the new National Park Service.

Muir reflected the Caring perspective in his efforts to understand the beauty and complexity of nature on its own terms and his advocacy for the protection of nature from unrestricted exploitation and commercial use by humans. Pinchot, the conservationist, and Muir, the preservationist, clashed publicly: Pinchot supported the grazing of sheep in Yosemite's meadows; Muir opposed this due to the destruction of grasslands. Pinchot supported the flooding of Hetch-Hetchy Valley, similar in its vistas to Yosemite, to provide water for San Francisco. Muir and others opposed Pinchot but lost these battles.[2]

By the mid-twentieth century, however, John Muir's Caring perspective had become increasingly influential. His focus on preservation informed the passage by Congress of the Clean Air Act of 1963, aimed at control of toxic air pollution, and the Wilderness Act of 1964, which protected millions of acres of federal land. This act also provided a definition of wilderness that Muir would have approved: "A wilderness, in contrast with those areas where man and his own works dominate the landscape, is hereby recognized as an area where the earth and its community of life are untrammeled by man, where man himself is a visitor who does not remain."

In 1970 Congress established the Environmental Protection Agency, charged with writing and enforcing regulations for the protection of the environment. This was followed by the Endangered Species Act of 1973 to protect species from extinction as a consequence of commercial development; the Clean Water Act of 1977 for the protection of rivers and streams from industrial, municipal, and agricultural pollution; and by similar legislation. This legislation guided by Muir's Caring perspective acted as a restraint on corporate and business interests reflecting the Loyal domination-of-nature and the Tactful preserve-for-human-use perspectives.

Pinchot's conservation perspective is a Weak Tactful standpoint, focusing on the value nature can have for humans; Muir's protectionist perspective is a Strong Caring standpoint that sees intrinsic worth in all living things. In recent decades, the Strong Caring standpoint on the environment has broadened to include a social justice dimension. The natural environment cannot be adequately protected without also addressing multiple human societal problems, including overpopulation, excess consumption, and waste and pollution. And these problems in turn afflict human communities that are poor, minority, and indigenous, thus raising significant issues of equality, fairness, and justice. From the Weak Tactful standpoint, however, additional environmental regulation and the movement for environmental justice threaten private property, corporate profits, and America's economic growth.

From the perspective of Weak Tactful conservationists, the statements and actions of Strong Caring preservationists about caring and community can appear naive, idealistic, and patronizing, yet forceful in the claim of common membership in a broader community (table 4.2). The efforts from the Strong Caring preservation standpoint to be sympathetic towards Weak Tactful's conservation standpoint may be viewed with mistrust and suspicion. Why is Strong Caring doing this for me, and what is expected in return? Weak Tactful is concerned about the reciprocal obligations that may be implied in an interdependent community, whereas Strong Caring is asking for little in return.

The attitudes and behaviors of the Strong Caring preservationists are grounded in the assumption that groups are defined through their relations with other groups. In the Strong Caring standpoint, the understanding of community is also shaped by the assumption that the primary motive for human action is to understand; that is, to construct meaning and significance in our lives, and to understand and appreciate the beauty, complexity, and worth of nature. A better understanding of our own identity and community must reflect the interdependent nature of identity construction. This is expressed through a caring commitment to others who are different from ourselves, including a caring commitment to protect the environment itself.

For Strong Caring there are dimensions of respect, caring, and responsibility towards other groups and relationships, and a commitment to striving to maintain and strengthen relationships. Strong Caring may consider the statements and actions of Weak Tactful to be self-centered, competitive, manipulative, menacing, and petty (table 4.3). Nevertheless, Strong Caring regards Weak Tactful with affection and concern and would like to care for Weak Tactful by involving this group, at some level, in the broader community.

Despite the inclusive intentions of Strong Caring preservationists, their actions can be interpreted by Weak Tactful conservationists as hostile efforts to destroy its identity and community, its control of nature, and its profits. Weak Tactful can defend itself against incorporation in Strong Caring's community by becoming hostile towards Strong Caring and by assuming negative characteristics that may make it less attractive as a recruit into this community. Weak Tactful can also become proactive, attacking Strong Caring's notions of community and even encouraging groups in that community to compete against each other, for example, to enter into conflicts over distribution of resources—a divide and conquer strategy.

From the standpoint of Strong Caring preservationists, the primary task is to help Weak Tactful conservationists become more mature and abandon their intentions towards competition, control, and domination of nature. The role of Strong Caring is one of teaching, mentoring, nurturing, and socializing as, for example, in the April 22nd celebrations of Earth Day, a global educational effort in support of the environment. Strong Caring must encourage Weak Tactful to trust Strong Caring, to believe that Strong Caring does not have competitive or aggressive desires to harm Weak Tactful.

This is not a simple matter of merely acting kindly towards Weak Tactful, for Weak Tactful would like to negotiate for a fair share of the resources, power, and prestige of Strong Caring. Recently, it has become commonplace for corporations, including the fossil fuel industry, to blur the line between the Tactful and Caring perspectives by branding themselves as ecologically and environmentally friendly. Strong Caring must find a way to balance the extension of freedom and responsibility towards Weak Tactful while at the same time retaining sufficient control to protect the integrity of the broader community and the natural environment.

While Weak Tactful conservationists and Strong Caring preservationists do share an understanding of the importance of a broader, shared community and of their mutual dependencies in that community, nevertheless they have different conceptions of how communities are organized. From the standpoint of Weak Tactful conservationists, we are all in this together, yet each person's primary responsibility is to watch out for him- or herself, not primarily to care for the Other. Thus, for Weak Tactful conservationists the concept of community is understood as a means towards the end of control and domination of nature by corporate and business interests, for example, uranium mining around the Grand Canyon, oil drilling in the Arctic National Wildlife Refuge, and additional coal, timber, and cattle-grazing leases in the national forests.

From the standpoint of Strong Caring, the concept of community is understood not as a means towards an end, as in the Weak Tactful standpoint, but as a positive goal in itself. The definition of community may be changed when this serves the goal of becoming more inclusive, of structuring the community so other groups may feel genuinely a part, as in the broadening of the environmental movement to include social justice issues. For Strong Caring preservationists, we are all in this together and we should watch out for each other, including watching out for the environment.

7

Working It Out Myself:
The Weak Detached Dialogues

Some things we prefer to think through and work out for ourselves: how to preserve our family's cultural and religious heritage and identity, whether it's best for our children to be vaccinated or not, and how America can best be protected and prosper in a world with many countries holding interests different from ours. These and similar standpoints can reflect the Detached perspective, defined like the Loyal perspective by an intrinsic, self-contained identity. The Detached perspective, however, is a sharp break from the Loyal and Tactful focus on competition and control. Instead, the Detached perspective has an intention to understand; that is, to construct meaning and significance in our lives.

What happens when people holding the Detached perspective—wanting to work things out for themselves—interact with those holding other perspectives? In this chapter, the four Weak Detached dialogues are presented, as

Weak Detached interacts with Strong Loyal, Strong Tactful, Strong Detached, or Strong Caring. Examples of the Detached perspective from chapter 1 include John Klope, the self-contained, independent Alaska gold miner; Amos Calendar, the Colorado cowboy who preferred living alone; and Edmund Steed, who immigrated to Maryland to live freely as a Catholic rather than under a Protestant majority. Examples from chapter 3 include Daniel Boone and Henry David Thoreau.

Dialogue 9. Weak Detached versus Strong Loyal
Cultural Identity versus Assimilation

The pattern of early European colonization of North America consisted in large part of diverse ethnic groups settling in different locations; for example, the English in New England and the southern colonies, the Dutch in the New York region, Quakers, Ulster Scots, and German Protestants around Philadelphia, the Spanish in Florida, Texas, New Mexico, and California, and the French in Louisiana. These groups established distinct communities to provide mutual support and to maintain their religious, linguistic, and cultural heritages and identities. This pattern continued through the eighteenth and nineteenth centuries, with Irish, Italians, Greeks, Hungarians, Poles and others settling into ethnic neighborhoods in America's urban areas. In the early twentieth century, Swedish and Norwegian immigrants settled primarily in the rural upper Midwest. This geographical pattern of settlement continues, with recent immigrants from Latin America, India, China, the Middle East, Southeast Asia, and elsewhere living together in distinctive ethnic communities.

Cultural identity is our understanding of belonging to a particular group, often defined by national origin, religion, or ethnicity. The dimensions of cultural identity can include language, religion, grooming and dress, food and drink, music and dance, occupational skills, and other shared traditions and practices. Ethnic communities in America have often been inward-looking and self-sustaining, with their own institutions and local economy, providing social support and a safe home for recent arrivals still seeking their place in American society. For members of these communities, opportunities to share one's heritage and tradition with others can provide a sense of connectedness and meaning in one's life. Many ethnic communities in America celebrate their African American, Chinese, German, Greek, Irish, Italian, Mexican, Native American, Polish, Scandinavian, Vietnamese, or other cultural heritage with events and annual festivals. These and similar ethnic communities, with a strong interest in maintaining and showing pride in their unique cultural identity, reflect a Weak Detached standpoint.

At the same time, immigrants to the United States reflect primarily a Weak Tactful standpoint. They know that to survive and get ahead, to become like Americans and live the American Dream, they must work together with many other Americans whose languages, traditions, and practices may be very different from their own. However, people on different occasions may hold two or more of the four perspectives, as illustrated by Nyuk Tsin, the Chinese immigrant to Hawaii, and Hans Brumbaugh, the German farmer who immigrated to Colorado. So the standpoint of immigrants to the United States is rightly described in dialogue 5 as Weak Tactful, but when the focus is narrowly on cultural identity, as here in dialogue 9, the standpoint can better be described as Weak Detached.

Hispanic and Latino Americans are about one sixth of the population of the United States. More than half are of Mexican origin, with smaller numbers coming from Puerto Rico, Cuba, the Dominican Republic, Central America, and South America. Many immigrants from Mexico and Central America live in New Mexico, California, Texas, Arizona, and Nevada; many from Puerto Rico and the Dominican Republic live in the Northeast. Los Angeles, Las Vegas, Chicago, Houston, Phoenix, San Diego and other cities have strong

Hispanic communities. Just as for other ethnic immigrant groups, these communities help maintain the religious, linguistic, and cultural heritage of Hispanics now living in the United States, for some families since the sixteenth century. These communities can also be important sources of social and economic support for more recent immigrants. A benefit of participating in these communities is maintaining one's Hispanic cultural identity, reflecting a Weak Detached standpoint.

Many other Americans view the existence of immigrant communities from a different perspective. They feel it is inappropriate for immigrants to settle into ethnic neighborhoods and attempt to maintain their own cultural identity. They argue that immigrants should set aside their original identity and strive to become quickly integrated into the culture of the United States, the country in which they are now living and working. This is the process of cultural assimilation or, as it has been called informally, the "melting pot." Many immigrants have, historically, given up their original ethnic identities and merged into a new, shared American society, lifestyle, culture, and identity. A unified and homogeneous American cultural identity, defined intrinsically and without reference to other national, religious, or ethnic groups, is the foundation of American feelings of nationalism, patriotism, and loyalty. To be an American is to be an American first and only, not to have one's allegiance split among cultural groups that are seen as competing against one another, for example, Hispanics versus Americans. This is a Strong Loyal standpoint.

Cultural assimilation appears very different from the Weak Detached and Strong Loyal standpoints. For Weak Detached immigrant groups, to be American is to participate in a society that is innovative and dynamic because it retains and respects its historical diversity of cultural traditions, values, and skills. Over time there is a sharing and blending of cultures, yet each retains many of its distinctive features. To be fully assimilated would mean to be indistinguishable from the dominant culture of the more than a third of Americans whose ancestry is German, Irish, and English; that is, Northern European, English-speaking, largely Protestant, and white. From the Weak Detached immigrant standpoint, the argument and the pressure for assimilation threaten the loss of their central cultural identity and values. Hispanics would argue that their focus on family rather than money, on community rather than individualism, is worth retaining.

From the Strong Loyal assimilation standpoint, the continued existence of any societal groups other its own is seen as divisive and threatening to its sense of what it means to be an American. For Weak Detached Hispanics, one can have an Hispanic cultural identity and be an American; American identity is enhanced by the inclusion of many different kinds of people. For Strong Loyal assimilationists, one must choose a cultural identity: either as the strange, competitive, threatening Other or as a loyal, patriotic American, but not both.

This dialogue between the Weak Detached focus on ethnic community and cultural identity and the Strong Loyal focus on assimilation and national identity is most clear in the debate over bilingual education, that is, teaching academic content and skills in two languages. Language can be a focus of tension and conflict because language is often central to our sense of cultural identity and because, from the Strong Loyal standpoint, language can be the most salient dimension of cultural difference between self and Other. Although many Hispanics in America are comfortable speaking both Spanish and English, most non-Hispanic whites understand little Spanish or none at all. Thus, Strong Loyal whites hearing Spanish spoken in public or in the media can find this alien, strange, and threatening.

Weak Detached advocates for bilingual education argue that children should be educated in their native language, Spanish, so they do not fall behind in reading, mathematics, and other subjects while they are also learning English. Further, they argue that if students are literate in their native language, they will find it easier to become proficient in English. In the context of twenty-first century globalization, being able to speak in two or more languages and communities is a high-level and marketable skill.

Strong Loyal opponents of bilingual education argue that teaching in Spanish delays children's learning of English and other subjects and, furthermore, impedes their assimilation into American society. They believe the unity of American society and its national identity depend on everyone speaking English as the common language. The persistence of other languages and cultural communities threatens this unity. Almost half the states have passed laws making English the official language for conducting government business. Opponents argue that these laws discriminate against immigrants who are still learning English. Advocates argue that these laws benefit immigrants by encouraging them to learn English more quickly and become integrated socially and economically into American society. In dialogue 5, Strong Loyal's standpoint towards immigrants is "Keep the Other out." Here, in dialogue 9, Strong Loyal's standpoint towards immigrants who are settled in America is "The Other must become like me, including speaking English."

The following paragraphs set forth the characteristic features of the Weak Detached versus Strong Loyal dialogue. For members of the Weak Detached ethnic group, the primary goal is to be left alone so they can pursue self-understanding inside the boundaries of their own community. The actions of Strong Loyal whites pressing for assimilation are viewed as intrusive, aggressive, dictatorial, and unprovoked (table 4.2). Indeed, the actions of Strong Loyal are difficult for members of Weak Detached ethnic communities to comprehend, for Weak Detached does not share the assumption that the primary intention for human action is to compete with and control others. While acknowledging the Strong Loyal white community has greater power, Weak Detached finds little to admire in Strong Loyal's actions and community; so Weak Detached has little desire to acquire the power and prestige that Strong Loyal feels it has. Weak Detached desires to remain independent and self-sufficient, and so feels besieged by the need to monitor its relationship with Strong Loyal.

A Strong Loyal individual or group will feel proud of the values and goals of its own community and see little worth in the values and goals of Weak Detached ethnic communities. Strong Loyal's feelings of nationalism, patriotism, pride, and self-righteousness support its refusal to yield any of the power and privilege associated with its own identity and community and acting with little regard for the integrity of others' lives and communities. The Strong Loyal nativist community regards any actions by Weak Detached ethnic groups—for example, continuing to speak their native language rather than English, or holding an annual ethnic festival—as a potential threat to its identity, community, power, and prestige, and feels justified in guarding against efforts by Weak Detached to increase its power and prestige. Strong Loyal may find it curious that Weak Detached does not initiate actions against Strong Loyal. Indeed, from Strong Loyal's perspective Weak Detached appears quite naive in failing to understand that the issues between the two groups are ones of competition, control, power, and survival.

In response to aggression from Strong Loyal, Weak Detached is likely to call for better understanding: "If we could learn more about each other, then we would be able to get along." Yet learning more, getting along, and reducing conflict are merely means towards Weak Detached's goal of being left alone. Strong Loyal is unlikely to find Weak Detached's request to be left alone appealing; indeed, the assertion of difference and the desire to remain separate can appear as arrogance and aloofness. From the perspective of Weak Detached, being separate is about being proud of one's cultural heritage. From the perspective of Strong Loyal, being separate is a threatening assertion of superiority, sufficient to motivate Strong Loyal to aggress against Weak Detached. Weak Detached doesn't want to engage in competition; for Strong Loyal, competition is the nature of group relationships.

Strong Loyal's lack of understanding of the intentions of Weak Detached, along with assertions by Weak Detached of its separateness from Strong Loyal, can lead to feelings of paranoia. Strong Loyal is likely to project its own intentions of control and domination onto the Weak Detached group, so Strong Loyal will understand the conflict as the Weak Loyal versus Strong Loyal type (dialogue 1). Strong Loyal can rationalize its aggression against and perhaps destruction of Weak Detached by emphasizing differences, rather than commonalities, between members of the two groups; that is, by building on the assumption of intrinsically defined identity.

The psychological distance between the groups can be increased by the use of stereotyping and derogatory terms, thus dehumanizing and removing an important barrier against attacking the other group. Indeed, there has been in America a long history of demeaning jokes and negative portrayals of immigrants as stupid, dirty, lazy, and violent. Unfortunately, because Weak Detached also holds to the same assumption of intrinsically defined identity, Strong Loyal's assertions of separateness and difference may well go unchallenged.

Dialogue 10. Weak Detached versus Strong Tactful
Religious Freedom versus Secularism

Minority religious groups that have disagreed with the views of the majority and established authorities have been central to the history of the United States. Among the first Europeans to settle in America were Pilgrims, Catholics, and Quakers escaping religious persecution in England and Huguenots fleeing Catholic hostility in France. Mennonites, Amish, and Shakers, also seeking religious freedom, followed in the eighteenth century. Separatist religious groups in the nineteenth century included Mormons (Latter-day Saints) and Jehovah's Witnesses, both of which experienced tension and conflict with majority Christians and American governments whose perspective in some cases could be described as Loyal. These minority religious groups reduced the potential for conflict by establishing their own communities separate from the powerful majorities opposing their religious beliefs.

Minority religious groups also established their own communities to resist social influences that conflicted with their religious practices. Many Quakers, Mennonites, and Amish are conscientious objectors to military service. Jehovah's Witnesses, also conscientious objectors, resist singing the American national anthem or saluting the flag. The Amish resist modern conveniences such as public grid electricity, telephones, and automobiles and school their children at home. In withdrawing from and minimizing competition with other groups and focusing instead on religious understanding and practice in their own communities, these groups reflect a Weak Detached standpoint. Their aim is to be free from constraints imposed by other religious groups or authorities; that is, to have religious freedom.

Majority religious groups in America have also broadened the concepts of religious tolerance and freedom. For example, the Maryland Toleration Act of 1649 protected Catholics and other Christians from having to conform to the Anglican tradition of the Church of England. The Virginia Statute for Religious Freedom, drafted by Thomas Jefferson in 1777 and enacted in 1786, guaranteed freedom of religion to people of all faiths. The latter was a precursor to the First Amendment to the Constitution, which prevents governments from establishing a state religion or otherwise preferring one religion to others and guarantees the right of Americans to follow the beliefs and practices of their religion. The result has been a flourishing of Christian denominations in the United States and thriving Jewish, Muslim, Hindu, Buddhist, Native American, and other religious communities.

State neutrality with respect to the religious beliefs and practices of individuals combined with the view that government decisions should not be influenced by any particular religious beliefs or practices constitute the principle of secularism. America's diverse religious groups, and atheists and agnostics, exist in a complex tension with each other and with the government, as they strive to maintain and advance their particular beliefs and practices while at the same time continuing to live and govern together. Secularism has been a useful procedure for negotiating these differences and reducing tensions among religious and atheist and agnostic groups and between these groups and the government. The First Amendment and the principle of secularism reflect a Strong Tactful standpoint (see also dialogue 2, fundamentalism).

There continues to be an intense dialogue between Weak Detached advocates for religious freedom and Strong Tactful supporters of secularism. Weak Detached religious minorities have cited the First Amendment in successfully challenging the imposition of certain laws and procedures by Strong Tactful secular governments and businesses. For example, accommodations are made for those with religious objections to particular laws: for conscientious objectors to military service and for those whose religious beliefs lead them to prefer home schooling in place of public schools. In addition, American law requires employers to accommodate the religious beliefs and practices of their employees. These accommodations may include work schedule changes for religious holidays or breaks for prayer, modification of job duties that conflict with religious beliefs, exceptions to an employer's dress or grooming requirements, or provision of private space for prayer or other religious observances.

On the other hand, religious accommodations are not required when these might cause undue hardship for an employer or infringe on the rights of other employees who do not share particular religious beliefs. What constitutes undue hardship for an employer or what constitutes infringement on others' rights can be difficult for employers, employees, and the courts to determine, reflecting the tension in the dialogue between Weak Detached advocates for religious freedom and Strong Tactful secularists. Some Christians charge that any limitations on how and when they can practice their religion amount to a "war on Christianity." This reflects a Weak Detached standpoint of feeling oppressed by a Strong Tactful secularism.

Nevertheless, the religion of Christianity continues to be privileged in America in many ways. For example, Christians can expect to have holidays from work to celebrate their religion, practice their religion openly without being questioned or challenged, have the media portray their faith accurately, and not be penalized for not knowing about other religions. And they can have Christianity be a part of their identity without others regarding it as the most salient aspect, for instance, being introduced as "my Christian friend." The secular Pledge of Allegiance was modified in 1954 to include the religious phrase "under God." "In God We Trust" appears on all American currency. Many Christians are comfortable with the balance between protections for religious freedom provided by the First Amendment and living in the United States as a secular country.

Here are the general features of Weak Detached versus Strong Tactful dialogues. For Weak Detached religious groups, the primary goal is to be left alone so they can pursue self-understanding, including religious practices, inside the boundaries of their community. The actions of Strong Tactful secularists are viewed as intrusive, manipulative, menacing, and unprovoked (table 4.2). Indeed, the actions of Strong Tactful are very difficult for Weak Detached to comprehend, for Weak Detached does not share the assumption either that the primary intention for human action is to compete with and control others or that both groups participate in a broader, shared community. Given a history of oppression, persecution, and violence directed at Weak Detached religious groups, there is a familiarity with control, competition, and winning as intentions for human action, but being familiar with is not at all the same as agreeing with.

The attitudes and behaviors of Strong Tactful secularists are grounded in the assumption that groups are defined through their relations with other groups. Yet, this understanding of the nature of community is shaped by the assumption that the primary intention for humans is to compete with and control others. For Strong Tactful any conflict is about competition and control and perhaps survival. Strong Tactful looks on Weak Detached's assertions of wanting to be left alone to seek self-understanding as being both naive, in failing to understand what their interactions are really about, and as unjustified indifference, aloofness, and alienation, in not acknowledging and perhaps even rejecting membership, at some level, in the broader community that Strong Tactful envisions (table 4.3); for example, challenging Strong Tactful's interpretation of the First Amendment to the United States Constitution.

Strong Tactful secularists will seek to add Weak Detached religious groups, in some sense, to their own community. The effort to recruit Weak Detached might involve attempts to undermine Weak Detached's sense of identity and community, efforts to convert Weak Detached to the beliefs, values, and identity of Strong Tactful's secular community, and negotiations aimed at securing Weak Detached's loyalty to Strong Tactful's community. From the standpoint of Strong Tactful, committed to a relational view of community, the mere fact of Weak Detached's insistence on disengagement may be a sufficient rationale for actions against Weak Detached. Strong Tactful always has its own particular sense of community, and so will have low tolerance for groups professing other potentially competing community identities and loyalties.

Weak Detached religious groups are likely to react strongly to any pressures from Strong Tactful secularists, perceiving these as serious threats to its own identity and community. From Weak Detached's standpoint, separation and an intrinsically defined identity are highly valued, and so any entanglements with Strong Tactful are to be strenuously avoided. Weak Detached is mindful that whatever Strong Tactful suggests about the importance and benefits of membership in a shared community is grounded in Strong Tactful's self-interests, including intentions of control and domination. Furthermore, in the pursuit of its own self-interest Strong Tactful is not above redefining the community and forming new alliances with groups other than Weak Detached. Weak Detached religious groups must understand that relationships with Strong Tactful secularists are always ad hoc and subject to revision.

Because Weak Detached religious groups and Strong Tactful secularists are exact opposites with respect to underlying assumptions of identity and intention, much potential exists for misreading each other's position. From the perspective of Weak Detached, Strong Tactful's position may be misread as a Strong Loyal position (dialogue 9). This misperception is especially likely given the history of many minority religious groups with oppression and violence consistent with the Loyal perspective. This may be all to the good, for it would lead Weak Detached to become more vigilant in protecting its identity and community.[1]

Dialogue 10. Weak Detached versus Strong Tactful
Vaccination Exemptions versus Requirements

Children in the United States are required to be vaccinated or immunized against preventable diseases before they are enrolled in schools. Vaccination is the administration of substances that will stimulate children's immune systems to develop resistance to infectious diseases including diphtheria, pertussis (whooping cough), tetanus, polio, measles, mumps, rubella, and varicella (chickenpox). The goals of vaccination are to provide children with immunity against preventable diseases and to provide communities with herd immunity.

Herd immunity occurs when most people have immunity to a disease, making the spread of the disease difficult, thus providing indirect immunity for those who are not immune. Herd immunity can lead to eradication of diseases including smallpox, polio, and measles.

Most states permit parents to opt out of children's vaccinations for medical or religious reasons. About a dozen states permit exemptions for personal philosophical reasons. Nationally, the rate of exemption from vaccination remains low, at less than two percent. In recent years the number of exemptions has been increasing and is now as high as seven percent in certain states. In some wealthy counties, the exemption rates can be eight to ten percent; in some expensive private schools, the exemption rates can be as high as seventy to eighty percent. High exemption rates expose larger numbers of children to outbreaks of infectious diseases. In addition, if the vaccination rate required for herd immunity is not met, then infants who are too young for immunization, children who have not been immunized for medical reasons, and older adults with compromised immune systems are at increased risk of infectious diseases.

Why do some parents choose to have their children exempted from vaccinations? These parents question the effectiveness, safety, and necessity of vaccines, arguing they contain harmful ingredients, cause serious side effects, and target diseases no longer serious or common in the United States. The counter-arguments are that vaccines prevent millions of cases of childhood illnesses, vaccine ingredients are safe, adverse reactions are rare, and serious and sometimes fatal diseases persist in the United States and globally. Parents who are opposed to vaccination of their children are rarely convinced by these counter-arguments. When people's perspectives, beliefs, and values are challenged, some become defensive. There can be a "backfire effect;" that is, arguments and evidence supporting vaccination can lead people to become more firmly opposed.

Parents who resist vaccination of their children reflect a

Weak Detached standpoint. From the Detached perspective, the focus is on maintaining a separate identity, with few connections to others outside one's group, and on constructing a meaningful life. Weak Detached parents do not have a close connection with or trust in authorities such as pediatricians, public health officials, teachers and scientists, pharmaceutical companies, and government agencies, including the Centers for Disease Control and the Food and Drug Administration. Instead, their aim is to be independent of presumed authorities and self-sufficient, evaluating the evidence on vaccines themselves, coming to their own conclusions, and sharing stories and opinions in their social network. Weak Detached parents strive to be good parents and protect the health of their children. For some, this can mean having their children eat only natural, organic foods and following alternative, holistic wellness advice rather than following modern medicine and its recommendations for vaccinations.

Vaccination procedures are designed to be the same for all children, with similar hypodermic needles, syringes, doses, and schedules. For some parents opting out of standardization can be a way to proclaim how their children are unique and special, like enrolling them in private schools rather than public schools, or providing them with the latest iPhone rather than a less expensive cell phone. The Detached focus on a separate identity apart from others can be consistent with becoming a "free rider," benefiting from a public good available to all members of society without contributing anything towards securing the public good. These parents calculate that they need not bother with vaccinating their own children because they will be protected by herd immunity when all the other children are vaccinated. These feelings of separateness and entitlement for one's children and lifestyle, consistent with the Weak Detached perspective, can be reinforced when entertainment celebrities participate in and endorse the anti-vaccine movement.

A further reason for supporting vaccination exemptions is

the belief that medical decisions for children should be made by parents and not by government. Government should not infringe on the freedom of individuals and families to choose their own medications, even if their choices might increase the risk of disease for their own children and for others in society. The view that individuals should be vigilant in protecting their freedoms from an intrusive and controlling government is consistent with the Detached perspective.

Yet, the arguments in support of children's vaccinations are often presented from a Strong Tactful standpoint. From the Tactful perspective, individuals and groups exist in interdependence with each other. When the issue is how to protect everyone in society, and especially children, from the risks and dangers of infectious diseases, then the interests of multiple groups must be taken into consideration. From the Tactful perspective there is an intention to control, and some would argue that public health requires compulsory vaccination laws. Others would counter, arguing that religious and philosophical views must be respected and individual freedoms must be protected.

As a result, vaccination policies in the United States reflect a balancing of these multiple interests. They are established by the individual states, not by the federal government. The options for exemption are varied, reflecting the diverse interests, negotiations, and agreements among the citizens of each state. At the same time, there must be a sufficient expectation for vaccination to ensure the maintenance of herd immunity inside each community. Vaccination has been an enormously successful public health achievement in the United States, not only saving lives and protecting children and adults from infectious diseases but also saving billions of dollars in the direct medical costs and indirect social costs of infectious diseases.

For members of the Weak Detached vaccination-exemption group, the primary goal is to be left alone so that they can pursue self-understanding inside the boundaries of their own community. The actions of the Strong Tactful vaccine-requirement group are viewed as intrusive, manipulative, menacing, and unprovoked (table 4.2). Strong Tactful looks on Weak Detached's assertions of wanting to be left alone to seek self-understanding as naive, in failing to understand what their interactions are really about, and as unjustified indifference, aloofness, and alienation, in not acknowledging and perhaps even rejecting membership, at some level, in the community that Strong Tactful envisions (table 4.3).

Strong Tactful will likely seek to add Weak Detached, in some sense, to its own community, to continue public education and other efforts to persuade Weak Detached parents to vaccinate their children. From the standpoint of Strong Tactful, committed to a relational view of community, the mere fact of Weak Detached's insistence on disengagement may be a sufficient rationale for actions against Weak Detached. Some pediatricians refuse to serve families who do not vaccinate their children, arguing that unvaccinated children put other children at risk.

Weak Detached is likely to react strongly to any pressures from Strong Tactful, perceiving these as serious threats to its own identity and community. From Weak Detached's standpoint, separation and an intrinsically defined identity are highly valued, and so any entanglements with Strong Tactful are to be strenuously avoided. Weak Detached must bear in mind that whatever Strong Tactful suggests about the importance and benefits of membership in a shared community is grounded in Strong Tactful's self-interests, including motivations of control and domination.

Because Weak Detached and Strong Tactful are exact opposites with respect to underlying assumptions of identity and intentions, there is much potential for misreading each other's position (see the perspectives matrix, table 3.1).

Dialogue 11. Weak Detached versus Strong Detached
Working Poor versus Rich

America's traditions and values are rooted in its small towns, where everybody knows who you are and knows your name. Walking along Disney World's early twentieth-century Main Street, you can exchange greetings with the mayor, a city councilor, and the fire chief. Everyone frequents the same barbershop and hair salon, the bakery and the restaurants, the jeweler and the department store; everyone rides the same train and attends the same theater. In Bedford Falls, the setting for the 1946 film *It's a Wonderful Life*, George Bailey, who runs the building and loan business, Henry Potter, the richest man and town, and the druggist, cab driver, cop, and other townspeople all know and talk comfortably with each other.

In *The Andy Griffith Show's* town of Mayberry, the residents include the sheriff, the mayor, an auto mechanic, a barber, a schoolteacher, the county clerk, a bank guard, a farmer, and others. The diverse characters in *The Simpsons'* town of Springfield include a middle-class family, the nuclear power plant owner, the state governor and the town mayor, the elementary school superintendent, principal, teachers, janitor, bus driver, and lunch lady, police officers, a bartender, judges, a restaurant owner, a barber, talk show host, lawyer, and many more who come together in various episodes.

In contrast, today most Americans live, work, and play in communities segregated by huge disparities in income and wealth. They rarely meet and interact with and do not understand those whose life prospects are markedly different. Roughly half of Americans live paycheck to paycheck, in poverty or near poverty, with no savings to fall back on if they lose their job or have a medical emergency. Roughly a quarter of Americans have jobs paying less than what is needed to live above the federal poverty line. Many of these families are forced to rely on food banks and government safety-net programs to get by. Wages for the working poor have remained stagnant for decades. The reasons include opposition to increasing the minimum wage, the weakening of labor unions, new labor-saving technologies and automation, a corporate focus on profits, and globalization. Workers worried about high unemployment and losing their jobs reluctantly work longer hours and accept lower pay.

Social mobility for Americans living in and near poverty is quite limited. Many continue to believe in the American Dream, that working hard will lead to getting ahead: owning a car and a home, taking a vacation every year, putting kids through college, saving for retirement. If they could see their situations improving, their perspective might be described as Weak Tactful (as described in dialogue 5, immigrants, and dialogue 7, disadvantaged). But due to lack of education beyond high school, few marketable job skills, and little relevant and responsible work experience, the working poor are stuck in low-wage jobs or underemployed and at high risk of unemployment. They live in dying communities with grossly inadequate funding for police, parks, and public transportation. Their belief in the American Dream leads many to blame themselves for not working hard enough. The prospects for their children, growing up in economically segregated neighborhoods with failing public schools, are not any better. The working poor feel subject to forces beyond their control, including rapid demographic, cultural, and technological changes. They have fallen out of the bottom of mainstream American society and feel alienated, disconnected, and powerless. This is a Weak Detached standpoint.

At the other extreme, a tiny percentage of Americans absorbs a hugely disproportionate share of all national income. The pay of CEOs of America's largest companies was once only a few times higher than the pay of an average worker. Now, CEO pay averaging millions of dollars a year is hundreds of times higher than what an average worker earns.

The earnings of other corporate executives and private investors have similarly skyrocketed in recent decades. Furthermore, a tiny percentage of rich Americans now controls more than half the wealth in America. Charles Murray, a fellow at the American Enterprise Institute, argues that a new upper class with a distinctive culture has emerged. The reasons are multiple, including the advantages for those who already have excellent educations and social connections in a time of rapid technological and globalization changes.

The reasons include, in addition, successful lobbying of federal and state governments to lower taxes, decrease regulation, and increase subsidies for corporations, thus increasing profits and benefits for the rich. And the reasons include successful lobbying to shape tax policies to be favorable for capital gains, hedge funds, partnerships, trusts, and other tax shelters and loopholes that only the rich can take advantage of (see chapter 9, the pro-business Tactful coalition). And the reasons include efforts to weaken and dismantle labor unions, resistance to increasing the minimum wage, paying workers less than they deserve based on their productivity, and paying workers less than they and their families need to live.

For example, most low-wage workers employed by the largest fast-food companies must rely on public assistance to get by, costing American taxpayers billions of dollars each year. Government safety-net programs to make up for low wages are essentially corporate welfare programs, allowing workers to be paid less than a living wage and maximizing corporate profits and benefits for the rich. Nicholas Kristof, Pulitzer-Prize winning op-ed columnist for *The New York Times*, pointed in March, 2014, to other public welfare programs benefiting corporations and the rich, including tax subsidies for private planes, vacation homes, and yachts and lower tax rates for capital gains.

Social mobility for rich Americans is also limited, except for the few who might fall back into the middle class. The perspective of the rich might be described as Tactful, if they had to take risks, compete, and work hard to attain their advantages. But continued success of the rich is largely guaranteed, through their social connections and access to financial and political power, through socializing and marrying primarily among their own social network, and increasingly through the inheritance of enormous wealth that reduces or eliminates the need to actually work. Thus, it would be unfair to describe the rich as competitive, ill-intentioned, or greedy, for the benefits of high income and wealth merely flow in a straightforward way to those who are already rich (as described in chapter 4, power and privilege). This enables the rich to easily live in exclusive neighborhoods, travel in private limousines and jets, and have access to private clubs and health care facilities.

The prospects for the children of the rich are also essentially guaranteed, starting with access to excellent public schools in affluent neighborhoods and to top private schools. Ample financial resources and affirmative action for alumni offspring ensure access to prestigious colleges, where making social connections is more important than what is learned, and to the very best graduate programs in business, finance, and law. Focused on enjoying life in their own financial, political, and social networks, the rich have little idea of what typical American workers must do to support themselves and their families. This perspective of the rich is best described as Strong Detached.

In contrast with the citizens of Bedford Falls, Mayberry, Springfield, and America's cities and towns in decades past, the working poor and the rich in America today no longer live in the same communities, send their children to the same schools, have the same life prospects, live and work in similar ways, have conversations together, or really know much about each other. The dialogue between these two groups, to the extent it exists at all, is a Weak Detached versus Strong Detached dialogue. The Weak Detached poor would like to live where there are good schools and job opportunities; the Strong Detached rich rig the system with residential zoning restrictions. The poor would like to respond to crime with better policing; the rich move to gated communities with private security guards. The poor would like increased funds for public schools; the rich enroll their children in private schools. The poor would like longer hours for public libraries and more branches; the rich buy their own books. The poor would like adequate funding for public parks; the rich go to weekend estates in the country. These examples are from Nicholas Kristof, writing in *The New York Times* in 2012.[2]

In summary, Weak Detached and Strong Detached have much in common—isolation from other groups and a striving for self-understanding—and so Weak Detached understands intuitively the standpoint of Strong Detached. From the perspective of Weak Detached, Strong Detached's greater power, privilege, and resources appear unearned and unjustified. In not recognizing the needs of Weak Detached and not offering to share ample resources, Strong Detached appears unreasonably aloof, insensitive, and tactless (table 4.2).

Nevertheless, because Weak Detached shares Strong Detached's perspective on independence and self-sufficiency, there is a reluctance to make any claim on these resources. Historically, the poor in America have had little antipathy towards the rich. Despite the recent surge in income and wealth inequality, there continues to be little social discontent. Consistent with their detached standpoint, the Weak Detached poor remain largely ignorant of, and so greatly underestimate, the true extent of inequality in America.

The Strong Detached rich are also largely ignorant of, and so greatly underestimate, inequality in America. If resources are sufficient for both groups, for example, minimally sufficient for the poor to get by (with food stamps, housing subsidies, and Medicaid), then conflict is unlikely. The Strong Detached rich view statements or actions by Weak Detached working poor as intrusive, self-serving, and unprovoked, and Weak Detached is seen as bothersome, aloof, and isolated (table 4.3). Both Weak Detached and Strong Detached wish foremost to be left alone and be able to ignore the other.

The Strong Detached rich feel little responsibility or obligation to contribute more with the aim of improving the opportunities and lives of Weak Detached poor. In contrast to other advanced economies, in America there has been relatively little concern on the part of the rich for the working poor. The two groups have a tacit agreement to leave each other alone. It is, however, in the interest of Strong Detached rich to remain vigilant and not permit Weak Detached poor to become stronger, through labor unions or political organizing, and thus perhaps challenge Strong Detached rich.

Even under the best of circumstances, when Weak Detached and Strong Detached are cooperating, this is a mechanical cooperation; for example, the following of a formula that yields a division of resources, rather than any long-term interest in maintaining the relationship. There is a technical compliance with what needs to be done, rather than a caring involvement with the other: "Tell me what I need to do and then when I do it, I'm done, I've paid my dues." There is no long-term interest in dominating, in forming alliances with, or in caring for the other group; each Detached group is willing to let the other go off alone.

An underlying theme in the Weak Detached versus Strong Detached dialogue is always the desire to remain separate, to not come into closer contact. Thus, either party may engage in ritualistic behaviors to avert any potential conflict, as in being polite, apologizing, or withdrawing. The rationale for these behaviors may be phrased in terms of "maintaining our good relationship," but the point is there is no relationship, and so the interest of both parties is in quickly minimizing any tension or conflict so that forming a closer relationship is unnecessary.

Dialogue 12. Weak Detached versus Strong Caring
Isolationism versus Idealism in Foreign Policy

Should the United States focus on its own problems and let other countries deal with theirs as best they can? Or should the United States help other countries deal effectively with their problems? In the past the United States helped Europe and Japan recover from World War II, helped reduce conflict in Northern Ireland, arranged a peace treaty between Egypt and Israel, helped bring about peace in the former Yugoslavia, and pushed Saddam Hussein out of Kuwait. Yet, expectations for American involvement in the world continue to arise in Sudan, Afghanistan, Libya, Syria, Ukraine, and elsewhere. Some have argued the United States can no longer serve as the policeman for the world.

What should be the principles guiding relations between the United States and other countries? Many Americans believe the United States should mind its own business and let other countries get along on their own. Cultural and economic separation and avoidance of foreign entanglements has been termed isolationism. Most Americans supported non-intervention and neutrality as World War I began and again, despite the success of German and Japanese advances, at the beginning of World War II until the attack on Pearl Harbor. Isolationists argue that giving military weapons and economic aid to other countries only intensifies conflicts and doesn't bring peace.

Many feel the United States is too involved in countries where we have no vital national interests and is trying too hard to solve all the world's problems. Instead, more attention and resources should be directed to solving problems at home, including improving education and health care, rebuilding transportation and other essential infrastructure, and strengthening the domestic economy and protecting American jobs. Participation in the United Nations and similar international organizations gives other countries too much control and threatens America's sovereignty. Isolationism, focusing on the interests and self-sufficiency of the United States and disregarding the needs of other countries, is an example of the Weak Detached standpoint.

On the other hand, many believe that America should promote democratic values in other countries, including freedom of expression and political participation, human rights particularly for women and children, and the growth of democratic movements and institutions. In addition, the United States should provide substantial economic assistance, including humanitarian aid to save lives and reduce the suffering of victims of natural disasters, wars, and famines. And the United States should provide development aid to increase access to education, medical care, food, and safe water; to reduce poverty and increase standards of living; and to stimulate long-term economic development. A long-term aim is to transform other countries politically through the extension of American values. Senator John McCain argues that American foreign policy must support human rights. "We are a country with a conscience. We have long believed moral concerns must be an essential part of our foreign policy, not a departure from it. We are the chief architect and defender of an international order governed by rules derived from our political and economic values."

The idea that a country's international relations should reflect its internal political philosophy—in the case of the United States, democracy, human rights, and respect and compassion for others—has been termed idealism. Idealism in international relations, attending to the needs and concerns of both the United States and other countries, illustrates a Strong Caring standpoint. Idealists argue that to have order in the world rather than chaos, to encourage justice in other countries and avert and mitigate tragedies, is ultimately in America's interest, too. This includes working cooperatively with other countries and in international organizations to solve global problems, for example, infectious diseases and environmental degradation, and to promote world peace. The

United States should use a combination of diplomatic, economic, political, and cultural tools to advance its political and ideological influence, respond to humanitarian needs, and work to maintain the global order.

Idealism may be contrasted with realism (or pragmatism), reflecting the Loyal perspective in foreign policy. Realism focuses on the use of economic strength and military power, acting unilaterally if necessary, to advance the self-interests of countries. The primary concern of realists is the use of power to defend against and contain America's potential enemies. What matters is whether the United States wins or other countries win and whether other countries side with the United States—are they friends or foes?—regardless of the extent of human rights, or lack thereof, in those countries.

Detached isolationism, Caring idealism, and Loyal realism may be contrasted with diplomacy (or internationalism), a Tactful perspective giving greater emphasis to being non-confrontational while negotiating multilateral military and economic partnerships, coalitions, and alliances that advance mutual, interdependent, long-term interests yet are still overall in the interest of the United States; for example, NATO, the United Nations, and the World Bank. From the Tactful perspective, other countries may still be seen as competitors but not as potential enemies.

For Weak Detached isolationists, the primary goal of foreign policy is for the United States to be left alone to pursue self-understanding and self-sufficiency inside the boundaries of its own community as opposed to participating in the international community. The actions of Strong Caring idealists can be difficult for Weak Detached isolationists to comprehend, for Weak Detached does not share the assumption that both the United States and other countries participate in a shared international community. From Weak Detached's isolationist standpoint, maintaining strong borders to block immigrants from other countries, minimizing international trade to protect American jobs, and slashing humanitarian aid and refugee assistance for other countries are all essential for protecting an intrinsically defined American homeland and identity. Separation from other countries is highly valued, so any entanglements with other countries, as Strong Caring idealists advocate, including supporting and participating in programs of the United Nations, are to be strenuously avoided.

The attitudes and behaviors of the Strong Caring idealist group are grounded in the assumption that groups are defined in large part through their relations with other groups. From the Strong Caring idealist standpoint, furthermore, the understanding of international community is strongly shaped by the assumption that the intention for human action is to understand, to construct meaning and significance in our lives. A better understanding of identity and community depends on recognizing the interdependent nature of identity construction, expressed through a caring commitment to others who are different. Strong Caring idealists may consider the statements and actions of Weak Detached isolationists to be self-centered, aloof, indifferent, disengaged, and immature (table 4.3). Strong Caring idealists are concerned that a policy of non-involvement would give a free pass to authoritarian governments in other countries to ignore human rights and imprison and torture dissidents.

From the standpoint of Weak Detached isolationists, the statements and actions of Strong Caring idealists about caring and community can appear naive, idealistic, and patronizing (table 4.2). In addition, Weak Detached may fear becoming entrapped in Strong Caring's notion of an interdependent international community and unable to defend its own conception of a unique and separate American identity and community. Thus, despite the good intentions of Strong Caring idealists, Weak Detached isolationists can interpret its actions as reflecting a hostile intention to destroy the identity and community of the United States.

For Strong Caring idealists there are dimensions of respect, caring, and responsibility towards other groups and relationships and a commitment to striving to maintain and strengthen relationships. From the standpoint of Strong Caring idealists, the United States should be a moral beacon for the international community. Domestically, a primary task is to help Weak Detached isolationists to mature and to become members, at some level, of the broader community. The role of Strong Caring is teaching, mentoring, nurturing, and socializing, helping Weak Detached to adopt an interdependent rather than a self-sufficient view of identity and community. The relationship between Strong Caring and Weak Detached does not involve potential conflict as in some other dialogues. Instead, moving forward can be a matter of Strong Caring discovering opportunities for Weak Detached to participate in and contribute to the international community that are not also threatening to Weak Detached's own sense of identity.

8

Looking Out for Others:
The Weak Caring Dialogues

Are human activities changing the Earth's climate and, if so, what should be done, if anything? What are the causes of homelessness in America? Whose responsibility is it to solve this problem? What's the best response to gun violence in America—passing sensible gun laws, increasing mental health services, or limiting the power of government? These are currently among the most explosive political issues in America. Often one side in these debates reflects the Weak Caring standpoint, the focus of this chapter. The other side often reflects the Loyal, Tactful, or Detached perspectives.

The Caring perspective is defined by an interdependent identity and an intention to understand. People and groups holding the Caring perspective aim to cooperate with others and look out for others. Examples from chapter 1 include Maxwell Mercy, the army captain in Colorado; Missy Peckham, the social worker in Alaska; Michael Healy, the revenue cutter captain in Alaska; and Hans Brumbaugh, the Colorado farmer. Examples from chapter 3 include Jane Addams and Eleanor Roosevelt.

Dialogue 13. Weak Caring versus Strong Loyal
Climate Change Mitigation versus Adaptation

The earth's climate system has warmed significantly since the Industrial Revolution and especially over the past century. Surface, atmospheric, and ocean temperatures have increased because of human burning of fossil fuels and the emission of greenhouse gases, primarily carbon dioxide and methane. The anticipated global warming effects include rising sea levels, expansion of deserts, melting of glaciers, permafrost, and sea ice, and more frequent weather extremes, including heat waves, droughts, and heavy rainfall and floods.

The impact on humans will vary regionally but include shortages of fresh water, decreasing crop yields and more hunger, increases in pandemic infectious diseases, abandoning populated areas due to rising sea levels, and increasing global conflict over scarce resources and a surge of climate refugees. In the United States, climate change is predicted to aggravate economic inequality, transferring wealth from sweltering Florida, Texas, and poor counties in the Southeast to well-off communities in the Northeast. The impact on other species will also be dire, as ocean acidification, earlier timing of spring events, shifts in temperature ranges, heat waves and wildfires, and loss of habitat lead to an unprecedented extinction of great numbers of plant and animal species.

One response has been an urgent campaign for mitigation; that is, reducing the extent of global warming and climate change by reducing the emission of greenhouse gasses. Programs for mitigation include increasing the efficiency of energy use, for example, through innovative manufacturing and transportation technologies and low-energy building design and insulation; decreasing the demand for energy by encouraging urban housing density, walking, and bicycling; wise use of heating and air conditioning and similar conservation measures; and shifting from fossil fuels to renewable, clean energy sources including solar, wind, hydro, and nuclear power. Taxes on energy and carbon can motivate energy users to reduce consumption and emissions. Advocates for mitigation, including William Nordhaus, Sterling Professor of Economics at Yale University, argue that the cost of reducing climate change now is less than the cost of responding to the impacts of climate change in the near future.

In 2015 representatives of the world's nations, meeting in Paris with leadership from the United States and China, committed themselves to programs to lower greenhouse gas emissions to avoid the devastating effects of global warming and climate change. Focusing on mitigation and putting the long-term interests of future human generations, inhabitants of poor and at-risk developing nations, and diverse habitats and species around the world ahead of America's short-term economic interests is an example of a Weak Caring standpoint. This Weak Caring mitigation standpoint understands that all groups of people, present and future, are mutually dependent with shared responsibilities for their actions and for the future of our planet.

A contrasting standpoint is to wait to see what might be the actual impacts of climate change and then adapt as necessary, for example, raising the height of sea walls or shifting to drought resistant crops. The stability and growth of the world economy depends on the energy currently provided by fossil fuels, including oil, natural gas, and coal. Major energy corporations and many countries have invested heavily in discovering and acquiring fossil fuel reserves and building the infrastructure for pumping, mining, refining, and delivering fossil-fuel energy for manufacturing and transportation and for lighting, heating, and air-conditioning of offices and homes. Alternative, renewable energy sources are inadequate to meet the existing demand for energy, much less what will be required in the decades ahead, especially as developing countries like China and India become more prosperous. It is unreasonable to disrupt the American and world economies and deny energy corporations an appropriate return on their investment, as advocates for mitigation of greenhouse gas emissions would do, merely because of vague and uncertain concerns about what might happen to the earth's climate in the future.

A quite different argument, also consistent with this adaptation perspective, is that the efforts toward mitigation of greenhouse gas emissions have been too little and too late to forestall the worst consequences of global warming and climate change. It is widely acknowledged, for example, that the 2015 Paris agreement is not by itself sufficient to forestall significant negative impacts of climate change, even assuming all the countries that are parties to the agreement achieve their proposed emissions reduction goals. In short, the adaptation perspective can be an argument both for waiting to see what the impacts of climate change might be and then adapting as necessary, and an argument that the mitigation strategy is a failure and so realistically we should wait and then adapt to the potential disaster of climate change as best we can.

This focus on adaptation to global warming and climate change is consistent with the Strong Loyal standpoint. The arguments are to support the status quo, in particular, to maintain existing control by corporations and countries over fossil-fuel resources and their extraction and distribution. No energy corporation or country heavily invested in fossil fuels for its own energy needs or for sale to others wants to be the first to adopt a mitigation strategy, commit to reductions in greenhouse gas emissions, and give up its presumed competitive economic edge against other corporations and countries. [1]

The Strong Loyal adaptation standpoint privileges its own corporate and national interests, without regard for the likely consequences of its actions on others, including the welfare of future generations destined to live in degraded environments, the economies of countries at high risk of climate disasters, and the habitats and prospects for numerous plant and animal species. From the Strong Loyal standpoint one asks, "Why should I sacrifice now for what might happen in an uncertain future and for distant others—people and species—with whom I have no relationship? If it eventually becomes necessary, humans will figure out how to adapt to any potential impact of climate change."

From the Weak Caring mitigation standpoint, identity and community are defined in part by a commitment to the integrity of others' identities and communities. A better understanding of oneself depends on recognizing the interdependent nature of identity construction. This understanding is expressed through a sincere interest in learning more about others and through the actions of caring for others, regardless of the extent to which people may be similar to or different from oneself. From the Weak Caring standpoint, the emphases of the Strong Loyal adaptation standpoint on self rather than other, and on competition, control, and domination, appear immature, aggressive, and perplexing. The Loyal assumptions about how individuals and groups are defined and what motivates humans are far removed from the Caring assumptions (table 4.3).

In contrast to the Weak Caring mitigation standpoint that all parties, present and future, are mutually dependent with shared responsibilities for their actions, the Strong Loyal adaptation standpoint is an example of cost externalizing; that is, shifting the indirect costs and moral responsibilities of fossil-fuel burning and climate change away from a self-contained, intrinsically defined self and onto third parties. These indirect costs are likely to include substantial increases in insurance costs for public and private buildings in coastal states; plummeting property values and tax receipts in communities at risk of sea level rise; tougher and more expensive building codes for areas at high risk of storm damage and flooding; and costs for cities and states to establish and administer disaster relief funds. For example, in 2013 New York City Mayor Michael Bloomberg proposed a $20 billion plan for adapting to sea levels rising two feet or more in the next forty years as a result of climate change, including new floodwalls and storm barriers and upgrades to power and telecommunications infrastructure.

The paragraphs that follow set forth the general features of the Weak Caring versus Strong Loyal dialogue. From the Strong Loyal adaptation standpoint, the values and goals of its own corporate and national community are worthy, whereas the values and goals of the Weak Caring mitigation advocates are not. Strong Loyal regards actions by Weak Caring as a potential threat to its identity, community, power, and prestige, and feels justified in guarding against any efforts by Weak Caring to increase its power and prestige. For example, Strong Loyal feels it must defend against Weak Caring's argument that most fossil fuel resources must be kept in the ground and so must be considered "stranded assets" that pose a substantial risk for investors.

Strong Loyal adaptation advocates may feel mystified and uncertain about the attitudes and behaviors of Weak Caring mitigation advocates, for the Caring perspective is maximally discrepant from the Loyal perspective (table 3.1). From Strong Loyal's standpoint Weak Caring appears quite naive and idealistic, in failing to understand that the issues between the two groups are ones of competition, control, power, and survival. Weak Caring's assertions that both groups are, at some level, members of a broader, shared global community and mutually dependent will be very difficult for Strong Loyal to hear and understand, given Strong Loyal's assumption of intrinsically defined corporate and national identities.

The actions of Strong Loyal adaptation advocates in continuing to expand extraction and marketing of fossil fuels can appear to Weak Caring mitigation advocates as domineering, aggressive, unprovoked, and immature (table 4.2). In response to these aggressive actions from Strong

Loyal, Weak Caring is likely to be initially surprised and confused, for Strong Loyal's actions are based on assumptions about identity and intention quite different from those of the Caring perspective.

Strong Loyal will take differences in viewpoints, behaviors, and assumptions to provide a rationale for control and domination. Weak Caring will take differences from Strong Loyal's assumptions as reasons for reaching out, seeking to better understand, and caring. Weak Caring strives to understand Strong Loyal as well as or better than Strong Loyal itself. The message Weak Caring wants Strong Loyal to hear is not a message of seeking power and privilege but rather a message of caring and cooperation. Weak Caring's message to Strong Loyal is one of love; but Strong Loyal's response is "Don't love me," for the message implies the two groups are interdependent and have something in common.

Strong Loyal's lack of understanding of the intentions of Weak Caring, along with suggestions by Weak Caring of shared membership in a common community, can fuel feelings of paranoia. Strong Loyal adaptation is likely to project its own intentions of control and domination onto Weak Caring mitigation, so Strong Loyal will understand the dialogue and conflict as Weak Loyal versus Strong Loyal (dialogue 1, business). Strong Loyal can be expected to engage in many of the same calculations and tactics as when Strong Loyal is opposed to Weak Loyal, including actions aimed at increasing psychological distance between the groups and dehumanizing the other (for example, accusations that Weak Loyal is waging a "war on coal"). In this context, the actions by the multinational oil and gas corporation Exxon to hide research evidence confirming the human impact on climate change and to fund climate-change denial groups are quite consistent with the Loyal perspective. Strong Loyal can rationalize its domination and perhaps the destruction of Weak Caring by emphasizing differences, rather than commonalities, between the two groups, by building on its own assumption of intrinsically defined identity.

Strong Loyal adaptation will likely hear the message of Weak Caring mitigation, with its implication that Strong Loyal and Weak Caring have common interests as members of a broader, shared global community, as a threat to the integrity of its own corporate and national identity and community and react accordingly. From the Loyal perspective, one belongs either with my community or with another community. One must choose between loyalty to one's corporation or country, on the one hand, and the environment of the future, on the other, but one can't be loyal to both at the same time. Strong Loyal's self-contained, self-sufficient nationalist identity is not consistent with cooperating and working together with other countries.

Weak Caring assumes the countries of the world are interdependent; collective action will be required to mitigate climate change. From the Caring perspective, community is always a both-and understanding: one belongs both to this community and to other communities. To be concerned and care for corporations, other countries, jobs, and the environment all at the same time is not contradictory. Thus, in addition to the issues of power and what motivates humans, the Strong Loyal versus Weak Caring conflict involves debate over the nature of community.

Dialogue 14. Weak Caring versus Strong Tactful
Supporting versus Not Supporting the Homeless

More than three million Americans experience homelessness every year. On any given night, the number of homeless Americans is more than half a million. Roughly two-thirds of the homeless sleep in emergency shelters or transitional housing. The remainder sleep on the street, in abandoned buildings, in cars and vans, or in tents and under tarps. The main reasons for homelessness are a lack of affordable housing, poverty, and unemployment and can also include mental health problems, abuse of alcohol and drugs, domestic violence, and medical bankruptcy. Almost half the homeless in America are women; about a third are children. About a tenth are veterans, many with substance abuse problems or suffering from disabilities.

The financial costs for American society are enormous. These include the salaries of law-enforcement officers to assist homeless people and to monitor and arrest them for nonviolent offenses such as trespassing, public intoxication, or sleeping in parks and the costs of jail stays, emergency room visits, and medical care. In addition, multiple nonprofit agencies collect and spend huge sums of money for food, warm clothing, and temporary shelter. The moral costs to American society of allowing women, children, and veterans to continue to be homeless are incalculable.

What can be done to solve the problem of homelessness in America? The traditional approach has been to provide immediate assistance with food and short-term shelter. The next step has been to link homeless people to health clinics and counseling programs that address mental health and substance abuse problems and to educational and skills training programs that increase employability. Providing homeless people with stable housing typically has been conditional on showing they can be good tenants; that is, being successful in substance abuse and mental health treatment programs and securing steady employment. Homeless people may pass through several levels of housing from public shelters to transitional housing and only eventually to an apartment or house in the community.

An innovative approach being implemented in several cities focuses on first providing stable housing, for example, an apartment, before engaging the homeless in programs leading to long-term solutions for their problems. It is difficult for people to make significant progress with mental health and addiction problems and find and hold a job if they remain uncertain where they will be sleeping from night to night. Stable housing can provide a base for homeless people to stay engaged with treatment programs. Having a permanent place to live makes it easier to participate in training for job skills, search for work and connect with employers, and get to work each day and successfully hold a new job.

Some families are given housing vouchers so they can afford their own apartment in the private market. And some not-for-profits and charitable foundations have bought buildings to develop into permanent housing, rather than continue to focus on providing short-term, transitional housing for the homeless. Although long-term, permanent housing may seem an expensive solution to homelessness, it often turns out to cost less than half the cost of emergency services for homeless people who are sleeping on the streets, in abandoned buildings, or in shelters and short-term transitional housing. The traditional approach and the housing first approach are consistent with a Weak Caring standpoint.

What are the obstacles to solving the problem of homelessness? People with a stable income and a secure place to live often assume they have nothing in common with those who are homeless. They believe incorrectly that homeless people are primarily men with mental health or substance abuse problems, or they are lazy and unwilling to look for work, or they are transients from elsewhere and not from the local community. Misunderstandings like these are reflected in laws intended to criminalize homelessness and make these people seem to disappear. Local ordinances may restrict people from resting in public places like bus terminals or libraries or sleeping on sidewalks or camping in parks. Focusing on perceived differences and failing to see potential similarities reflects the self-contained identities of the Detached and Loyal perspectives. A Detached attitude of indifference toward homeless people or a Loyal attitude of disdain may also lead to harassment and violence directed against homeless people.

The primary obstacle, however, is resistance to providing the financial resources Weak Caring advocates for the homeless believe would solve the problem. The number of affordable housing units has sharply decreased in recent decades. The reasons include reductions in federal incentives for affordable housing and urban gentrification resulting in higher property values and displacement of low-income families. At the same time, the number of people living in poverty has increased, reflecting the long-term stagnation of hourly wages insufficient to pay for housing, the deinstitutionalization of the mentally ill, and steep funding cuts in America's social safety net (dialogue 11, working poor). The number of people needing affordable housing now exceeds by millions the number of affordable housing units in America. One solution is for government to provide the resources to build and rehabilitate housing for people with the lowest incomes. Another solution is for government to provide rental assistance, for example, housing vouchers for people with the lowest incomes to increase their range of housing options.

The resistance to providing these resources is grounded in the idea of the American Dream, that is, America as a country where people who work hard will be successful and get ahead. Conversely, people who are homeless didn't try hard enough in school, haven't tried hard enough to get a job, didn't work hard enough to hold onto a job, are losers and not winners. From this Strong Tactful standpoint, homelessness is the fault of those who failed to take advantage of opportunities, lacked initiative in getting and holding a job, and made poor lifestyle choices involving drugs and alcohol. Receiving government support for housing should be earned, not viewed as a basic right. In addition, from the Strong Tactful standpoint, homeless people already receive substantial food, housing, and medical benefits from the government, for which they are not giving back to society by working, so they have chosen to live as free riders.

The funding resistance is based in the recognition that homeless people and everyone else are interdependent members of the same American society. Affordable housing and rental assistance for the poor are seen as a real cost to the rest of society, threatening funding for schools and other public services and higher taxes. It's a zero-sum game. These implicit assumptions of interdependent relations and intentions to compete and win in a zero-sum game reflect the Strong Tactful standpoint. (Advocates for the homeless would counter, "The home mortgage interest tax deduction is a substantial government subsidy to property owners. Renters and the homeless don't get this government benefit.")

Here are the general features of the Weak Caring versus Strong Tactful dialogue. The attitudes and behaviors of Weak Caring advocates for the homeless are grounded in the assumption that groups are defined through their relations with other groups. Their understanding of community is strongly shaped by the assumption that the primary intention for human action is to understand, to construct meaning and significance in our lives. A better understanding of our own identity and community depends on recognizing the interdependent nature of identity construction and expressing this through a caring commitment to others who may appear to be different from ourselves.

From the Weak Caring standpoint, there are dimensions of respect, caring, and responsibility towards other groups and a commitment to strive to maintain and strengthen relationships. All individuals and groups in a community are interdependent and so homeless people should be understood as an integral part of communities and not as a nameless, faceless "they." Weak Caring advocates view homelessness in America as reflecting not the failures of individuals but instead economic downturns and poverty, the lack of affordable housing, and inadequate funding of mental health and substance abuse treatment programs.

The attitudes and behaviors of Strong Tactful funding opponents are also grounded in the assumption that groups are defined through their relations with other groups. However, this understanding of community is shaped by the assumption that the primary intention for humans is to compete with, to control, and to win against others. The concept of community is understood not as a goal in itself, but rather as a means toward the end of control and domination. For Strong Tactful, as from the Loyal perspective, any conflict is about competition and control and perhaps survival. Strong Tactful views Weak Caring homeless advocates as a potential threat, yet also as naive and idealistic. For Strong Tactful to agree to funding for the homeless would be to agree to a cost for themselves with no obvious gain.

There is potential for common ground between Weak Caring homeless advocates and Strong Tactful funding opponents, for both assume that groups are defined through their relations with other groups. The key difference is that Strong Tactful expects to manipulate relationships with others for its own self-interest. Weak Caring, however, understands relationships as involving dimensions of respect, caring, and responsibility that transcend any short-term self-interest. From the Strong Tactful standpoint, Weak Caring homeless advocates must be either with Strong Tactful or not. Thus, Strong Tactful views Weak Caring, in their support of the homeless, as unreliable and untrustworthy. Weak Caring homeless advocates, in contrast, view Strong Tactful funding opponents as lacking compassion, manipulative, menacing, and overbearing, yet as potentially enriching the broader life of the community should they participate more fully. Weak Caring would say, "If you aren't part of the solution, you're part of the problem."

Dialogue 14. Weak Caring versus Strong Tactful
Civility in Speech versus
Speech for Winning on Campus

Freedom of speech is essential for American democracy. Government by the people is based on voting by citizens who are informed and knowledgeable, through the unconstrained flow of information and ideas, with no concerns over censorship or retaliation for what is said. Freedom of speech is not unlimited, however, when it conflicts with other values and rights or has the potential to harass, intimidate, or harm people. Legislatures and courts have struggled to establish clear boundaries between freedom of speech, on the one hand, and restrictions against harming the reputation of individuals with false statements (defamation or slander), disturbing the peace and public order and inciting violence (misdemeanor or felony), distressing or threatening to harm another person (harassment and intimidation), urging people to rebel against the government (sedition), and willfully lying in court (perjury), on the other.

Freedom of speech requires a responsibility to maintain civility. Civil discourse includes listening with respect to what others are saying, being prepared to defend what one says with arguments and evidence, willingness to compromise and to change one's mind, and not engaging in bullying or hate speech. Hate speech intimidates or incites discrimination or violence based on people's race, religion, ethnicity, gender, disability, sexual orientation, or other attributes (perhaps reflecting a Loyal standpoint, as in dialogue 3). The responsibility for civil discourse does not ensure, however, that speakers are always polite and well-mannered. Controversial issues can generate strong feelings and statements; having our beliefs, values, and attitudes challenged can be painful. Indeed, some would argue that a liberal education at America's colleges and universities should rightly include discomfort for students as their assumptions and beliefs are examined and challenged. Supporting freedom of speech and civil discourse and opposing hate speech is consistent with both the Tactful and the Caring perspectives.

Yet, on several American college and university campuses, there has been vocal support for policies to restrict offensive speech. Opponents, pointing to the First Amendment, argue that there should be no limitations on speech. America's campuses sometimes appear forced to make difficult choices: between a welcoming educational community or ensuring academic freedom, between protecting a campus's core values or supporting open inquiry and debate, and between discouraging offensive speech or ensuring freedom of speech for all.

What, then, is the basis for this controversy over offensive speech and freedom of speech on America's campuses? It arises from the difference in intention between the Caring perspective, oriented toward understanding and cooperation, and the Tactful perspective, oriented toward controlling the world and achieving success.

From the Caring perspective, the purpose of an educational community is to enhance the mutual respect and understanding of its members through sharing a wide range of perspectives and experiences, including differing views on political and moral issues. The formal mission statements of many of America's colleges and universities include being an inclusive community and respecting cultural diversity.[2] In this context, it is essential that all students and other members of the campus community feel welcome, their backgrounds and experiences are respected, and others listen with respect and open minds when they express their views.[3]

Given these Caring goals of understanding and cooperation, statements that are perceived as rude or offensive—for example, that demean an individual's race, gender, sexual orientation, or religion—can be destructive to the integrity of the community and its aim of enhancing understanding for all. Similarly, statements that are seen as reflecting implicit hierarchies, the projection of power, and unearned privilege can be seen as efforts to control the course and outcomes of public conversations, maintaining the status quo and benefiting those already in power. The impact of rude or offensive speech can be to discourage the participation of students who may, for other reasons, already feel marginalized, vulnerable, or oppressed. These students and others may feel reluctant to speak out on controversial issues or to say to opponents, "What you said offended me."

For some students and groups (for example, racial, ethnic,

gender, or religious minorities), fears of incivility, bullying, harassment, and intimidation can lead to withdrawing from campus discussions (and perhaps adopting a Weak Detached standpoint). And students, like people in general, do not think or argue as clearly when they are insulted, under stress, treated unfairly, or feel emotionally uncomfortable. Fewer viewpoints are aired, positions on issues become polarized, and discussions are shaped more narrowly than would otherwise be the case. When this happens, opportunities for the sharing of ideas, discussing and debating important values and policies, and engaging in critical thinking, vital not only on America's campuses but also for American democracy, are lost.

From Weak Caring's standpoint, there should be restrictions on the ability of the privileged and powerful to use their freedom of speech to control the agenda and outcome of classroom discussions and public debates. In particular, speech that turns people against each other not because of what they think but because of who they are—their race, ethnicity, gender, or religion—should be strongly discouraged. Thus there have been calls for policies to discourage offensive speech and, in a few cases, speaker invitations and campus events have been cancelled for the sake of maintaining civility and the integrity of the educational community. From the Weak Caring standpoint, the focus is on encouraging and strengthening civil discourse and discouraging offensive and intellectually sloppy speech, and maintaining and strengthening an educational community that welcomes people of diverse views, backgrounds, and experiences with the aim of increasing mutual respect and everyone's understanding.

In contrast, from the Strong Tactful standpoint, oriented toward controlling the world and achieving success, freedom of speech is essential in ensuring that the best arguments and evidence on all sides can be presented and therefore that the truth will win out. Free speech is a useful tool for competing in discussion and debate, advancing and winning arguments, and maintaining and increasing power and privilege. From the Strong Tactful standpoint, the idea of freedom of speech should be broad, including the right to say what some people may take as offensive and to not be concerned with protecting the feelings of others.

Discussion and debate in a democracy can involve intense arguments over proposals to move forward from what is commonly believed and from the status quo, often advanced and advocated with words that can be raucous, rancorous, bruising, and ugly. The appropriate response to speech that some may find offensive is not to limit that speech but, instead, to listen carefully and then respond with more rational and eloquent speech that successfully challenges what has been said. The response to offensive speech may also include asserting that the speaker is ignorant, offensive, insulting, racist, and sexist. This is the Strong Tactful argument for unconstrained freedom of speech in order to find the truth and to win.

Strong Tactful would add that freedom of speech is the principal means for arguing against abusive power and privilege and for advocating unpopular positions; for example, positions for civil rights or against war that may be opposed by a populist majority or the government. Free speech has been a useful tool for exposing corruption, for empowering disenfranchised groups, for shaming bullying politicians, and for preventing the powerful from silencing dissent. This includes the ability of the disempowered and marginalized to speak out against the powerful and privileged and others with whom they may have disagreements, to tell those in power what they may not want to hear. Excessive concerns about civility, including shielding students from ideas they may find offensive, should not be used as a rationale for limiting speech. From the Strong Tactful standpoint, there should be no restrictions on freedom of speech in a fair and open competition among diverse groups and interests and ideas in American society.

In short, students, faculty, and campus administrators

should consider their goal in a given speech situation. Do they want people to feel welcome and not be offended, be encouraged to share their ideas openly, come to a consensus and mutual understanding, and strengthen the campus community, consistent with the Weak Caring standpoint? Or is the goal for one group or idea among many with competing interests to win, to be successful over the others, for the truth to win out regardless of who may be hurt, consistent with the Strong Tactful standpoint? The answer to this question—are we seeking social justice or truth?—will guide opinions on whether there should be more or fewer limitations on speech.

Weak Caring and Strong Tactful do share an interest in civility, mutual respect, being intellectually challenged, and searching for truth. However, for Weak Caring the balance is toward the former, on not being rude, offensive, bullying, harassing, or intimidating. For Strong Tactful the balance is toward the latter, on robust debate, seeking the truth, and winning regardless of whether some might take offense or feel hurt. Perhaps the balance should be determined by whether potentially offensive speech is directed toward people and groups with relatively less or more power and privilege in the speech situation. In short, Strong Tactful's support for unrestrained freedom of speech does not justify offending or bullying the vulnerable and powerless; yet, the right to freedom of speech does empower Weak Caring (and Weak Loyal, Weak Tactful, and Weak Detached) to speak truth to and perhaps shame and offend the powerful.

Here are the general features of the Weak Caring versus Strong Tactful dialogue. The Weak Caring civility-in-speech standpoint is committed to maintaining and strengthening relationships. The definition of the campus community includes the goal of becoming more inclusive, so that all individuals and groups may genuinely feel they belong and all ideas are represented. From Weak Caring's standpoint, restrictions on speech are necessary.

When people say things that are offensive and that reflect implicit hierarchies and the use of power, this appears to

Weak Caring as an effort to hijack the conversation, to turn the speech goal from mutual understanding and cooperation to a contest in which there are multiple losers and only one winner. Indeed, this may in fact be what Strong Tactful desires. Thus, Weak Caring can view Strong Tactful as manipulative, menacing, and overbearing (perhaps misreading Strong Tactful's insistence on freedom of speech as a Strong Loyal standpoint), yet at the same time as potentially enriching both in terms of relationships and in the search for truth (table 4.2).

Strong Tactful's speech-for-winning standpoint is also grounded in the assumption that groups are defined through their relations with other groups. However, this understanding is shaped by the assumption that the primary intention for humans is to compete against and control others and to win. Thus for Strong Tactful the concept of community is understood not as a goal in itself, but rather as a context in which manipulation and negotiation lead toward the end of control and domination. For Strong Tactful, with the singular aim of winning, Weak Caring must be either on Strong Tactful's side or opposed.

Given Strong Tactful's standpoint, Weak Caring's call for restrictions on offensive speech may sound like an attempt to control the debate and win against Strong Tactful. This would be a misperception, of course, for Weak Caring is concerned with understanding, not winning. Strong Tactful views Weak Caring as a potential threat (perhaps misreading Weak Caring as Tactful or Loyal), yet also as naive and idealistic (table 4.3).

It's possible that Strong Tactful hears an insistence on limitations on offensive speech as an effort to hijack the conversation, to turn the speech goal from ascertaining what is the truth of a matter—who will win the debate—to a goal of mutual understanding and cooperation. Indeed, this may be what Weak Caring desires, to reduce the level of conflict, to promote a cooling-off period, and to prevent a dialogue with Tactful from degenerating into a conflict with Loyal.

Dialogue 15. Weak Caring versus Strong Detached
Gun Control versus Gun Rights

The United States ranks number one among advanced countries in gun deaths for each citizen. Civilian gun ownership in the United States is the highest in the world. The killing by guns of tens of thousands of Americans every year, including many women victims of domestic violence and several children killed each day on school playgrounds and in their neighborhoods, has been described as a public health epidemic. Active shooter incidents, the killing of people in a confined space such as a school, theater, or church, are increasingly common. The costs of responding to frequent gun tragedies, providing emergency medical care for gun victims, enhancing security screening at public buildings, hiring more armed security guards, and living a more stressful and fearful life are incalculable. Americans cannot be secure when most citizens are armed and have the ability to kill anyone in their vicinity in a few seconds.

Many Americans believe it is a responsibility of government to prevent needless deaths and ensure the safety of the public. To this end, they support requiring stricter background checks for the purchase of guns and ammunition; limiting the availability of military-style weapons, armor-piercing bullets, and high-capacity magazines; requiring trigger locks and safe gun storage; and increasing the availability of mental health services. They argue that the Second Amendment right to bear arms must be balanced by Americans' First Amendment right to peaceably assemble without fear of gun violence in schools, theaters, workplaces, churches, shopping malls, and other public places. Their argument for more strict controls on guns in order to decrease the number of gun deaths in America is consistent with the Weak Caring standpoint. Advocates for gun control recognize that all segments of American society are affected by gun violence. Solutions must be a shared responsibility and broad-based, not directed toward particular groups like hunters or target shooters who might feel threatened by restrictive gun policies and regulations.

Opponents of increased regulation of guns, in contrast, argue that easy access to gun ownership is essential in the defense of freedom. First, all Americans have the right to defend themselves, their families, and their homes against criminals and intruders and, in rural areas, animal predators. Because criminals are often armed with guns, law-abiding citizens must be armed as well. Second, "a good guy with a gun" could make active shooter incidents far less deadly, by disabling or killing the shooter long before the police can arrive. (Gun control advocates would note that armed citizens have rarely been effective in such incidents and can make matters worse.) Third, if the military became unable to defend America, for example, following a devastating nuclear attack, then the defense of America and its freedoms would depend on large numbers of civilians adequately armed with military-style assault weapons. Similarly, in the event of a breakdown of American society, for instance, following destruction of the electrical grid by terrorists, survival would depend on having guns and ample ammunition.

Fourth, and perhaps the most important argument in the current debate, many Americans do not trust their own government. They believe the federal government already controls too much of their daily lives. They fear the government is aiming to take Americans' rights away one by one, including taking away their guns, until they are no longer living in a democracy but in a tyrannical police state. The main protection against this happening is for civilians in America to be adequately armed to defend themselves against a tyrannical government. Guns are the most effective protection for essential rights of American citizens such as freedom of speech, freedom of assembly, freedom of the press, and freedom of religion. A populist version of this argument is that it is affluent and powerful Americans who would like to have all the guns taken away from less privileged Americans.

These arguments for protecting gun rights reflect a Strong Detached standpoint, a view of oneself as weak, besieged, and vulnerable (table 3.2). Having guns and ammunition changes the view of self from weak and dependent to strong and self-sufficient. The supporters of gun rights are not arguing for having guns in order to aggressively compete and win against other groups (as might be argued from the Loyal perspective). They are arguing merely to be left alone and, to that end, for the right to defend themselves against multiple others, including criminals, intruders, active shooters, invaders, and a federal government out to destroy Americans' freedoms. This Strong Detached gun control standpoint gains strength through extensive National Rifle Association lobbying and financial support from gun manufacturers.

The paragraphs that follow set forth the characteristic features of the Weak Caring versus Strong Detached dialogue. From the Weak Caring standpoint, advocates for both gun control and gun rights live together in the same American communities. These communities as a whole should be the focus of concern. For Weak Caring gun control advocates, there are dimensions of respect, caring, and responsibility towards other groups and relationships, plus a commitment to maintain and strengthen relationships. For these reasons, they support gun control and safety measures that could reduce America's current epidemic of gun violence. Weak Caring is concerned that without strong gun control measures, millions more guns will be sold as Americans seek to protect themselves and their families, more public buildings will be forced to adopt airport-style security measures, and American communities will require more frequent patrols by heavily armed security guards and police. Weak Caring gun control advocates view Strong Detached gun rights advocates as self-centered, insensitive, and apathetic yet nevertheless as enriching and as deserving of being included in the broader community (table 4.2).

For members of the Strong Detached gun rights group, the primary goal is to be left alone so they can pursue self-understanding within the boundaries of their own community. From the Strong Detached standpoint, other individuals and groups are of little interest. The actions of Weak Caring gun control advocates are viewed as intrusive, self-serving, naive, idealistic, and vexatious (table 4.3). Requiring stronger background checks and denying gun purchases to extensive lists of citizens requiring surveillance are viewed as excessive government intrusion (and may raise constitutional issues). Because of their lack of engagement with other groups, Strong Detached gun rights advocates may be insensitive to the needs of others and not have a good sense of their own standing relative to other groups. For example, while being powerful and privileged they may at the same time deny their own privileged status.

From the standpoint of Weak Caring gun control advocates, Strong Detached gun rights advocates are all talk and no action. There appears to be an intention towards understanding, but it is focused on self-understanding rather than mutual understanding. Thus Strong Detached gun rights advocates appear aloof, uninvolved, and patronizing (table 4.2). Strong Detached's assumption that groups are defined intrinsically may lead it to feel offended by Weak Caring's claim that both are members of the same community. Strong Detached gun rights advocates do not want to be associated with weakness or other perceived negative characteristics of Weak Caring gun control advocates or be engaged in a community defined more broadly than itself and so responds, "We have nothing in common."

Strong Detached's modes of relating to other individuals and groups include focusing on its own self-sufficiency, especially if gun rights are maintained so individuals and communities can be protected, and avoiding engagement with others. Strong Detached is likely to try to erect barriers against interactions with Weak Caring and procedures to prevent Weak Caring from accruing additional resources and power, for example, success with legislative efforts to increase control of guns and reduce gun violence. Weak Caring supports blocking people with disabling mental health issues from buying handguns; Strong Detached opposes this and similar efforts to limit the availability of guns.

Dialogue 16. Weak Caring versus Strong Caring
Friends versus Friends

In *Christmas Eve on Sesame Street*, the Muppets Bert and Ernie realize they have no money to buy gifts for each other. Bert secretly trades his prized paper clip collection for a soap dish for Ernie's rubber ducky. Meanwhile Ernie gives away his rubber ducky to obtain an empty cigar box to hold Bert's paper clips. This Sesame Street story, which received an Emmy Award for Outstanding Children's Program, is based on *The Gift of the Magi*, a 1905 O. Henry story that has been widely adapted. In O. Henry's story, a young couple, Della and Jim, realize they have no money to buy Christmas gifts for each other. Della has her beautiful long hair cut and sold so she can buy a platinum fob chain for Jim's heirloom watch. Meanwhile, Jim has sold his watch to buy tortoise shell combs for Della's hair.

The importance of Bert and Ernie for *Sesame Street* is to show that two people, even with quite different personalities, can still be good friends and, in this Christmas story, make significant personal sacrifices for the benefit of the other. Similarly, Della and Jim represent two people with different interests who are still willing to sacrifice what is personally important for the happiness of the other. In each story, the identities of the characters are interdependent; that is, the characters define themselves in part through their friendship with each other. The intentions of the characters are not to compete and win, but to understand, cooperate with, and support and care for each other and maintain and strengthen their mutual friendship. Bert, Ernie, Della, and Jim are excellent examples of the Caring perspective.

The friendships of Bert and Ernie and Della and Jim,

despite marked differences between them as individuals, involve similar amounts of power and privilege. Illustrating dialogue 16, however, requires examples in which one person or group has relatively more power or privilege than another, so that the dialogue can be fairly described as Weak Caring versus Strong Caring. It will be helpful to first consider how friendships and caring are understood from the Loyal, Tactful, and Detached perspectives.

From the Loyal perspective, friendships are conditional on a shared *membership* and identity, agreement about who we are and how others are different, about what we have in common that others do not share with us. To be friends means we are both members of, proud of, and loyal to the same family, sports team, candidates for office, political party, sexual orientation, racial or ethnic or religious group, or country. When we are members of the same group, we feel a sense of solidarity with each other, a feeling of us versus them or in-group versus out-group. To care means that we look after our own, that we look after those who are like us. If this condition of similarity no longer holds, if we no longer agree on the defining boundary between ourselves and Others, then we are no longer friends. Differences of membership or opinion now become salient and so we dislike and compete against each other. The breakups of friendships based in the Loyal perspective are described with terms such as renounce, reject, sever, and shun.

From the Tactful perspective, friendships are *utilitarian*, that is, conditional on what we can do for each other. To be friends means we support each other in pursuit of a common goal, for example, playing or working on the same team. "I come up with great practical solutions for our problems at work, but my friend is well-organized, a detail person, and better at implementation." Yet, people often pursue different goals or sometimes the same goals with different levels of commitment. So to be friends can mean we have resources that may be exchanged in support of our own goals. "I'm a good listener when my friend needs to talk; and I count on my friend to fix my car." To care means we are concerned for those who are or who may become useful for us. If this utilitarian basis for friendship no longer holds, for example, we feel the other can no longer support us or the short-term goal has been achieved, we may nevertheless continue to stay in contact and remain friendly. Indeed, it is good to have many friends and "contacts" on social-networking sites, any one of whom might become useful in the future toward advancing our careers. Meanwhile, our friendship may be described not as having broken up but rather as dormant or having lapsed, faded, paused, or been suspended.

From the Detached perspective, friendships are more often *superficial*. To be friends means that we know each other slightly, that we are somewhat familiar with each other, that we are acquaintances, that we may be friendly but we are not really actually friends. Perhaps we go to Starbucks around the same time each day and sometimes see each other and briefly talk. Or perhaps we see each other at the grocery store or the post office and have a brief conversation. Or perhaps we interact primarily online on Facebook or other social media. But someone who appears to be seeking a relationship involving more closeness and intimacy may be seen from the Detached perspective as bothersome and intrusive; wearing headphones while we are out in public can be a defense against interacting with others. Similarly, from the Detached perspective one takes care not to bother other people or intrude on their privacy. More important than deep friendship is authenticity, knowing yourself, being yourself, managing your reputation, and fine-tuning your Facebook profile. From the Detached perspective, the ending of a friendship is described not as a breakup but instead with words such as avoid, escape, ghost, and "unfriend."

From the Caring perspective, friendships are *unconditional*. To be friends means our own identities and communities are interdependent with the identities and communities of others, regardless of similarities or differences between ourselves and others. Friends can be very different from one another--consider Mary Matalin and James Carville, George W. Bush and Bill Clinton--although a consequence of being friends is that they may become more similar. From the Caring perspective, other individuals and groups are regarded as worthy and as enriching our own lives. Friendships necessarily involve dimensions of respect, responsibility, and caring.

In short: From the Loyal perspective, friendships are primarily a confirmation of our own identity and group membership; our identity imposes conditions or limits on who we can be friends with. From the Tactful perspective, friendships are important as a means toward personal goals; the potential usefulness of others guides who one remains friends with and stays in contact with. From the Detached perspective, friendships are superficial and short-lived. From the Caring perspective, friendships are not the means but rather the goal. Friends are always there when we need them. The intention is to understand ourselves and others and to maintain and strengthen friendships.[4]

From the Caring perspective, to care means to appreciate and have a strong interest in others, to be concerned for their well-being, and to accept responsibility and act for the benefit of other individuals and communities. The focus of caring actions is primarily on others rather than oneself, in contrast to the other three perspectives. However, given the interdependence of self and others, all who are involved in the relationship become the beneficiaries of caring. A challenge, from the Caring perspective, is to care not merely for what is in our own interest and the groups to which we belong, but also to care for others with whom we may appear to have little in common, to care for someone or something beyond ourselves and our own group.[5]

Thus the challenge is for people to care for others of a different gender, race, ethnicity, and religion than their own; to care for the well-being of people in social classes different from their own; to care for species and environments other than their own; and so forth. From the Loyal, Tactful, and

Detached perspectives, a key question is how my community—my nation, my religion, or my ethnicity—can be dominant over yours, can interact with yours in a way that is most advantageous to mine, or can remain apart from yours. From the Caring perspective, our communities have been constructed through a mutually dependent and historical process. The key question is how the continuing engagement of our communities can renew and strengthen opportunities for more dialogue, greater understanding, and mutual enrichment.[6]

There is, however, the disparity in power and prestige in a Weak Caring versus Strong Caring dialogue that must be addressed. These differences in power may be along the same dimension—for example, one friend has greater material and emotional resources, or skills, abilities, and expertise, or moral character and determination, and the other friend has less. Differences between friends may also lie in different dimensions. For example, one friend has strong leadership abilities, and the other friend has strong moral character. From the other three perspectives, differences in power and prestige can be among the reasons friendships break up, fade away, or fail to develop. When friendships are conditional, utilitarian, and superficial, breakups are allowed to happen. From the Caring perspective, however, for friendships to break up is not an option. The primary concern and responsibility is to maintain and strengthen the friendship and so appropriate terms include hang together, support each other, reconcile, reunite, and love.

In a potential conflict between Weak Caring and Strong Caring, each looks for ways to yield and to do what is best for the other. Instead of putting our own interests first, we put the other's interests first. Of course, it is sometimes difficult to know what is in the best interest of the other, and so a responsibility from the Strong Caring standpoint is to strive to understand what may be the true interests of others. In this regard, the Golden Rule—treat others as you would like to be treated—may not be a sure guide towards acting responsibly.

What I would like in a given situation, perhaps reflecting my self-contained Loyal or Detached perspective, may be quite different from what another would like. Furthermore, my thoughtful and Tactful understanding of another's situation may be quite different from the understanding of someone actually in that situation. A better guide to caring and acting responsibly may be to ask others how they would like to be treated and what they would prefer in a given situation and then act accordingly. Strong Caring thus has a responsibility to create conditions of trust under which others feel free to express their true interests.[7]

Knowing the other is likely to yield and perhaps sacrifice for the good of the relationship—as Bert and Ernie and Della and Jim did—both Weak and Strong Caring are likely to make minimal demands on the other. While Strong Caring may be quite willing to redistribute and share resources, Weak Caring may be resistant to accepting resources that appear to be unearned or for which there is no clear way to give back. Thus Strong Caring may view Weak Caring as resistant, naive, and idealistic, yet at the same time as having potential for enriching the relationship and the broader community. Weak Caring, in contrast, may similarly view Strong Caring as overbearing, naive, and idealistic, yet as potentially nurturing and enriching if both can cooperate within the broader community. Weak Caring will recognize that Strong Caring appears to have Weak Caring's best interests at heart, even if what is suggested is not yet what Weak Caring most desires to do. Children generally recognize that their parents have the children's best interests at heart, even if what is suggested is not yet what they most desire to do.

For Weak Caring and Strong Caring to move forward in their relationship, they can strive to listen carefully to each other, learn from each other and understand the other's situation, demonstrate respect for the other's standpoint, redefine the situation to emphasize their interdependent relationship, and seek additional resources both can share (see table 3.4). Although initially one of the individuals or groups may be stronger than the other, both are enabled to become stronger through their cooperative interactions. The question before Caring friends is primarily one of how to better understand each other and best cooperate to their mutual advantage despite the fact that one may have more power and privilege than the other.[8]

Looking back, the sixteen dialogues have been arranged into four chapters focusing on the weaker standpoints in each of the dialogues; that is, the Weak Loyal dialogues, the Weak Tactful dialogues, and so forth. Yes, the chapters could have been arranged to focus on the stronger standpoints, for example, the Strong Loyal dialogues, the Strong Tactful dialogues, and so forth. Readers may gain additional insight into the character of the four perspectives by skimming across chapters 5, 6, 7, and 8 and focusing on the strong standpoints for each of the perspectives. For example, review the Strong Loyal standpoints in chapters 5, 6, 7, and 8; and then the Strong Tactful standpoints in chapters 5, 6, 7, and 8; and so forth.

Looking ahead, Part III addresses the question of what light the four perspectives and the sixteen dialogues might shed on America's changing political scene. We begin our romp through American political parties, the dangers of political polarization, and potential political realignment in chapter 9 by asking what the relationship might be between the four American perspectives—Loyal, Tactful, Detached, and Caring—and America's two dominant political parties, the Republicans and the Democrats.

Part III

America's Changing Political Scene

9

Four Perspectives but Only Two Political Parties

The 2016 presidential election was, of course, a contest between America's dominant political parties. Yet much of the conflict and drama of 2015 and early 2016 took place within these two parties, in their presidential primaries. The Republican primaries pitted mavericks and outsiders such as Ted Cruz, Marco Rubio, and Donald Trump against moderates and insiders such as Jeb Bush, Chris Christie, John Kasich, and George Pataki. Similarly, the Democratic primaries were a close contest between an independent, revolutionary outsider, Bernie Sanders, and a well-established insider, Hillary Clinton.

Columnist David Brooks, writing in *The New York Times* shortly in advance of the 2016 election, described the Republican Party as "a coalition of globalization-loving business executives and globalization-hating white workers. That's untenable." And Brooks described the Democratic

Party as "a coalition of the upscale urban professionals who make up the ruling class and less-affluent members of minorities who feel betrayed by it. That's untenable, too."

These within-party conflicts continue after elections are over. Political factions can thwart the passage of Congressional legislation and appointments of Cabinet officers and judges. In late 2016 Frank Bruni wrote in an op-ed for *The New York Times*, "The path ahead is all the trickier because the campaign has widened fault lines not only between Republicans and Democrats but also within each camp. . . . it feels as if we're coming out of this election with four parties: the Paul Ryan Republicans, the Freedom Caucus, the establishment Democrats, and the Elizabeth Warren/Bernie Sanders brigade. . . . Meet the new paralysis, same as the old paralysis. Potentially, worse."

David Brooks, also writing shortly after the 2016 election, highlights the fault lines within the political parties and similarly identifies *four* principal groups: "A system dominated by two party-line powers gives way to a system with a lot of different power centers. Instead of just R's and D's, there will be Trump-dominated populist nationalism, a more libertarian Freedom Caucus, a Bernie Sanders/Elizabeth Warren progressive caucus, a Chuck Schumer/Nancy Pelosi Democratic old guard."

Can the four perspectives—Loyal, Tactful, Detached, and Caring—shed light on contemporary politics in America and on these conflicts both between and within the dominant political parties, the Republicans and the Democrats? What is the relationship between these four perspectives and the attitudes and values of American citizens and voters? Recognizing that people have a choice of not merely two political parties but four perspectives makes the American political scene more understandable and more fascinating.

There are three main dialogues in American politics: The two major political parties have long been involved in a Weak Tactful versus Strong Tactful dialogue (dialogue 6); one of the parties is currently engaged in a Weak Loyal versus Strong

Tactful dialogue (dialogue 2); and the other party is engaged in a Weak Caring versus Strong Tactful dialogue (dialogue 14). The Strong Tactful standpoint is present in all three dialogues, so we begin with the Tactful perspective and then move to the Loyal and Caring perspectives in American politics.

Two Tactful Business and Political Coalitions

Power in Washington, DC, is held and exercised by coalitions of business and political interest groups. Their members include corporate, business, and Wall Street executives and political leaders who have been around Washington, DC, long enough to become powerful and well-connected with one another; big-money political donors; and media pundits and personalities. Their members also include more than 10,000 lobbyists representing demographic constituencies and interest groups; for example, ethnic minorities, children, and the aging; advocates for education, health care, civil rights, unions, guns, and the environment; and economic sectors including agriculture, energy, aerospace, pharmaceuticals, banking, health care, insurance, telecommunications, tobacco, and many more.

These coalitions compete to gain jobs for elected and appointed officials, high-level bureaucrats, and federal judges who will be favorable to their interests. They also compete to have privileged access to information about how the government makes decisions and distributes its resources, including who will benefit from $4 trillion in annual federal spending. And they compete by closely following the legislative, judicial, and executive activities of government. They engage in extensive lobbying to influence how laws and regulations are written, interpreted, and enforced for the benefit of these business and political groups. For example, the federal tax code has been written to provide deductions and special favors that benefit corporations and wealthy families. The actions of these Tactful coalitions reflect what political scientist Francis Fukuyama describes as processes of "repatrimonialization," the capture of the federal government by elite networks of families and friends, and "rent-seeking," manipulation of the political system to increase private wealth without producing any new wealth for society as a whole.

The Tactful perspective is defined by the assumptions of interdependent identity and intention to compete and control. In competing against others yet at the same time understanding the need to negotiate, compromise, and work together, these business and political coalitions share a solidly Tactful perspective. They view themselves as moderates, the pragmatic center of American politics, the Establishment, uniting rather than dividing, concerned for American society as a whole, willing to compromise in order to solve problems and serve the greater good, and trusting and confident in government and America's future.

Two of these Tactful business and political coalitions— America's two major political parties—play dominant roles on the American political scene and especially in Washington, DC. Both argue for the importance of a strong American economy and for effective government programs. However, the first of these Tactful coalitions represents primarily business interests, from small businesses to banking and investment institutions and large corporations. The goals of this *pro-business Tactful coalition* include lowering taxes, cutting government regulation of markets, and reducing the size of government.

The second Tactful coalition represents children, youth, and the aging; ethnic minorities and middle class workers and their families; and educated professional and government workers at many levels; for example, teachers, university professors, and government employees. The goals of this *pro-government Tactful coalition* include government programs to improve education, health care, job skills, and civil rights for more Americans and to protect the environment.

Both of these Tactful coalitions are routinely described as core, centrist, moderate, and pragmatic. These business and political coalitions are comfortable with the status quo from which they benefit. For example, the median wealth of members of Congress is $1 million. So these groups rarely seek substantial changes in laws or policies. They are open to listening, learning, and changing policies when necessary yet reluctant to move too quickly, for maintaining good long-term relationships with others and holding onto power in Washington, DC, are central and significant Tactful values and goals.

Dialogue 6. Weak Tactful versus Strong Tactful

The pro-business Tactful coalition and the pro-government Tactful coalition are engaged in a Weak Tactful versus Strong Tactful dialogue. Which coalition is stronger depends on which one controls Congress and the presidency. Each sees the other as a group to compete against, to manipulate, and to persuade in order to increase its own power. At the same time, the other is viewed as a potential partner to negotiate and compromise with (tables 4.2 and 4.3). Many issues are at stake in this dialogue: Does Wall Street help or hurt the economy? Is the economic system generally fair or does it favor powerful interests? Is government doing too much or should it do more to solve problems and help needy Americans? Can peace best be assured through military strength or through good diplomacy?

Although the dialogue between these two Tactful coalitions reflects serious competition over control and power in America, this is not a Loyal dialogue but a Tactful dialogue. The two Tactful coalitions aim to get along with each other. A concrete example of the dual Tactful emphases on control plus interdependence, on competition plus connectedness, is the Civil Rights Act of 1964. The support of Everett Dirksen, the Republican senator from Illinois, was instrumental in passing Democratic President Lyndon Johnson's civil rights proposals. A second example is the friendship in the 1980s between Republican President Ronald Reagan and Democratic Speaker of the House of Representatives Tip

O'Neill. Reagan and O'Neill were highly partisan leaders of opposing political parties and adversaries on issues of taxes and government spending. Yet, they were also good friends who met often to discuss the day's political events and share stories. Their bipartisan collaboration enabled passage of the Social Security Amendments of 1983 and the Tax Reform Act of 1986.

A recent example of Tactful competition and friendship involves Orrin Hatch, Republican senator from Utah, and Ted Kennedy, Democratic senator from Massachusetts. Although they represented opposing political parties, their friendship and collaboration led to passage of the Americans With Disabilities Act in 1990 and the State Children's Health Insurance Program in 1997. A fourth example is the agreement in 1993 by war hero and Republican Senator John McCain and antiwar activist and Democratic Senator John Kerry that there was no evidence that Americans remained in Vietnamese prisons, opening the way to diplomatic recognition and a true ending of the war. A fifth example is the successful passage of the Bipartisan Budget Act of 2013, the result of extensive discussions and compromises between Republican Representative Paul Ryan from Minnesota and Democratic Senator Patty Murray from Washington.

These examples illustrate the Tactful inclination to listen and learn from others, engage in coalition building and logrolling (exchanging political favors and votes to gain passage of legislation of interest to each other), and compromise on short-term goals for the greater long-term good of America. Weak Tactful political leaders are comfortable with their minority role as "the loyal opposition"; that is, opposing the policies and actions of the Strong Tactful majority yet remaining faithful to government as an institution and to the responsibility of governing. The two Tactful business and political coalitions aim to get along with each other.

The Loyal and Pro-Business Tactful Movement

From the Tactful perspective identity and community—and power in Washington—can be strengthened by joining with other individuals and groups. Thus, the pro-business and the pro-government Tactful coalitions are motivated to seek the support of others who may be holding the Loyal, Caring, or Detached perspectives. Among the tactics Tactful may employ are, first, arguing there is a shared perspective on the issues (even if this is not the case); and second, persuading others to adopt the Tactful perspective, to accept negotiation and compromise as reasonable political tactics. Third, Tactful may attempt to strike deals, exchanging support and votes on important Tactful issues for support and votes (or promises of support and votes) on significant issues from the Loyal, Caring, or Detached perspectives.

The Loyal perspective is defined by assumptions of self-contained identity and intention to compete and control. From the Loyal perspective, one is proud of and committed to one's identity and community, including one's family, religion, local school, neighborhood, sports team, ethnic heritage, America's military, and the United States as a nation. And one wants to work hard and get ahead and be more powerful than others, who are viewed by Loyal as less worthy and threatening. Those holding the Loyal perspective see themselves as standing apart from those who are different; for example, those whose race, ethnicity, or religion might be different, or whose sexual orientation might be different, or recent immigrants whose culture and history in America might be different. They also view the United States as unique and standing apart, proudly independent and self-sufficient, in competition with and threatened by other countries, but always the top-ranked country in the world.

Those who hold the Loyal perspective aim to stay in control through maintaining core values, often including deeply held religious values, and through military strength. The strong support Loyal people have for their own identity, community, and values involves a commitment to tradition and the status quo and an aversion to change and whatever might be new and different. In recent decades those holding the Loyal perspective have been suspicious of and resistant to globalization and free trade, changing roles and increased opportunities for women and minorities, women's access to contraception and abortion services, rapid cultural changes such as same-sex marriage, judicial decisions that might constrain religious practice, changes in energy use and lifestyle because of climate change, and in general to the findings and recommendations of scientists. Social and cultural changes such as these have the potential to increase doubts about traditional beliefs and values and thus threaten the identity and long-term prospects for Loyal individuals and communities.

A political movement including those holding the Loyal perspective and the pro-business Tactful perspective has played a central role on the American political stage for several decades. Sometimes described as "the Ronald Reagan coalition," it has included Loyal national-security hawks and Christian fundamentalists, on the one hand, and pro-business Tactful interests, on the other. This movement was constructed on the foundation of Richard Nixon's "Southern strategy," which aimed to attract white voters who were resentful of federal civil rights legislation. This Loyal and Tactful movement has endured because both have benefited and increased their power through their relationship with the other. The pro-business Tactful interest groups have been able to increase their strength in local, state, and national elections with the support of millions of additional voters holding the Loyal perspective.

In turn, the Loyal interest groups have benefited from support the pro-business Tactful coalition has provided for traditional Loyal issues, including resistance to expanded civil rights for women, minorities, and gays and lesbians and opposition to contraception and abortion. Loyal and pro-business Tactful voters have also been unified in their opposition to policies of the pro-government Tactful coalition. Loyal religious and political leaders find that being aligned with the pro-business Tactful coalition may open doors and increase their influence in Washington, DC, and also provide access to big-money donors and increase visibility in the national media.

Dialogue 2. Weak Loyal versus Strong Tactful

Political movements often involve not only commonalities of interests but also an underlying divergence of interests. Conflicts between the divergent interests of Loyal voters and the pro-business Tactful coalition reflect a Weak Loyal versus Strong Tactful dialogue. Weak Loyal may view Strong Tactful, with its powerful Washington, DC, base, as manipulative, threatening, and deceitful. In contrast, Strong Tactful may view Weak Loyal as immature, aggressive, and rebellious (tables 4.2 and 4.3).

The political issues dividing the Weak Loyal group and the pro-business Strong Tactful coalition are numerous: Weak Loyal has a strong nativist stance against legal status for undocumented immigrants who they believe are taking their jobs (dialogue 5, immigrants). Strong Tactful, in contrast, believes deporting millions of undocumented immigrants would be unrealistic. From Strong Tactful's standpoint, many immigrants are highly skilled work colleagues and neighbors, while the unskilled immigrants working for low wages provide Strong Tactful with affordable child care, yard work, hotel rooms, restaurant meals, and other services. Weak Loyal is open to banning Muslims from entering the United States, while Strong Tactful feels constrained by the Constitution's protections for religious freedom (dialogues 2 and 10).

Weak Loyal is opposed to social and cultural changes that encourage racial and ethnic diversity and inclusion and to increased rights and opportunities for women, such as contraceptive, abortion, and reproductive health services, and for gays and lesbians and transgendered people. In the past,

Strong Tactful was willing to at least tacitly support these Weak Loyal positions. More recently, Strong Tactful and its business allies are recognizing that recruiting and retaining the best employees requires not tolerating discrimination. From the Strong Tactful business standpoint, Weak Loyal positions on issues of diversity and inclusion are now seen as a threat to corporate brand and market share, as a potential liability, and so not in their self-interest to continue supporting.

Several issues at stake in this Weak Loyal versus Strong Tactful dialogue divide the American middle class from a more affluent class. Weak Loyal does not have a stake in lowering tax rates for the wealthy, bailing out banks that are too big to fail, deregulating the banking and investment industry, weakening consumer protection regulations, or free trade with Latin American and Asian countries, whereas Strong Tactful business interests are likely to benefit from these policies.

Weak Loyal tends to be interested in protecting Social Security and Medicare and raising the minimum wage. Strong Tactful, in contrast, advocates for fiscal responsibility, smaller government, and less government regulation. This means privatizing Social Security, cutting back on Medicare and Medicaid funding, and not raising the minimum wage. In short, Weak Loyal may see pro-business Strong Tactful as not supporting middle class workers with higher wages and more jobs and instead merely pushing an agenda that works best for an affluent elite.

In presidential primaries, Weak Loyal has favored candidates who present themselves as independents or outsiders or anti-Establishment, as not being long-term incumbents or coming from "inside the Beltway"; for example, Donald Trump. Strong Tactful has favored presidential candidates who have legislative- or executive-branch experience and long-standing mutually beneficial relationships with other Washington, DC, business and political insiders; for example, Senate Majority Leader Bob

Dole, Governor George W. Bush, Senator John McCain, and Governor Mitt Romney.

Finally, a major issue in the Weak Loyal versus Strong Tactful dialogue concerns what tactics are appropriate in the Washington, DC, competition for influence, resources, and power. From the Loyal perspective, the most familiar tactics are focusing on differences with others and competing, attempting to control, and aggressing against others (table 3.4). Thus, for Weak Loyal it is essential to stand up for one's values and principles, to be confrontational, to always be a winner, and even, if necessary, to block votes on federal spending bills and shut down the government. Cooperation, legislative bargaining, and compromise are viewed as betrayal of core values and principles. It is not surprising that Weak Loyal members of Congress announced, as Barack Obama was being inaugurated in 2008, that they would not cooperate with any of his initiatives. Nor that Weak Loyal senators announced, in early 2016, that they would not hold hearings on any candidate nominated by President Obama to fill a Supreme Court vacancy.

In contrast, from the Tactful perspective the most familiar tactics are to negotiate, to attempt to persuade, and to form coalitions. From the Strong Tactful standpoint, it is important to maintain respect for the institution of government and to strive to enable government and business to work well together. John Boehner illustrated this fundamental respect for democratic institutions when he was Speaker of the House of Representatives. Those with a Strong Tactful standpoint recognize that in a democracy one can't get one's own way every time, one can't be assured of always winning every argument. Strong Tactful is uncomfortable with Weak Loyal's confrontational tactics, which can undermine the compromises, agreements, and mutual respect and trust that are essential for bipartisan and pragmatic solutions and for preserving democracy in America. Underlying this difference in tactics are assumptions of separateness, self-sufficiency, and hierarchy, "I win, you lose," on the one hand, and assumptions of interdependence, compromise, and pragmatism, "how do we get this done," on the other.

The Caring and Pro-Government Tactful Movement

The Caring perspective is defined by assumptions of interdependent identity and intention to understand; that is, to construct meaning and significance in one's life. From the Caring perspective, one's own identity and community depend on the well-being of others' identities and communities. Those holding the Caring perspective are concerned less with self and more with respecting others and cooperating, although the assumption of interdependence means that concerns for self and others are not separate. These concerns are often broadly framed, for example, concerns for the well-being and integrity of American society as a whole, and concerns for people in other countries and for the global environment.

The goals of those with a Caring perspective are to have American society and its institutions work for the benefit of everyone, not just a fortunate and affluent elite. Improvement, strengthening, and significant changes are necessary across a broad range of American institutions and governance, including education, health care, criminal justice, energy, and transportation. Those holding a Caring perspective are focused on who is benefiting least and most and what obstacles in society and government impede a better society. The Caring list of major concerns includes economic inequality, the excessive influence of individual and corporate wealth on government decision-making, and threats to the stability and integrity of democratic processes in America. People with a Caring perspective view themselves as open-minded, sympathetic to and understanding of the ideas and behaviors of others, and willing to take up new ideas and engage in reforms without being unduly bound by tradition.

A political movement including those holding the Caring and pro-government Tactful perspectives has existed since the 1930s. Franklin Roosevelt's New Deal supported farmers, union workers, the poor, and the unemployed with government programs that stimulated the economy. Bill Clinton's New Democrat or Third Way coalition brought Caring advocates for middle class families, minorities, and the poor together with pro-government Tactful advocates for economic growth. The Caring members of this movement have focused on improving education, health care, civil rights, and social justice for more Americans and on protecting the environment. The pro-government Tactful members of this movement have sought improvements of the American economy through deregulating agriculture and other economic sectors, eliminating barriers to global trade, balancing the federal budget, and reducing the deficit.

Caring advocacy groups and political leaders find being aligned with the pro-government Tactful coalition can open doors and increase their influence in Washington, DC, and also provide access to big-money donors and greater visibility in the national media. The pro-government Tactful coalition has increased its strength in local, state, and national elections with the additional support of millions of Caring voters.

Dialogue 14. Weak Caring versus Strong Tactful

Nevertheless, as in all movements, there can be a divergence of interests between the Caring perspective and the pro-government Tactful perspective. From the Caring perspective, the focus is on cooperating with and respecting others; from the Tactful perspective, the focus is on negotiating with and persuading others (table 3.4). From the Weak Caring standpoint, those with a Strong Tactful standpoint are seen as manipulative, overbearing, and deceitful (table 4.2); from the Strong Tactful standpoint, those, with a Caring perspective are seen as naive, idealistic, and easy to persuade (table 4.3).

Weak Caring is concerned that Strong Tactful has neglected its commitment to government policies that benefit the middle class and the poor. Strong Tactful has become too comfortable working closely with Wall Street, Silicon Valley, and corporate interests. Weak Caring would like a stronger push for policies and programs that would decrease income and wealth inequality, including quality child care, affordable housing, affordable health care, paid family and medical leave, better funding for public schools, investments in education and job retraining, and a minimum wage that is a living wage.

And Weak Caring would like a stronger push for exposing and punishing corporate corruption, curtailing the influence of wealthy donors in elections and in Washington, DC, and moving more rapidly toward responding to climate change. In short, Weak Caring sees Strong Tactful as not supporting the middle class and instead as pushing an agenda that works best for an affluent elite. Weak Caring would like to pull Strong Tactful from its underlying intention to compete and control toward an intention to understand, cooperate, and care and toward a social justice agenda.

Strong Tactful, in contrast, is not interested in the risks of rapid social change. The highly educated professionals and managers are comfortable with the status quo and enjoy the lifestyle and benefits they feel they have earned. From the Tactful perspective, the familiar tactics are to negotiate, attempt to persuade, and form coalitions and be content with small steps in a positive direction, but not to engage in fundamental transformations or radical social changes in the economy or in government. Strong Tactful does speak out against discrimination and inequality, but Weak Caring views such talk as merely allowing Strong Tactful to feel good about itself while nevertheless failing to act. Strong Tactful views Weak Caring as idealistic and asking for the impossible; Strong Tactful offers in return pragmatism, competence, and experience.

In presidential primaries, Weak Caring has favored candidates with a strong social justice agenda; for example, Bernie Sanders. Strong Tactful has favored presidential candidates who have legislative- or executive-branch experience and long-standing mutually beneficial relationships with other Washington, DC, business and political insiders; for example, Hillary Clinton. Underlying these differences are the contrasting assumptions of the Caring and Tactful perspectives: assumptions of understanding and cooperation with others, on the one hand, and assumptions of competition and control of others, on the other.

In short, two major political parties reflecting two competing coalitions dominate the American political scene: a pro-business Tactful coalition (the Republican Party) supported by Loyal voters, and a pro-government Tactful coalition (the Democratic Party) supported by Caring voters. The differences in perspectives inside these broad movements may lead to intense conflicts over values and goals. When it comes to winning national elections, neither movement can be confident of the support and votes of its own diverse members. Thus, both these broad movements reflecting the first three American perspectives—Tactful, Loyal, and Detached—must seek additional support from voters holding the fourth, Detached perspective. How the two Tactful coalitions can appeal for the support of Detached voters in order to win elections is the topic of the next chapter.

10

Winning Elections with Detached Voters

Imagine you are a candidate running for a seat in the US House of Representatives. Many potential voters in your district live in or near poverty, with no savings to fall back on in an emergency. They have been stuck in low-wage jobs for decades and, with no education beyond high school, have little chance of moving ahead. Many rely on food banks and government safety-net programs to get by. Factories have closed, jobs have been lost, and their town is dying. There is not adequate funding for police, fire safety, public schools, and drug treatment. These voters feel alienated, disconnected, and powerless. Yet, many continue to believe in the American Dream, that if they work hard they will be able to get ahead. They value being independent and self-sufficient and working things out for themselves. They are proud of their families and hometown and ethnic heritage and traditions. Many of these potential voters have adopted a Weak Detached standpoint (dialogues 9, cultural identity, and 11, working poor).

Today you are canvassing door-to-door in your

congressional district, introducing yourself and listening to voters' concerns. You have only a couple of minutes and two or three sentences to make your pitch for why people should vote for you. Which would be your best argument, the most memorable and with the greatest impact on potential voters? First, "I've served for many years on the town council and in the state legislature. I have experience and I know how government works. Vote for me and I can get things done." Second, "I understand what you are up against—the outside groups and government policies that have taken jobs away from this community. Vote for me and I will fight for you. I'll bring back jobs and make this a winning community again." Third, "I understand what you are up against. But know that you are not alone. Many other Americans in other communities are facing similar challenges. If we all work together politically, we can make America better for everyone."

Your difficulty in deciding on the best pitch to gain the support of Detached voters is similar to the difficulty faced by the pro-business Tactful and pro-government Tactful coalitions—the Republicans and the Democrats—in their competition in state and national elections. Also described as independent voters or swing voters, Detached voters now represent between a third and half of the American electorate—more than either Republicans or Democrats—and so cannot be ignored. In this chapter, the approaches that Tactful, Loyal, and Caring politicians may use to gain the support of Detached voters are described. The chapter concludes with recent Pew Research Center findings showing how the four perspectives are reflected in the attitudes and values of American citizens and voters today.

The Detached perspective is defined by assumptions of self-contained identity and intention to understand; that is, to construct meaning and significance in life. From the Detached perspective, identity and community are strengthened by being isolated from others and striving for self-understanding. People and groups may adopt the Detached perspective for different reasons. For some, choosing to be independent, to be self-sufficient, and to live apart from mainstream American society is the means to being true to one's own cultural, religious, or philosophical values, in the tradition of Daniel Boone or Henry David Thoreau. For others the adoption of a Detached perspective can feel forced because of financial setbacks and struggle and cultural alienation from mainstream society. These people have been displaced by economic crises and recessions, technological changes, injuries and chronic illness, globalization and outsourcing, and employers' rising expectations for education and training, job-relevant skills, and on-the-job experience.

For these Detached groups, there never was—or no longer is—an intention to compete with others, try to get ahead, and be successful in the American economic system. The focus is, instead, on trying to survive with few resources. They want to be self-sufficient in a local economy and get by with only marginal income (dialogue 11, working poor). And the focus is on understanding one's own situation and extracting meaning and significance for oneself and one's family and community. For many, this means striving to be a good worker, a good provider, a good spouse, and a good parent. Yet, the inability to maintain steady employment, obtain a home mortgage, provide for children's college expenses, afford health insurance premiums and copays, and save for retirement may signal personal failure at these goals. For many Detached individuals and families, their sense of purpose, identity, and community is seriously threatened or lost.

Some Detached individuals and families may be angry and rail against an economic system that is not a level playing field, with rules written and enforced by an affluent elite, that benefits only those who are already wealthy and the powerful business, professional, and political class. They may also feel the traditions and values of their community are being mocked by a privileged cultural and media elite who view those holding the Detached perspective as ignorant, racist, rednecks, losers, in the way, flyover country, and no longer relevant in modern America. Those holding a Detached perspective can feel excluded, left out, marginalized, voiceless, and ignored by mainstream America and the political establishment. In return, they tend to be distrustful of government, are less likely to register or vote, and don't bother discussing government or politics.

Direct Appeals from Tactful Coalitions to Detached Voters

Can the pro-business Tactful coalition and the pro-government Tactful coalition gain the support of Detached voters? Tactful views Detached as unsophisticated and alienated, yet extremely useful in terms of their potential votes. But actually gaining these votes can be difficult. Tactful and Detached are at opposite corners of the perspectives matrix (table 3.1). They differ on assumptions of control versus understanding and on assumptions of separateness versus interdependence. Detached views Tactful as bothersome, manipulative, and threatening (tables 4.2 and 4.3). Detached views both of the Tactful coalitions as conspiracies of greedy and corrupt career politicians, government bureaucrats who want to control people, and corrupt and privileged Wall Street and corporate executives who live in Washington, DC, New York City, and Silicon Valley bubbles.

In a direct appeal to Detached voters, the pro-business and pro-government Tactful coalitions can argue for their own position and against the other, that is, engage in public Weak Tactful versus Strong Tactful media campaigns in order to persuade Detached voters. The pro-business Tactful coalition argues that government bureaucracy is the problem and business efficiency is the solution; and the pro-government Tactful coalition argues that corporate greed and corruption is the problem and good government is the solution. "I have experience and I know how government works. Vote for me and I can get things done." From the perspective of Detached voters, however, the two Tactful coalitions, sharing the opposite corner of the perspectives matrix (table 3.1), appear indistinguishable, equally unfamiliar, equally out of touch with the concerns of Detached voters, equally illegitimate and dysfunctional politically, and equally unlikable.

The more important dialogue that Detached individuals see is between themselves as Detached prospective voters and the Tactful political parties and candidates. For this reason, Tactful can try to gain the support of Detached voters by claiming to be on their side, that is, appearing to have adopted the Detached standpoint against the Strong Tactful standpoint of other career politicians, against the affluent corporate and cultural elite, and against the government itself. Thus, Tactful politicians commonly portray themselves as outsiders campaigning against incumbents, inside-the-Beltway politicians, the federal government, and the Establishment. As Ronald Reagan said in his inaugural address, "government is the problem." Ronald Reagan, Nancy Pelosi, Donald Trump and many others have routinely promised to "drain the swamp" in Washington, DC.

Some political analysts have questioned why Detached voters, in voting against government programs from which they likely benefit, are seemingly voting against their own self-interests. One reason is that Detached voters—both Weak and Strong—are less likely to discuss government and politics with family and friends and so can be less knowledgeable; for example, in a 2017 survey a third of Americans didn't know that the Affordable Care Act and Obamacare are the same. And when they vote, Detached voters—both Weak and Strong—may be more likely to vote "for the best person" rather than for either political party or specific policies or programs.

More important from the Detached perspective, however, is that safety-net programs discourage self-sufficiency and encourage dependence on government. "My family and neighbors have earned our benefits, but many others aren't worthy or deserving and are not like us. They are getting a free ride with these government benefits." Voting against safety-net programs and career politicians is a vote against perceived Tactful government intrusion and control of people's lives and a vote for Detached values of self-sufficiency, independence, and freedom.

Tactful's Indirect Appeals from the Loyal Perspective

A more successful strategy for the Tactful coalitions to gain the support of Detached voters is to appeal indirectly from the Loyal or Caring perspectives. Each of these differs from Detached on only one of the underlying assumptions of identity and intention (and not on both assumptions, as in the case of Tactful). The first and easier appeal is to build on assumptions that Detached may already hold in common with Loyal or Caring. The second and more difficult appeal is to convert Detached to a new assumption, to convince Detached to adopt the Loyal or Caring perspectives.

So, for example, Tactful's indirect appeal to Detached voters from the Loyal perspective will first build on the assumption of separateness shared by Detached and Loyal. Adopting the Loyal perspective, politicians tell Detached voters that their financial struggles and feelings of alienation are not their own fault. Rather, they have been victimized by Others who are different: powerful interests who are controlling the government and the economic system, racial minorities and others receiving government assistance—line-cutters—who create an economic burden, undocumented immigrants who are taking jobs away from Detached workers and changing how America looks, people in other countries who have unfairly stolen America's factories and jobs, and a culture of liberal political correctness threatening Detached's core values and principles. The powerful Tactful coalitions in Washington, DC, politicians say from the Loyal perspective, are looking after their own interests but have abandoned the American middle and working classes.

Second, an indirect appeal from the Loyal perspective will attempt to move Detached voters from their intention to understand to an intention to compete and control. The best way to respond to these external threats to Detached communities is, from the Loyal perspective, to take control, be in charge, and be a winner. This means cutting taxes to shrink the size and power of government; attacking corrupt and incompetent political leaders; opposing civil rights for minorities, immigrants, and others who appear different; opposing globalization, international trade, and American military entanglements abroad and having a more isolationist foreign policy; and doing what is necessary to provide jobs and economic opportunities for real, patriotic Americans.

All of this can be phrased to appeal to the values of those with a Detached perspective; you can be independent, self-sufficient, and free and have a better life if we can first get rid of government intrusion and other external forces and groups that have brought about the problems you are dealing with. "I understand what you are up against—the outside groups and government policies that have taken jobs away from this community. Vote for me and I will fight for you. I'll bring back jobs and make this a winning community again." This indirect appeal by Tactful to Detached from the Loyal perspective is not without risks nor guaranteed successful, however. Those holding a Loyal perspective often present themselves as proud and righteous, but Detached voters may perceive them as intrusive, immature, and aggressive (tables 3.3 to 3.5).

Tactful's Indirect Appeals from the Caring Perspective

Tactful's indirect appeal to Detached voters from the Caring perspective will first build on their common underlying intention to understand (rather than to compete and control). Adopting the Caring perspective, politicians may say to Detached voters that their financial struggles and feelings of alienation are not their own fault. Rather, they have been victimized by others who are competitive and controlling: greedy Wall Street bankers and corporate CEOs who have rigged the economic system, corrupt politicians who do the bidding of lobbyists and wealthy campaign donors, the top 1% who are benefiting the most from the productivity of Detached workers, and a powerful elite who have little understanding or sympathy for the lives of Detached workers and their families.

Second, an indirect appeal from the Caring perspective will attempt to move Detached voters from the assumption of separateness to an assumption of interdependence (table 3.1). This means convincing Detached voters that their financial struggles and alienation are not unique to their own communities but are shared throughout American society and that "we are all in this together." How the economic system and government are currently structured contributes to the displacement of not only Detached workers and their families but also many other families and communities throughout America. The powerful Tactful coalitions in Washington, DC, are looking after their own interests but have abandoned the American middle and working classes.

Several of these statements may not appear very different from what Loyal politicians would tell Detached voters. However, there is a critical difference in the underlying messages. Loyal politicians tell Detached voters the problems in your lives are caused by Others whose *identities* are different. Caring politicians tell Detached voters their problems are caused by those whose *intentions* are different. Consequently, proposed solutions from the Loyal and the Caring perspectives can be quite different.

The Caring solution is not to shrink and weaken government or attack those who are different or engage in international trade wars—as Loyal may suggest—but instead to work together to reform government to be more responsive to the needs of all Americans and managed more effectively to bring about desired results. Similarly, the economic system needs to be reformed so the benefits of workers' increased productivity are shared more broadly and fairly across all American families and communities, rather than benefiting only an already wealthy and powerful corporate elite. "I understand what you are up against. But know that you are not alone. Many other Americans in other communities are facing similar challenges. If we all work together politically, we can make America better for everyone."

Caring politicians may also express attitudes of concern and sympathy, looking out for the needs of Detached voters and their families and communities. They may promise to make sure government programs will protect them, and to fight for the rights of Detached voters and families and stand up for them. This can be a tricky appeal, however, because people holding a Detached perspective may view Caring programs and policies aimed at helping the poor as bothersome and smothering. Detached voters may perceive Caring politicians as intrusive, naive, and idealistic (tables 3.3 to 3.5). At the core, Detached voters want to be independent and self-sufficient, not be taken care of, and not be recipients of charity from those with more power.

Better, then, is for Caring to build its appeal on the shared assumption of understanding and cooperation. Caring can tell Detached, for example, that the means to becoming more independent and self-sufficient is learning how the economic system and government work, playing a more active role in the community and politics, working together with others to influence and shape the economic system, making government work better for all, pushing for more spending on schools and health care, and doing whatever is necessary to provide jobs and economic opportunities. These solutions from the Caring perspective require making progress on broad issues of social structure, including inequality, health care, and education.

In the contest between the pro-business and pro-government Tactful coalitions for the support of Detached voters, the indirect appeal from the Loyal perspective may be easier and more resonant. Detached and Loyal already share the assumption of separateness; that is, identity is self-contained. The focus is always oneself and one's community in opposition to those who appear different. For someone holding the Detached perspective to convert to the Loyal perspective requires merely changing from an intention to understand to an intention to compete, control, and be successful. The solution to my pain is to win against Others who are different and hurting me, who closed my factory and took my job, who are threatening my safety, who ripped me off, who took advantage of me. In short, by opposing others who appear to be different, I can quickly be on the path to success and become a winner. As Donald Trump said in the 2016 presidential campaign, "We're going to win so much. You're going to get tired of winning."

Appealing to Detached voters from the Caring perspective may be more difficult. Both perspectives share the assumption of an intention to understand. For someone holding the Detached perspective to convert to the Caring perspective requires changing from a self-contained identity to an identity of interdependence with others. The solution to my pain is to be concerned not just for myself but also for Others who are different from me and in pain and for us to work together and support each other. As Hillary Clinton said during the 2016 presidential campaign, "We're stronger together." Clinton also considered "Progress For All," "Fighting for Fairness," and "Moving Ahead Together" as campaign slogans. In short, Detached voters are being asked to care not only for themselves but also for other individuals, families, and communities who may appear different. *For many, this can be a giant leap.*

Pew Research Center Political Groups

Do the four perspectives—Loyal, Tactful, Detached, and Caring—actually reflect the political attitudes and values of the American electorate? The short answer is yes. A detailed answer is provided by the Pew Research Center in a report titled "Beyond Red vs. Blue" with findings from a survey of 10,000 Americans. A statistical procedure (cluster analysis) was used to create eight relatively homogeneous groups based on answers to more than 70 questions concerning political attitudes and values. Conservative and liberal groups are presented as partisan anchors of a single dimension, with the remaining diverse groups arranged awkwardly between these two. The findings are more understandable, however, when presented in terms of the four American perspectives on political issues.

The Pew Research Center groups represent relatively stable types of people, while the four perspectives are flexible points of view that people can hold and change. Nevertheless, an alignment of the Pew groups and the four perspectives is straight-forward, as shown in table 10.1: Steadfast Conservatives reflect the Loyal perspective (about 12 percent of Americans); Business Conservatives, Solid Liberals, and Faith and Family Left reflect the Tactful perspective (39 percent); Young Outsiders, Hard-Pressed Skeptics, and Bystanders reflect the Detached perspective (37 percent); and Next Generation Left reflects the Caring perspective (12 percent). The justification for this alignment is presented in the following paragraphs.

Loyal perspective. The Pew Research Center identified one group, Steadfast Conservatives (about 12% of the American population), whose attitudes and values are consistent with the Loyal perspective. These voters are critical of government and socially conservative. They believe politicians should stick with their positions and not compromise, the United States stands above other countries

Table 10.1. Pew Research Center "Beyond Red vs. Blue" Groups

Loyal	**Detached**
Steadfast Conservatives	Young Outsiders, Hard-Pressed Skeptics, Bystanders
Tactful	**Caring**
Business Conservatives, Solid Liberals, Faith and Family Left	Next Generation Left

in the world, government is doing too many things better left to businesses and individuals, government aid to the poor does more harm than good, the government in Washington, DC, cannot be trusted to do what is right, Americans should pay less attention to problems overseas and concentrate more on problems at home, US efforts to solve problems around the world usually end up making things worse, free trade agreements are bad for the United States, undocumented immigrants now living in the United States should not be eligible for citizenship, same-sex marriage should be opposed, the right of Americans to own guns should be protected, Americans should not have to give up privacy to ensure safety from terrorism, the best way to ensure peace is through military strength, honor and duty are core values, and they often feel proud to be Americans (all of these findings are from the Pew report).

Steadfast Conservatives are likely to be older, white, evangelical Protestant, and live in the South. In short, the Loyal perspective of Steadfast Conservatives is to see themselves as standing apart from other countries, the poor, immigrants, and gays and lesbians. At the same time, they aim to stay in control through maintaining core values and military strength.

Tactful perspective. Three groups identified in "Beyond Red vs. Blue" reflect the Tactful perspective. Business Conservatives (10%) are critical of government, like Steadfast Conservatives, but differ in their support for business and immigration reform. Business Conservatives believe the United States stands above all other countries, as Americans we can always find ways to solve our problems, Wall Street helps the American economy more than it hurts, the US economic system is generally fair to most Americans, government is doing too many things better left to businesses and individuals, government aid to the poor does more harm than good, the government in Washington, DC, cannot be trusted to do what is right, America should be active in world affairs, problems around the world would be worse without American involvement, free trade agreements are good for the United States, undocumented immigrants should be eligible for citizenship if they meet certain requirements, the right of Americans to own guns should be protected, the best way to ensure peace is through military strength, honor and duty are core values, and they often feel proud to be Americans. Business conservatives are likely to be older white men, and likely to have some college education or be college graduates.

Solid Liberals (15%) in the Pew report have liberal attitudes toward government, the economy, business, and foreign policy as well as social issues. They believe elected officials should compromise with people they disagree with, the country's best years are ahead, America's success has been due to its ability to change, Wall Street hurts the American economy more than it helps, the economic system in the United States unfairly favors powerful interests, the government should do more to solve problems, government aid to the poor does more good than harm, the United States should be active in world affairs, free trade agreements are good for the United States, undocumented immigrants should be eligible for citizenship if they meet certain requirements, gays and lesbians should be allowed to marry legally, the best way to ensure peace is through good diplomacy, and government should do more to help needy Americans. Solid liberals are likely to have some college education or be college graduates.

The third Tactful group, Faith and Family Left (15%), is a racially and ethnically diverse group. It has confidence in the government's ability to address American social issues. These voters believe the country's best years are ahead, government should do more to solve problems, problems around the world would be worse without American involvement, free trade agreements are good for the United States, undocumented immigrants should be eligible for citizenship if they meet certain requirements, and same-sex marriage should be opposed. Faith and Family Left voters are likely to be older, black, Protestant, and live in the South.

In short, the Tactful perspective of Business Conservatives, Solid Liberals, and Faith and Family Left is evident in their positive attitudes toward trade with other countries and toward citizenship for undocumented immigrants. The Tactful perspective is also evident in their openness to change and willingness to compromise in order to solve problems, and in their trust and confidence in government and America's future.

Detached perspective. Three groups identified in the Pew survey reflect the Detached perspective. These groups are less likely to follow what's going on in government and public affairs, and they are more likely to identify as Independents than Republicans or Democrats. Thus their attitudes and values are more mixed and contradictory than for the other groups.

Young Outsiders (14%), like the Steadfast Conservatives and Business Conservatives, favor limited government. Yet, they also have more liberal attitudes on social issues. Young Outsiders believe the economic system in the United States unfairly favors powerful interests, government is doing too many things better left to businesses and individuals, government aid to the poor does more harm than good, the government in Washington, DC, cannot be trusted to do what is right, Americans should pay less attention to problems overseas and concentrate more on problems at home, US efforts to solve problems around the world usually end up making things worse, the right of Americans to own guns should be protected, Americans should not have to give up privacy to ensure safety from terrorism, and government can't afford to do much more to help needy Americans.

Hard-Pressed Skeptics (13%) are financially battered and support government programs for the poor, yet at the same time are critical of the government's performance. They are dissatisfied with the way things are going in America today. They believe America can't solve many of its important problems, Wall Street hurts the American economy more than it helps, the economic system in the United States unfairly favors powerful interests, government aid to the poor does more good than harm, the government in Washington, DC, cannot be trusted to do what is right, Americans should pay less attention to problems overseas and concentrate more on problems at home, US efforts to solve problems around the world usually end up making things worse, free trade agreements are bad for the United States, undocumented immigrants should not be eligible for citizenship, same-sex marriage should be opposed, Social Security benefits should not be reduced, Americans should not have to give up privacy to ensure safety from terrorism, and government should do more to help needy Americans. Hard-Pressed Skeptics are likely to have a high school education or less and have a low income.

The third Detached group, characterized by the Pew Research Center as Bystanders (10%), includes people who are not registered to vote and do not attend to politics. Members of this group believe America can't solve many of its important problems, America's success has been due to its ability to change, the economic system unfairly favors powerful interests, the government should do more to solve problems, Americans should pay less attention to problems overseas and focus more on problems at home, free trade agreements are good for the United States, undocumented immigrants should be eligible for citizenship if they meet certain requirements, gun ownership should be controlled, and the best way to ensure peace is through good diplomacy. Bystanders are likely to have a high school education or less, to have a low income, and to be video or computer gamers.

In short, Detached Young Outsiders, Hard-Pressed Skeptics, and Bystanders have attitudes and values that reinforce their feelings of separation from the American economy and government and from immigrants and people in other countries. In the context of the mainstream media's single dimension of left versus right political polarization, these three groups would be viewed as independent voters or moderates, standing midway between conservatives and liberals, agreeing with some attitudes and values of each. However, aligning the Pew Research Center groups with the four perspectives makes clear that these *Detached voters have attitudes and values in direct opposition to those of Tactful groups* such as Business Conservatives and Solid Liberals (perspectives matrix, table 3.1). *These Detached voters are focused more on understanding than on competition and control, and more on separateness and self-sufficiency than on interdependence.*

Caring perspective. Next Generation Left (12%), young, affluent, and liberal on social issues, reflects the Caring perspective. Members of this group believe elected officials should compromise with people they disagree with, the country's best years are ahead, America has been successful because of its ability to change, government aid to the poor does more good than harm, the government can be trusted to do what is right, the United States should be active in world affairs, problems around the world would be worse without American involvement, the United States should have a stronger relationship with China, free trade agreements are good for the United States, undocumented immigrants should be eligible for citizenship if they meet certain requirements, developing alternative energy sources should be an important priority, gays and lesbians should be allowed to marry legally, and the best way to ensure peace is through good diplomacy. The young members of this group are likely to have some college experience or be college graduates. The Caring perspective of Next Generation Left is evident in its optimism, openness to change, and engagement with and concern for others including the poor, gays and lesbians, undocumented immigrants, other countries, and the environment.

How durable are the pro-business and pro-government Tactful coalitions in Washington, DC? Is the Loyal and pro-business Tactful movement productive and sustainable? Is the Caring and pro-government Tactful movement productive and sustainable? Or, is increasing political polarization in Washington, DC, with its damaging effects and threat to America's future as a democracy a sign of an impending realignment among these political movements? Political polarization and the potential for political realignment are explored in the next chapter.

11

Political Polarization:
Causes, Consequences, Responses

Many Americans are accustomed to being starkly divided between opposing sides, in their support for rival National Football League teams; for example, the Baltimore Ravens versus the Pittsburgh Steelers, the Dallas Cowboys versus the Washington Redskins, the New England Patriots versus the New York Jets, or the Chicago Bears versus the Green Bay Packers. Other sports teams also have their legions of fans whose enthusiasm and loyalty are unquestionable, who would never consider the possibility of supporting another team. Committed fans gain a sense of identity and belonging by joining with others to support their team. They don't have to think about which team to support; fans don't really have a choice and often their family and friends don't either.

Unfortunately, some sports fans can become, well, fanatics, no longer merely enthusiasts but instead now possessing excessive and irrational passion for their team.

Especially if the home team loses and the final score is close, brawls among fans, serious injuries, and arrests for violence increase markedly. Unruly fan behavior and violence in and around stadiums, particularly in the parking lots, is now a major concern of the NFL and local police and security forces. For these fans, there has been a shift from enjoying the competition among teams and good sportsmanship, even if the home team loses, to an intense focus on loyalty to the home team and on winning. Their perspective has shifted from Tactful to Loyal.

Similar to sports fans, many Americans gain a sense of identity and belonging by joining with others to support one of our two dominant political parties. They don't have to become as informed or think as deeply about complex issues or policies—such as immigration or climate change—as long as they know where their own party and its leaders stand—a convenient mental shortcut. Similar to sports fans, they can disagree strongly about whether the United States is heading in the right direction and what changes would be best for America's future. Yet, they understand that elections and votes in Congress are sometimes won by the other side and that accepting this and moving on is essential for the future of American democracy. Historically, politics in America has been a Weak Tactful versus Strong Tactful dialogue (as described in chapter 9).

Unfortunately, political polarization in America is similar to the fanaticism of fans who put loyalty to their home team and winning before good sportsmanship. Now many Americans put loyalty to political party and winning before commitment to country and democracy. They are certain that their own political party is right on the issues and the other is wrong and they distrust and dislike those who are on the other side. Politicians and citizens alike think, talk, and vote without regard for evidence or logic or the merits of particular issues or candidates for office or even their own self-interest, but merely because of their identification with and loyalty to their own political party. This increasing polarization has reduced much of American politics to a rigid and destructive Weak Loyal versus Strong Loyal dialogue. Loyal political standpoints are defined by self-contained identities, intention to compete, control, and win, pride in one's own political party and identity, and a view of others as unworthy and threatening.

Conversation, discussion, and debate regarding critical issues in society is an American tradition; what is new is that these conversations are becoming increasingly polarized. According to a Pew Research Center report, "Political Polarization in the American Public," the proportion of Americans who are extremely liberal or extremely conservative in their views has increased, while the proportion whose views are moderate and centrist has decreased. Many American citizens and voters, media observers and personalities, and elected officials and political leaders now see everything in terms of only two opposing sides: my side, always right, and the other side, always wrong.

The rise of talk radio, cable television, the internet, and social media has contributed to this polarization. Although Americans now have access to more and diverse sources of information, they tend to focus on media featuring views consistent with what they already believe; some get their political and government news from liberal sources such as CNN, NPR, and MSNBC; others get theirs from conservative sources such as Fox News and local radio and television sources. Political polarization threatens the foundation of credible, commonly held information required for rational discussion and reaching consensus in American politics.

Dialogue 1. Weak Loyal versus Strong Loyal
Polarization in American Politics

Conversations about political issues in America increasingly reflect a Weak Loyal versus Strong Loyal dialogue, the most oppositional of the sixteen dialogues. Each political party feels proud and self-righteous, convinced that its own values and goals are worthy and those of the other are not. Each party is unwilling to yield the power and privilege associated with its own identity and community, while acting with little or no regard for the integrity of others' lives and communities.

Commenting on "the feeling of many Americans that our politics are totally stuck," Pulitzer-Prize winner and columnist for *The New York Times* Thomas Friedman has written, "The nonstop fighting between our two political parties has left many Americans feeling like the children of two permanently divorcing parents. The country is starved to see its two major parties do hard things together again." Breaking away from this destructive Weak Loyal versus Strong Loyal dialogue and moving towards other perspectives and dialogues can be difficult. In contrast, for each of the other three perspectives and fifteen dialogues, at least one of the sides is motivated to understand, cooperate, or compromise with the other.

Why is the polarized Weak Loyal versus Strong Loyal dialogue more and more common in American political discussion and debate? First, the Loyal (Steadfast Conservatives) and pro-business Tactful (Business Conservatives) movement in Washington, DC, is engaged in a Weak Loyal versus Strong Tactful dialogue (as described in dialogue 2, chapter 9). Given Loyal's customary tactics of open confrontation, no cooperation, and no compromise, pro-business Tactful can feel pressured to abandon negotiation, persuasion, and coalition building and imitate Loyal's confrontational tactics. Thus, this Weak Loyal versus Strong Tactful dialogue can easily deteriorate into the damaging and intractable Weak Loyal versus Strong Loyal dialogue (tables 4.2 and 4.3). Indeed, some argue that in recent years Steadfast Conservatives have gained the upper hand in this dialogue; that is, they now occupy the Strong Loyal standpoint; for example, the Tea Party and the Freedom Caucus in the US Congress.

Second, the dialogue between the pro-business Tactful coalition (Business Conservatives) and the pro-government

Tactful coalition (Solid Liberals) has traditionally been a Weak Tactful versus Strong Tactful dialogue (dialogue 6, chapter 9), with their relative power depending on who controls Congress and the presidency. However, as the Loyal and pro-business Tactful movement engages more and more in the confrontational maneuvers of the Loyal perspective, this Weak Tactful versus Strong Tactful dialogue is at risk of deteriorating into the damaging and intractable Weak Loyal versus Strong Loyal dialogue. For example, in early 2016 Republican senators refused to hold hearings and vote on any candidate nominated by President Obama to fill a Supreme Court vacancy. As a result, in early 2017 Democratic senators engaged in a brief filibuster in opposition to a Supreme Court candidate nominated by President Trump.

Third, the Tactful coalitions have a strong impetus towards maintaining good relations, engaging in discussion and negotiation, and avoiding confrontational tactics. Nevertheless, at the same time the pro-business Tactful and pro-government Tactful coalitions do have conflicting political interests and intentions towards gaining more power and prestige. If Strong Tactful pushes too hard on its agenda, this may violate the traditions, conventions, or rules for interactions in the broader, shared communities of Congress and the American political scene. For example, if one Tactful coalition controls both Congress and the presidency, it may neglect to work cooperatively with the other Tactful coalition. The Weak Tactful versus Strong Tactful dialogue (dialogue 6) can then deteriorate into the stressful Weak Loyal versus Strong Tactful dialogue (dialogue 2) and subsequently into the polarizing and destructive Weak Loyal versus Strong Loyal dialogue (dialogue 1).

Political Polarization Threatens America's Future

What are the consequences of increasing polarization? Discussion of important issues facing American society has become more partisan, reflecting the political ideologies and commitments of the two Tactful coalitions, and often angry and bitter. People are less willing to compromise and are more insistent on getting their own way. People do not listen carefully to those who hold views contrasting with their own; indeed, they are often ignorant of, misinformed about, and dismissive of those views. Complex issues are frequently oversimplified when forced to fit into the framework of only two political positions. Simplistic and misleading representations of the issues become obstacles to fruitful discussion, to productive legislative collaboration, and to the crafting of workable solutions that can solve critical problems and move America forward.

These consequences are visible in the United States Congress. Passage of effective legislation requires a Tactful perspective, including thoughtful deliberation, open-mindedness, willingness to compromise, and bipartisan agreements among legislators. Yet recently members of Congress have struggled with even routine tasks of governance such as approving budgets and raising the debt ceiling. Instead, politicians in Washington, DC, now interact primarily through partisan activist organizations, special interest advocacy groups, think tanks, and the many influential lobbyists representing corporations and the wealthy. The legislative leaders now focus on fine-tuning their message wars and holding symbolic votes—for example, to repeal Obamacare, to affirm that climate change is human-caused, to send more troops to Iraq or Syria, to defund Planned Parenthood, to support strong background checks for gun purchases—to create sharp contrasts between the two dominant Tactful coalitions that may influence the next election. Political image and branding have become more important than facts, loyalty to partisan coalitions more important than loyalty to country.

The inability of Congress to address significant problems facing American society has been described as political stalemate, deadlock, and gridlock. Continual bickering and ineffectiveness has eroded the American public's respect for

Congress and, more broadly, has led many Americans to have less trust in government. While partisan political leaders and the media are espousing and fighting each other's extremist positions, moderate voices have lost influence and power in Washington, DC. This broad climate of angry polarization and mistrust of government undermines the open exchange of information and ideas and respectful discussion and debate among family members, neighbors, coworkers, and citizens that is essential for America to function and endure as a democratic society.

Americans are concerned about the consequences of polarization for the future of the United States. At the close of 2015, journalist Anna North asked readers of *The New York Times* what they felt was the greatest challenge facing the United States. Polarization ranked among the top five challenges (the others were climate change, money in politics, education, and inequality). In 2014, political scientist Francis Fukuyama described the decay of the American political system, and observed that "With sharp political polarization, this system is less and less able to represent majority interests but gives excessive representation to the views of interest groups and activist organizations that collectively do not add up to a sovereign American people."

Only a small fraction of Americans currently feel that the pro-business Tactful and pro-government Tactful coalitions are responsive to their concerns. An increasing number of Americans, especially younger Americans, no longer identify with either of the major political parties. In the past two decades, the proportion of voters who identify as Republican has declined to about one quarter of the electorate. The proportion who identify as Democrat has remained constant at about one third of the electorate. Most striking is that the proportion identifying as independent—that is, as Detached—has increased to about 40 percent of the electorate.

So there are now more Detached independents than either Republicans or Democrats. They represent a substantial proportion of the American electorate that is dissatisfied with what the two, dominant Tactful coalitions can offer. Another indication that Americans would like to move beyond the two partisan positions is low voter turnout. In recent presidential elections, only about half of eligible voters have actually voted.

The increasingly heated dialogues within the two Tactful coalitions are further evidence that differences and tensions on the American political scene are more complex than the current polarized political climate would suggest. The Loyal and pro-business Tactful movement is engaged in an internal Weak Loyal versus Strong Tactful dialogue over numerous issues that divide them (dialogue 2, chapter 9). Strong Tactful business leaders see the social and cultural conservatism of Weak Loyal voters as potentially harmful to their economic interests. And Loyal working-class voters do not have the same economic interests as pro-business Tactful politicians who favor smaller government, cuts in programs benefiting the middle class, and tax cuts for the wealthy.

Similarly, the Caring and pro-government Tactful movement is engaged in an internal Weak Caring versus Strong Tactful dialogue over the numerous issues that divide them (dialogue 14, chapter 9). Caring voters are concerned that pro-government Tactful politicians have neglected their long-standing commitment to government policies benefiting the middle class and the poor. The consequences of political polarization, including legislative gridlock, declining trust in government, and failure to address America's problems, will shape America far into the coming decade.

Ineffective Responses to Political Polarization

"Let's face it. The American political system is broken," Nicholas Kristof, Pulitzer-Prize winning op-ed columnist for *The New York Times*, wrote in 2014. "Politicians have figured out what works for their own careers: playing to their base, denouncing the other side, and blocking rivals for getting credit for anything." In short, increasing polarization in American politics, decreasing identification of voters with the two traditional Tactful coalitions (the Republican and Democratic parties), declining voter participation in elections, and increasing stress and conflict within the Tactful coalitions all make clear that seeking to represent and understand issues in American society with only two sides is no longer adequate.

The American electorate is searching for and thinking in terms of additional perspectives beyond those offered by the two Tactful coalitions. Indeed, some pundits, pointing to the Tea Party, the Freedom Caucus, Occupy Wall Street, and other populist movements, suggest that a political realignment is already well underway in America. Harvard historian Jill Lepore, writing in *The New Yorker* in 2013 on extremist voices in the media and on the internet, notes, "What's really going on could be anything from party realignment to the unraveling of the Republic."

The pundits disagree, however, on whether this political realignment involves evangelical Christians versus liberal-leaning Christian and secular voters; working class versus professional, affluent, and elite voters; economic nationalists versus cosmopolitan globalists; white nationalists versus Black, Hispanic, and other minorities; American heartland interests and values versus East and West Coast entrepreneurial and technological interests; business interests versus social justice interests; voters without college degrees versus college graduates; state and local control versus the federal government; boomers versus millennials; men versus women; rural versus urban voters; or other contrasting viewpoints. Whatever the future holds, this great diversity of political interests will be more understandable in a framework of four American perspectives rather than being squeezed into the traditional dichotomy of right versus left, conservative versus liberal.

Pundits, concerned politicians, and dismayed and outraged citizens have made three suggestions for how to respond to political polarization in the United States. Unfortunately, all three are ineffective and unacceptable non-starters. The first has been widespread calls for compromise and negotiation, finding common ground, meeting in the middle, bipartisan solutions, overcoming our differences, reaching across the aisle, working together, getting along, agreeing to disagree, electing moderates, making government work, and so forth. For example, columnist for *The New York Times* David Brooks called in 2017 for a political establishment with "people who actually know about public policy problems. . . . who have had gradual, upward careers in government and understand the craft of wielding power. . . . who know how to live up to certain standards of integrity and public service" and who conduct themselves "in office as if nation is more important than party."

These are all actually calls for returning to America's historic Weak Tactful versus Strong Tactful political dialogue as this existed between Ronald Reagan and Tip O'Neill in the 1980s and between Orrin Hatch and Ted Kennedy in the 1990s (described in chapter 9). Unfortunately, these calls are in denial of the problem: American politics is trapped in a Weak Loyal versus Strong Loyal dialogue. Every issue is cast in polarized self versus other, black versus white terms; and the intention on both sides is always to win, never to compromise.

A second suggestion has been, "Get used to it." Jane Mansbridge, Harvard professor and past president of the American Political Science Association, wrote in *The Washington Post* in 2016 that "political polarization is here to stay." She argues that none of the causes of polarization— gradual party realignment, closer elections, and inequality—is likely to change. Also writing in 2016, Arthur C. Brooks, president of the American Enterprise Institute, laments that "there is a Polarization Industrial Complex in American media today, which profits handsomely from the continuing climate of bitterness."

A third suggestion has been to propose structural changes in America's political institutions. In general, these changes would be difficult if not impossible to implement; for example, changing the Constitution to rebalance federal and state power, redistricting to combat gerrymandering, increasing turnout in primaries, and having senators chosen by state legislatures. An article in *The Atlantic* by Russell Berman, "What's the answer to political polarization in the U.S.?" offers these and similar proposals. None of these is likely to solve the problem of political polarization.

Changing How We Think and Talk about Politics

Damaging consequences of political polarization threaten America's future as a democracy. The best solution is to change how people think and talk about issues in American society. "*The solution starts not with institutions but with individuals*," writes Arthur C. Brooks, president of the American Enterprise Institute, in *The New York Times*. "We look too much to political parties or Congress to make progress, but not nearly enough at our own behavior. You can't single-handedly change the country, but you can change yourself."

The way forward—including being prepared to understand and participate in a forthcoming political realignment—is to recognize that there are not merely two partisan positions but in fact four perspectives on issues in America: Loyal, Tactful, Detached, and Caring. These four perspectives, grounded in people's assumptions about identities and intentions, have persisted throughout American history. They have powered our economic and social progress, and enabled Americans to better understand ourselves and others.

Why does recognizing four perspectives matter? If we see only two partisan positions, we are tempted to ignore the complexities of American issues and crush everything that is said and written into one or the other partisan stance. This risks misrepresenting and ignoring the beliefs and values of many thoughtful people. When they feel their views aren't reflected in the two dominant positions, they feel left out, drop out of civic discourse, lose trust in government, and stop voting.

The four perspectives do not describe fixed and stable types or categories of people. Instead, the perspectives are flexible and changeable, depending on who we are in dialogue with and the particular issues. For example, how people who hold the Tactful perspective view others, behave towards others, and are perceived by others will reflect whether the others' perspective is Loyal, Detached, or Caring (tables 3.3. 3.4, and 3.5).

How the Tactful civic leader of a small town perceives, behaves towards, and is perceived by others could reflect whether the civic leader is interacting with, for example, a Loyal small business owner, a Detached community poet, or a Caring social worker. The civic leader may adopt a Loyal perspective when confronting an industrial polluter or a Caring perspective when inviting refugees to settle in the town.

The four perspectives are flexible and changeable, depending on whether one's power—control over material and emotional resources, expertise and leadership abilities, determination and moral character, or legitimacy and access to information—is relatively weak or strong when compared with others in the dialogue. For example, although the same two perspectives are involved, a Weak Loyal versus Strong Tactful dialogue will unfold differently than a Weak Tactful versus Strong Loyal dialogue. A conversation between the Loyal owner of a small startup business and the town's long-established and respected Tactful civic leader will unfold differently than a conversation between a Tactful civic leader recently elected in a close vote and the Loyal factory owner who employs many of the town's residents (tables 4.2 and 4.3).

The power of an individual or group can be greater or lesser, depending on who we are in dialogue with and the particular type of power at play. So, for example, a Tactful civic leader with influence and control over zoning regulations and building permits may be more powerful than a younger Loyal business owner who hopes to open a new bar and restaurant. But the same Tactful civic leader may be less powerful than a Caring social worker with a network of professional friends who share a determination to advocate for subsidized housing for the homeless.

In the concluding chapter, seven suggestions for how to have a conversation about politics provide a clear path for moving beyond political polarization by thinking and talking from the four American perspectives—Loyal, Tactful, Detached, and Caring.

Moving Beyond Political Polarization

"Our country is finally moving in the right direction."
"No, our country is seriously off track!"
"The most important issues facing our country are immigration and terrorism."
"No, the most important issues are foreign policy, inequality, and climate change!"

How can we have a conversation about politics without getting drawn into divisive arguments? This question arises not only during stressful Thanksgiving dinners but throughout the year with our families and friends, in our communities and workplaces, and in the media and all levels of government. The temptation for some is to step aside, to become detached, to avoid discussing politics: "Disagreeing with others makes me uncomfortable. And talking about politics is pointless. You can never agree. Political talk annoys me and wears me out."

What's important, however, is not to abandon the field

and leave political discussion and debate and decisions about America's future to others. "Debating, like voting, is a way for people to disagree without hitting one another or going to war," Harvard historian Jill Lepore writes in *The New Yorker*. "It's the key to every institution that makes civic life possible, from courts to legislatures. Without debate, there can be no self-government." The most urgent problem in American civic life, Jonathan Zimmerman, professor of history of education at the University of Pennsylvania, writes in *The Atlantic*, is our inability to communicate with people who do not share our opinions. He argues that our schools aren't doing enough to teach young people how to engage civilly with other Americans over divisive issues. Conversation, communication, dialogues, discussion, and debate--these are the topics of this concluding chapter.

"The most important problem confronting the United States," writes Roger Cohen, columnist for *The New York Times*, is that "Tens of millions of Trump opponents cannot communicate with tens of millions of his supporters. There is no viable vocabulary. There is no shared reality." How did the notion arise that political positions could be arranged along a single dimension, anchored by the labels right and left, conservative and liberal? During the French Revolution, those who sat on the right in parliament supported tradition, the monarchy, hierarchy, and the church, while those who sat on the left supported the revolution, the republic, equality, and secularization. Now, more than two centuries later, most Americans cannot explain what these labels mean in the context of contemporary politics. Nor is there consensus among distinguished scholars on the current meanings and utility of these political labels. Unfortunately, these labels—right, left, conservative, liberal—continue to be powerful: they make us identify with our political tribe, stop thinking, and double-down.

So to have sensible conversations about politics and move beyond political polarization, we must abandon these worn-out labels and start anew with a familiar, impartial vocabulary that everyone understands. The first step is to recognize that Americans hold not two partisan positions but four perspectives on the issues: Loyal, Tactful, Detached, and Caring. Is the reality of four perspectives too complex, too challenging as a framework for talking about politics? Not at all! American barbershop quartets sing in four-part harmony, as do iconic American vocal groups with top chart hits. Surely we can strive for similarly beautiful harmonies and remarkable and memorable outcomes in our political conversations.

It's a mistake to ignore the real complexity of American issues and crush everyone's thoughts and opinions into only two positions, right versus left, conservative versus liberal. And it's a mistake to try to understand the American political scene by focusing on who people are—identity politics—and their ages, genders, education, race or ethnicity, occupations, wealth, geography, or political party affiliation. The four American perspectives do not describe fixed and stable types or categories of people. Instead, the perspectives are flexible and changeable, depending on who we happen to be talking with and the particular issues. We can't change who we are, but we can change how we think and talk with one another.

Seven Suggestions for Conversations About Politics

In short, moving beyond political polarization and ensuring America's future as a democracy requires considering far more closely what we are assuming and thinking as individuals and how we can do a better job of sharing our ideas and opinions with those whose views are different from ours. Here are seven suggestions for how to have joyful, engaging, and productive conversations about politics. These suggestions provide a clear path for moving beyond political polarization by thinking and talking from the four American perspectives—Loyal, Tactful, Detached, and Caring.

(1) *Most important, clearly identify your own perspective*

on the issue at hand. Some may be tempted, given the concrete illustrations in chapters 5 through 8, to align themselves with the perspective that appears most consistent with their stand, pro or con, on many of those issues. However, perspectives can be changeable, depending on the particular issue. A more productive strategy is to first identify a perspective to shy away from, because being aligned with this perspective would make us feel too uncomfortable, especially if called out and challenged by our family, friends, or colleagues. Second, identify an aspirational perspective, one that seems most consistent with the values and attitudes we feel that we hold and to which we would like to be true.

Having done this, we still must identify the perspective that we are adopting on the issue of immediate concern. For example, we may have concluded that the Detached perspective has limited applicability and the Tactful perspective is an aspirational ideal, yet find the facts and our feelings on a particular issue mandate adopting a Loyal perspective or a Caring perspective. A simple question to ask is, do I want to be in charge, get along with others, work this out myself, or look out for others? When in doubt, consider the underlying assumptions regarding identity and intentions (chapters 2 and 3).

(2) *Of equal importance, clearly identify the perspective of the other person in the conversation.* Recognizing there are not two positions but four perspectives opens up possibilities for more nuanced, effective, and productive dialogues. Identifying the other's perspective will be difficult and perhaps impossible to do well, if we believe there are only two points of view, our own, the right one, and the other's, the wrong one. Perhaps on a particular issue the participants in the dialogue have without adequate thought adopted two inappropriate perspectives, for example, Loyal and Caring. Yet, the remaining two perspectives, Tactful and Detached, may better reflect one or both of their concerns on the immediate issue. In other words, with only two perspectives at play, one must be right, the other must be wrong. With four

perspectives at play, it's possible that both participants in the dialogue should reassess their standpoints and arguments.

Why is it important to determine where the other is coming from? Merely setting forth our own views on an issue is rarely effective in convincing others that ours is the better position and so they should yield. Nor is attacking the assumed views of the other helpful in moving a conversation forward to a productive conclusion. Nor is looking at actual data necessarily useful towards finding common ground, for people often focus only on what they feel to be supportive data, reinterpreting the data from their own perspective, and neglect what might be inconsistent.

Much more effective in resolving conflicts is to reframe our own arguments in terms of the perspective, attitudes, and values that are important for the other side. This is, for example, what politicians holding the Tactful, Loyal, and Caring perspectives do in trying to gain the support of Detached voters (as illustrated in chapter 9).

However, this tactic will not be effective if we misunderstand the other's perspective. For example, a Tactful civic leader may attempt to persuade a business owner by arguing in terms of the other's assumed Loyal values. But suppose the business owner is anticipating retirement and now views the world from a Detached or Caring perspective? Or, a Tactful civic leader preparing to meet with a constituent regarding a proposed policy should consider whether that person is a Loyal business owner, a Detached poet, or a Caring social worker in order to have a productive conversation.

Success in correctly identifying the other's perspective can require asking good questions that draw the other out. For example, a good conversation may include statements such as the following: "This is what I hear you saying," "This is how what you are saying sounds to me," and "Let me try to say this back to you. Is this correct?" A good conversation requires listening carefully and striving to understand what the other person is saying, not using this time to think about what you will say when it is your turn. And having a good conversation requires distinguishing between the person and what the person is saying. When in doubt about what the other's perspective might be, consider the underlying assumptions regarding identity and intentions (chapters 2 and 3).

It's always possible that the other person has some reasonable, valid points and something useful to offer. "The beauty of politics," David Brooks, columnist for *The New York Times*, wrote in 2016, is that "it involves an endless conversation in which we learn about other people and see things from their vantage point and try to balance their needs against our own." Brooks' insight is remarkably similar to how caring friends move forward in their relationship (dialogue 16): they strive to listen carefully to each other, learn from each other and understand the other's situation, demonstrate respect for the other's standpoint, and redefine the situation to emphasize their interdependence.

Critical Thinking Is About Ourselves, Not Others

(3) *Do not assume that people, including yourself, are committed to holding the same perspective on all issues.* The four perspectives are not stable types or fixed categories of people, but rather are points of view that people can hold and change, depending on the issue. A Tactful civic leader may be in conflict with a Loyal business owner on some economic issue, but discover that the same person holds a Caring perspective on another, unrelated social issue. The same is true for ourselves, that is, we can hold any of the four perspectives depending on the issue. We may hold a Loyal perspective when negotiating a business contract, a Tactful perspective when chairing a school board meeting, a Detached perspective when composing a new poem or song, and a Caring perspective when coaching a youth sports team.

The flexibility to change from one perspective to another, and so change the structure of a dialogue, can be advantageous both for resolving otherwise intractable conflicts and for creating opportunities for the future.

Suppose a group of civic leaders is engaged in a Weak Tactful versus Strong Tactful dialogue over whether a manufacturing company should receive tax reductions as an incentive for locating a new factory in the town. The course of the dialogue and its resolution would be improved if one of the participants changes from the Tactful to the Caring perspective and suggests that the tax incentives be matched with a commitment to hire a percentage of new factory workers from among current town residents.

The challenge for people and groups is to consider whether their current perspective is the most appropriate, or whether the content of the issue and the other's perspective call for adopting another of the three remaining perspectives. Changing from one perspective to another means, of course, that the conversation will have shifted to another of the sixteen dialogues, perhaps a dramatic and a positive turn in a conversation about politics. Being flexible regarding our own perspectives, and having the courage to consider adopting one of the other three, requires critical thinking.[1]

Critical thinking is commonly misunderstood to mean presenting arguments and evidence that expose the flaws in another's position, that justify rejecting what the other believes and says, and that will convince the other of the rightness of our own position. To the contrary, the essence of critical thinking is not criticism of others' ideas but rather being critical of our own thinking, reflecting on our own assumptions and perspective, strengthening our own understanding of the issues, and holding our own thinking to a higher standard.

It's not reasonable to expect other people or groups in a dialogue to change their perspective unless we can be open-minded about the possibility that our own perspective ought to be abandoned and replaced. Sometimes our favorite sports team plays badly and deserves to lose. Sometimes our favorite political party is on the wrong side of important issues. Sometimes we must examine the evidence and the options and think for ourselves—including discovering our mistakes and blind spots—and not always go along with whatever our "home team" political party dictates.

What changes with experience and growing older is not a tendency to adopt any one of the four perspectives in preference to the others. Rather, what changes is having a greater familiarity with all four perspectives—Loyal, Tactful, Detached, and Caring—and a greater capacity to assess the appropriateness of each for a given issue. What's important to me here? To be in charge, get along with others, work this out myself, or look out for others?

Engaging in critical thinking and shifting perspectives when appropriate is like being wise. To be wise is to hold the attitude that knowledge is fallible and to strive for a balance between knowing and doubting. To be wise is to remain open to the arguments and merits of other perspectives and to be flexible in adopting a new perspective when this is appropriate. We regard other people as wise when they say or do something that leads us to see a situation in a new way, when they cause us to change our perspective on an issue.[2]

(4) *Take care to avoid misperceptions of others' perspectives and to forestall misperceptions by others of your own perspective.* The other's perspective is more likely to be confused with a nearby perspective in the same row or column of the perspectives matrix (table 3.1) than with a perspective on the diagonal. For example, Loyal is likely to misperceive Tactful as Caring, for both share the assumption of interdependence, but not as Detached. Similarly, Loyal is likely to misperceive Detached as Caring, for both share the intention to understand rather than to control, but not as Tactful. Loyal is most likely to misunderstand Caring (and vice versa), for these two perspectives are at odds on the assumptions of both self-definition and intention. Similarly, misunderstanding is more likely between Tactful and Detached than with nearby perspectives in the matrix.

An example of the potential misperception of one's perspective by another arises in dialogue 9, Weak Detached cultural identity versus Strong Loyal assimilation (chapter 7).

A Weak Detached cultural minority could misread the Strong Loyal cultural majority's position as Tactful, and thus be overly confident that learning more about each other, negotiating and compromising, including yielding to Strong Loyal's expectations and demands, may reduce tensions between the two groups. Weak Detached is willing to live and let live; Strong Loyal is not willing to compromise with groups that threaten its self-contained identity and community. A second example is dialogue 10, Weak Detached religious freedom versus Strong Tactful secularism. Here, Weak Detached may misread Strong Tactful as Strong Loyal and so be overly suspicious and defensive regarding the possible motivations of the other.

A third example of misperception of one perspective by another is dialogue 7, Weak Tactful disadvantaged versus Strong Detached privileged (chapter 6). In this dialogue, Weak Tactful disadvantaged is likely to interpret Strong Detached privileged as Strong Loyal, and Strong Detached is likely to misinterpret Weak Tactful as Weak Loyal. When both happen simultaneously, dialogue 7 degenerates into dialogue 1, Weak Loyal versus Strong Loyal, a conflict in which the greater power usually wins. When in doubt about the perspective of the other, consider the underlying assumptions regarding identity and intentions (chapters 2 and 3).

It can be important to forestall misperceptions of our own perspective by others. Unfortunately, people tend to view the attitudes and behaviors of others from their own perspective. For example, Loyal is likely to project its intentions of competition and control onto those who hold the Tactful, Detached, and Caring perspectives (tables 3.3 and 3.4). Thus, from Loyal's perspective, many situations will be understood as Weak Loyal versus Strong Loyal dialogues, when in fact this may not be the case. Furthermore, groups initially holding perspectives that could fairly be described as Tactful, Detached, or Caring may feel forced, in the course of defending their own identity and community from attack, to adopt the Loyal perspective (for example, dialogues 5, immigrants, and 9, cultural identity). It can be prudent to consider whether the other is correctly perceiving our own perspective in a dialogue.

Who Are Our Allies? Who Can Mediate?

(5) *When engaged in a dialogue and trying to persuade the other, consider where you may find allies who could help.* Of course, those who share our own perspective are likely allies (but not always). What is noteworthy, however, is that supportive alliances based on a shared perspective can be quite independent of the actual content of particular issues. For example, Weak Tactful advocates for expanding minority voting rights (dialogue 6) and Weak Tactful advocates for working women (dialogue 7) would benefit by sharing analyses of opponents' perspectives and working together to construct persuasive and effective counter-arguments.

Similarly, Weak Caring advocates for climate change mitigation (dialogue 13) and Weak Caring advocates for the homeless (dialogue 14) would benefit from sharing and supporting each other's analyses, arguments, and tactics, even though these issues are markedly different in content. Other examples of diverse interest and advocacy groups that share perspectives and would benefit by working more closely might include Strong Loyal big business (dialogue 1) and Strong Loyal adaptation to climate change (dialogue 13); and Strong Detached privileged (dialogue 7) and Strong Detached rich (dialogue 11).

The perspectives matrix (table 3.1) suggests where those holding any one perspective may find allies among the other three. Potential allies are found in the same rows and columns, where another perspective shares an underlying assumption of self-definition or intention, but not at the diagonal, where the opposite perspective shares neither of these two assumptions. Those holding the Loyal perspective on some issue are likely to find allies among those holding the Tactful and Detached perspectives but not those holding the

Caring perspective. A Loyal business owner pushing for reductions in government regulations is likely to find allies among nearby Tactful civic leaders and Detached poets but not among far-removed Caring social workers.

(6) *Consider which people and groups can serve as mediators in dialogues in which those most directly engaged are having difficulty moving forward.* Mediators can arrange conversations, ask questions and clarify perspectives, and negotiate compromises and agreements. Tactful is well positioned to mediate conflicts in a stressful dialogue between Loyal and Caring. Tactful shares a row or a column, that is, one of the two basic assumptions, with each of Loyal and Caring. Thus, Tactful partially understands these two perspectives and may be able to interpret the values and aims of each for the other. Similarly, it is not surprising that Detached is also well positioned to mediate conflicts between Loyal and Caring. So, for example, in a conflict between a Loyal business owner and a Caring social worker, both a Tactful civic leader and a Detached poet could serve as mediators.

(7) *Recognize that people and groups sometimes get locked into perspectives and standpoints due to historical circumstances in their lives, including losses and gains in power and privilege.* For example, it's likely that many of America's working poor feel that forces beyond their control have caused them to fall out of mainstream American society. Maintaining the Tactful perspective and pursuing the American Dream no longer seem like options. Instead, they feel locked into a Weak Detached standpoint (dialogue 11 and chapter 10).

As a second example, success in accumulating property and wealth, political connections and influence, and visibility and status might be taken as confirmation that one's consistently held perspective has in fact been the best among the four. If the Strong Detached standpoint (for example, dialogue 7, male workplaces; or dialogue 15, gun rights) has worked well in the past, why consider changing one's perspective now? Nevertheless, the appropriateness of a perspective depends both on the particular issue at hand and on the perspectives held by others in the dialogue.

In addition, the events of our lives may contribute to a bias towards one or another of the two underlying assumptions that define the four perspectives. Someone who has developed a preference for what is familiar versus what is new and different, for what is certain versus what is uncertain, or for what has worked in the past rather than untested alternatives may be inclined towards the assumption that groups are self-contained, defining themselves intrinsically and not through relations with other groups (and so have a bias towards Loyal or Detached). In contrast, someone who has developed a preference for what is innovative versus what is traditional, for what is bold versus what is safe, and for what may be a better approach versus what has been adequate in the past may be inclined towards the assumption that groups are interdependent, defined through their relations with each other (and so have a bias towards Tactful or Caring).[3]

Similarly, the events of our lives may lead someone to develop a preference for either an intention to control or an intention to understand. Having an interest in improving the material situation for one's family and community may be consistent with an intention to compete with and control others (and have a bias towards Loyal or Tactful), whereas having an interest in expanding one's creative or spiritual potential or strengthening relationships with others may incline one towards an intention to construct meaning and significance in one's life (Detached or Caring).

The damaging consequences of political polarization threaten America's future as a democracy. Simplistic and misleading representations of the issues become obstacles to fruitful discussion, to productive legislative collaboration, and to the crafting of workable solutions that can solve critical problems and move America forward. The remedy for political polarization is not to change the structure of our political institutions. The best solution is to change how we think and talk about issues in American society; that is, to focus on conversation, communication, dialogues, discussion, and debate. How people talk with each other is more important than who they are. Americans must recover how to talk sense about politics; that is, to have thoughtful, productive conversations without getting drawn into divisive arguments.

Recognizing four perspectives—not two partisan positions—and as many as sixteen possible dialogues on the issues greatly expands the public space and the diversity of voices for discussion and debate in American society. Thoughtful Americans who feel frustrated as their ideas and values are misrepresented and blocked by the dominant political stances—right versus left, conservative versus liberal—can feel empowered to re-engage in reasonable discussions and argue openly and convincingly for what they believe. Providing space for more actors and voices on the public stage will facilitate more accurate presentations of complex issues and the emergence of novel, workable solutions that would not otherwise have been envisioned. Thinking critically in a framework of four perspectives—Loyal, Tactful, Detached, and Caring—will enable families, friends, voters, and the media to move beyond political polarization and think broadly, creatively, and constructively about the challenges for America's future.

Acknowledgments

My ideas on how people think and talk about political issues developed from teaching American Pluralism, a course on the changing demographics of American society, and numerous conversations with University at Buffalo faculty as we designed and taught that innovative course, especially Jeannette Ludwig, and with the many inquisitive and concerned students who enrolled. I have been fortunate to participate in programs of the Association of American Colleges and Universities, which aims to advance high-quality, meaningful, and inclusive undergraduate education. During two decades, I benefited greatly from the enthusiasm, insights, and teaching skills of AAC&U leadership and countless engaged and dedicated colleagues. The interest, questions, and helpful suggestions of Ann Farmer improved an early draft of the manuscript.

Elizabeth Lyon has been a caring mentor, collaborator, advocate, and editor. She led me to expand the vision of what my writing could become and pressed me repeatedly to connect with readers by adding more feeling, engaging stories, and examples to my abstract concepts and academic wording. Throughout, I have been amazed at how Elizabeth's suggestions to add or delete only a few words have markedly improved my writing and clarified what I was trying to communicate. This book is vastly different and more engaging because of her commitment and effort. I hope that we might have an opportunity to work together again.

Notes

Chapter 1

1. Michener's novel *Hawaii* is the source for John Whipple (pages 285 to 439) and Nyuk Tsin (427-932); *Centennial* for Maxwell Mercy (291-425), Amos Calendar (432-639), Hans Brumbaugh (501-768), and Paul Garrett (833-873); *Chesapeake* for Edmund Steed (70-119) and Rosalind Steed (236-291); *Texas* for Earnshaw Rusk (666-791) and Floyd Rusk (784-897); and *Alaska* for Michael Healy (329-363), John Klope (375-522), Missy Peckham (406-740), and Tom Venn (406-854).

Chapter 3

1. The distinction between instrumental and strategic action, on the one hand, and communicative action, on the other, is described in Habermas, 1982, 234-237; Habermas, 1984, 284-295; and Furth, 1983, 184-185.

Chapter 4

1. The outline of various kinds of power draws upon Dahl, 1968.
2. Tables 4.2 and 4.3 were constructed as follows. Initially, from each perspective all of the other perspectives and standpoints are viewed similarly. For example, from the Loyal perspective, all other perspectives and standpoints are viewed as wrong and unworthy, as shown in table 3.3. The same two descriptive terms—wrong and unworthy— appear as the first two terms in each set of five for

dialogues 1, 2, 3, and 4 in table 4.2 and dialogues 1, 5, 9, and 13 in table 4.3. And each of the perspectives, regardless of whether the standpoint is strong or weak, is initially viewed the same from all other perspectives and standpoints. For example, the Loyal perspective is always viewed as immature and aggressive as shown in table 3.5 and in the third and fourth terms for dialogues 1, 5, 9, and 13 in table 4.2 and dialogues 1, 2, 3, and 4 in table 4.3. The fifth term in each set is unique for each of the thirty-two standpoints.

Chapter 6

1. The Protestant versus Catholic conflict in Philadelphia in the 1840s in dialogue 5 is described more fully in Feldberg, 1980, and Meacham, 1994, 172-173.
2. The perspectives in dialogue 8 on how humans conceive of their relationship to the environment are similar to the images presented in Meacham, 1991b. The Tactful conservation perspective is comparable to "ecological disasters." The Caring preservation perspective is comparable to "living with nature." The ideas in dialogue 8 are also presented with additional examples in Meacham, 1994, 177-178.

Chapter 7

1. Both dialogue 10 and a discussion of religious dialogues in Meacham, 1994, 176-177, draw on Driver, 1987, a theologian who writes about relations between Christianity and other religions. Driver's "exclusivism" corresponds to the Loyal perspective, "inclusivism" to the Tactful perspective, and "pluralism" to the Detached perspective. Driver also advocates acknowledging the multiplicity of religious faiths while preserving the integrity of each (page 213), pondering the integrity of religions not our own (page

217), and committing ourselves to the Other—all consistent with the Caring perspective.

2. For an excellent analysis of the issues raised in dialogue 11, see Reich, 2015.

Chapter 8

1. The perspectives in dialogue 13 on how humans conceive of their relationship to the environment are similar to the images presented in Meacham, 1991b. The Caring mitigation perspective is comparable to "living with nature." The Loyal adaptation perspective is comparable to "domination of nature." A fourth image, "neglect," is comparable to the Detached perspective.

2. Questions are raised in dialogue 14 about what may be the purposes of educational communities. Meacham and Barrett, 2003, surveyed the mission statements of America's leading colleges and universities. Many of these statements include being an inclusive community and respecting cultural diversity.

3. Meacham, 1995, offers suggestions for conversations that respect the integrity of students' positions, consistent with the Caring standpoint described in dialogue 14.

4. The four kinds of friendship in dialogue 16 are consistent with Meacham, 1991a, who distinguishes between "false cooperation," grounded in the orientation towards success of the Loyal and Tactful perspectives, and "true cooperation," grounded in the sincere interest in the other and mutual understanding of the Caring perspective.

5. Meacham, 1999, contrasts five challenges of caring: being cared for, caring for ourselves, caring for others, caring together with others, and caring for others from whom we differ. This last challenge is consistent with the Caring standpoint in dialogue 16.

6. Meacham, 2015, argues that America's colleges and universities should require all students to become more

familiar with and knowledgeable about the religion of Islam.

7. This critique of the Golden Rule is by Jürgen Habermas, as described by McCarthy, 1978, 326. Meacham and Emont, 1989, provide suggestions for how people can work together to create conditions of trust, as described in dialogue 16, and solve everyday problems.

8. Mayeroff, 1990, provides an excellent elaboration of the Caring standpoint as described in dialogue 16.

Chapter 12

1. Meacham, 1995, describes procedures for how to engage students in discussion of controversial issues, a skill they must have as citizens in a democratic society.

2. A detailed discussion of the nature of wisdom and how it may change as we get older is in Meacham, 1990.

3. Meacham and Boyd, 1994, 70-71, present preliminary ideas on a developmental sequence from a local identification with family, heritage, heroic figures, and nationality to a broader concern for society as a whole including succeeding generations.

Bibliography

Berman, Russell. "What's the answer to political polarization in the U.S.?" *The Atlantic*, March 8, 2016. http://www.theatlantic.com.

"Beyond Red vs. Blue: The Political Typology." Pew Research Center, Washington, DC, June 26, 2014. http://www.people-press.org/2014/06/26/the-political-typology-beyond-red-vs-blue/.

Brooks, Arthur. "Bipartisanship isn't for wimps, after all." *New York Times*, April 9, 2016. http://www.nytimes.com.

Brooks, David. "The governing cancer of our time." *New York Times*, February 26, 2016. http://www.nytimes.com.

Brooks, David. "Time for a realignment." *New York Times*, September 9, 2016. http://www.nytimes.com.

Brooks, David. "The future of the American center," *New York Times*, November 29, 2016, http://www.nytimes.com.

Brooks, David. "The alienated mind." *New York Times*, May 23, 2017. http://www.nytimes.com.

Bruni, Frank. "Why this election terrifies me." *New York Times*, November 5, 2016. http://www.nytimes.com.

Cohen, Roger. "Americans, let's talk." *New York Times*, May 30, 2017. http://www.nytimes.com.

Dahl, Robert A. "Power." In *International Encyclopedia of the Social Sciences* (Vol. 12), edited by D. L. Sills, 405-415. New York: Macmillan Company & Free Press, 1968.

Driver, Thomas F. "The case for pluralism." Chap. 12 in *The Myth of Christian Uniqueness*, 203-218. New York: Orbis, 1987.

Feldberg, Michael. "The Philadelphia Native American riots of 1844: The Kensington phase." Chap. 1 in *The Turbulent Era: Riot and Disorder in Jacksonian America*, 9-23. New

York: Oxford University Press, 1980.

Friedman, Thomas. "Trump and the Lord's work." *New York Times*, May 4, 2016. http://www.nytimes.com.

Fukuyama, Francis. *Political Order and Political Decay*. New York: Farrar, Straus and Giroux, 2014.

Furth, Hans. "A developmental perspective on the societal theory of Habermas." *Human Development* 26 (1983), 181-197.

Habermas, Jürgen. "A reply to my critics." In *Habermas: Critical Debates*, edited by John B. Thompson and David Held, 219-283. Cambridge, MA: MIT Press, 1982.

Habermas, Jürgen. *The Theory of Communicative Action*. Vol. 1. *Reason and the Rationalization of Society*. Translated by Thomas McCarthy. Boston: Beacon Press, 1984.

Kristof, Nicholas. "A failed experiment." *New York Times*, November 22, 2012. http://www.nytimes.com.

Kristof, Nicholas. "A nation of takers?" *New York Times*, March 26, 2014. http://www.nytimes.com.

Kristof, Nicholas. "America's broken politics," *New York Times*, November 5, 2014. http://www.nytimes.com.

Leiss, William. *The Domination of Nature*. Boston: Beacon Press, 1972.

Lepore, Jill. "Long division: Measuring the polarization of American politics." *New Yorker*, December 2, 2013. http://www.newyorker.com.

Lepore, Jill. "The state of debate." *New Yorker*, September 19, 2016. http://www.newyorker.com.

Mansbridge, Jane. "Three reasons political polarization is here to stay." *Washington Post*, March 11, 2016. http://www.washingtonpost.com.

Mayeroff, Milton. *On Caring*. New York: HarperPerennial, 1990.

McCain, John. "Why we must support human rights." *New York Times*, May 8, 2017. http://www.nytimes.com.

McCarthy, Thomas. *The Critical Theory of Jürgen Habermas*. Cambridge: MIT Press, 1978.

McIntosh, Peggy. "White privilege: Unpacking the invisible knapsack." In *Race, Class, and Gender in the United States* (6th edition), edited by Paula S. Rothenberg, 188-192. New York: Worth Publishers, 2004.

Meacham, John A. "The loss of wisdom." In *Wisdom: Its Nature, Origins, and Development*, edited by Robert J. Sternberg, 181-211. Cambridge: Cambridge University Press, 1990.

Meacham, John A. "Conflict and cooperation in adulthood: A role for both?" In *Bridging paradigms: Positive Development in Adulthood and Cognitive Aging*, edited by Jan D. Sinnott and J. C. Cavanaugh, 87-98. New York: Praeger, 1991a.

Meacham, John A. "The concept of nature: Implications for assessment of competence." In *Criteria for Competence: Controversies in the Conceptualization and Assessment of Children's Abilities*, edited by Michael Chandler and Michael Chapman, 43-64. Hillsdale, NJ: Lawrence Erlbaum Associates, 1991b.

Meacham, John A. "Identity, community, and prejudice." *Journal of Adult Development* 1, no 3 (1994): 169-180.

Meacham, Jack A. "Conflict in multiculturalism classes: Too much heat or too little?" *Liberal Education* 81 (1995): 24-29.

Meacham, Jack A. "Connecting life-course challenges of caring with the college curriculum." *Journal of Adult Development* 6, no 3 (1999): 53-161.

Meacham, Jack A. "Islam is essential for general education." *Journal of General Education* 64, no 1 (2015): 56-64.

Meacham, Jack A. and Crystal Barrett. "Commitment to diversity in institutional mission statements." *Diversity & Democracy* 7 (2003): 6-9.

Meacham, John A., and Cynthia Boyd. "Expanding the circle of caring: From local to global." In *Interdisciplinary Handbook of Adult Lifespan Learning*, edited by Jan D. Sinnott, 61-73. New York: Greenwood Press, 1994.

Meacham, John A., and Nancy C. Emont. "The interpersonal basis of everyday problem solving." In *Everyday Problem Solving: Theory and Applications*, edited by Jan D. Sinnott, 7-23. New York: Praeger, 1989.

Michener, James A. *Hawaii.* New York: Random House, 1959.

Michener, James A. *Centennial.* New York: Random House, 1974.

Michener, James A. *Chesapeake.* New York: Random House, 1978.

Michener, James A. *Texas.* New York: Random House, 1985.

Michener, James A. *Alaska.* New York: Random House, 1988.

Murray, Charles. "Trump's America." *Wall Street Journal*, February 12, 2016. http://www.wsj.com.

Nordhaus, William. *The Climate Casino: Risk, Uncertainty, and Economics for a Warming World.* New Haven: Yale University Press, 2013.

North, Anna. "The biggest challenges of 2016." *New York Times*, January 6, 2016. http://www.nytimes.com.

"Political polarization in the American public." Pew Research Center, Washington, DC, 2014. Retrieved from http://www.people-press.org/2014/06/12/political-polarization-in-the-american-public/.

Reich, Robert B. *Saving Capitalism: For the Many, Not the Few.* New York: Knopf, 2015.

Sampson, Edward E. "The debate on individualism: Indigenous psychologies of the individual and their role in personal and societal functioning." *American Psychologist* 43 (1988): 15-22.

Zimmerman, Jonathan. "Civic education in the age of Trump." *The Atlantic*, April 9, 2016. http://www.theatlantic.com.

Index

MAY 1 7 2018

CPSIA information can be obtained
at www.ICGtesting.com
Printed in the USA
LVOW10s1934200318

570510LV00012B/1166/P

9 780999 297612